MONTEVERDI

Orfeo / La favola d'Orfeo

The Return of Ulysses / Il ritorno d'Ulisse in patria

The Coronation of Poppea / L'incoronazione di Poppea

English National Opera

45

ENO

continued inside back cover

1264
100k

Anthony Rolfe Johnson as Ulysses in David Freeman's 1989 production for ENO, conducted by Paul Daniel and designed by David Roger (photo: Laurie Lewis)

This Opera Guide is sponsored by

The Operas of Monteverdi

Opera Guide Series Editor: Nicholas John

Calder Publications Limited
Riverrrun Press Inc.
Paris · London · New York

Published in association with English National Opera

COPYRIGHT DATA

Published in Great Britain, 1992, by
John Calder (Publishers) Limited
9-15 Neal Street, London WC2H 9TU

Published in the U.S.A., 1992, by
Riverrun Press Inc., 1170 Broadway,
New York, NY 10001

BRITISH LIBRARY CATALOGUING IN PUBLICATION DATA
Monteverdi, Claudio, *1567-1643*
    The operas of Monteverdi.—(English National Opera guides; 45)
    I. Title   II. Series
    782.1092

ISBN 0-7145-4207-5

LIBRARY OF CONGRESS CATALOGING-IN-PUBLICATION DATA
Monteverdi, Claudio, 1567-1643.
    [Operas. Librettos. English & Italian]
    The Operas of Monteverdi.
    208p 21.6cm.—(Opera guide: 45)
    Librettos of the operas Orfeo, Ritorno d'Ulisse in patria, and L'Incoronazione di Poppea in Italian with English translations by Anne Ridler with commentary.
    ISBN 0-7145-4207-5
    1. Operas—Librettos.   2. Monteverdi, Claudio, 1567-1643.   Operas.
    3.—Analysis, appreciation.   I. Ridler, Anne, 1912- . II. Series.
    ML49.M75R52   1992 <Case>
    782.1'026'8—dc20
                                                        91-32133
                                                            CIP
                                                            MN

English National Opera receives financial assistance from the Arts Council of Great Britain.

Typeset in Plantin by Spooner Typesetting & Graphics, London NW5.

Printed in Great Britain by Billing & Sons, Worcester.

CONTENTS

LIST OF ILLUSTRATIONS

Cover design by Anita Boyd
Frontispiece: Anthony Rolfe Johnson as Ulysses at ENO, 1989 (photo: Laurie Lewis)

Monteverdi, Opera and History

Iain Fenlon

Prominent composers from d'Indy to Berio, via Respighi, Hindemith and Maderna, have been strongly attracted by Monteverdi's *Orfeo*, to the extent of making editions and free adaptations of the score. Yet for all the musical appeal of a work that has come to be thought of as the first true opera, it is important to distinguish what is new about it and what is traditional. Many of its stylistic and formal aspects are derived from existing models (madrigals, instrumental ritornellos and various kinds of stage music), traditions to which Monteverdi himself had contributed. We should not be misled by textbook labels into believing *Orfeo* represents a radical break with his previous music, for much of the writing is rooted in styles that were current at the Mantuan court when the composer arrived from his native Cremona at the end of the 1580s. At the same time, *Orfeo* cannot simply be explained as the logical development of Monteverdi's training and career at the Gonzaga court, since it is also clearly influenced by Florentine experiments with sung drama, and especially by Jacopo Peri's *Euridice*, first performed in 1600 and subsequently published. To point to precedents and influences is not to play down the impact of *Orfeo*, which effectively heralds the spread of the new theatrical style outside Florence. Nor can there be much question of its extraordinary boldness, particularly in matters of formal design, or of Monteverdi's powers of synthesis, which forged the language of the work from a wider range of musical resources and expressive techniques.

Unusually for an opera of this period, the composition of *Orfeo* is documented and can be traced in a series of letters between two members of the Mantuan ruling house, Francesco and Ferdinando Gonzaga. As well as informing us about the pitfalls that befell the preparations for the first performance, these letters give an insight into some of the practical constraints, and at a more general level they underline the intimate nature of the first staging. Nineteenth-century notions of opera, together with the list of instruments printed at the front of the score, have often combined to produce rather grand performances, in opera houses on large stages with large choruses and instrumental ensembles. But other evidence suggests that *Orfeo* was first given in a small room, and this may explain the different endings given in Monteverdi's score and in Alessandro Striggio's libretto. The libretto, which is known to have been available to the audience at the first performance, adheres quite closely to the ending in Angelo Poliziano's fifteenth-century version of the legend, which is in turn derived from Ovid and Virgil, but the published score of 1609 substitutes a happy ending in which Apollo descends to rescue Orpheus. This scenographically more complicated *dénouement*, requiring a machine to effect Apollo's descent, probably reflects a later performance.

As a chamber work designed for performance before members of an academy, *Orfeo* is cast in the same social mould as the early Florentine operas, and this influence goes deeper than superficial similarities of function and audience to embrace important details of dramatic shape and musical language. Both composer and librettist took as their starting-point Peri's *Euridice* with its text by Ottavio Rinuccini. This is not to say that there is no stylistic difference between the recitative of the two works: Monteverdi's is rhythmically more ingenious, more flexible in its pace, than anything to be found in *Euridice*. At the same time it is also less abstract, more inclined to heighten the sense of individual words by using stock devices drawn from the language of the polyphonic madrigal, than Peri's rather experimental and formulaic writing. In terms both of bass-line movement and of harmonic progression Monteverdi's style is also more adventurous and wide-ranging.

These recitative sections are often framed within set pieces, most of which are based on theatrical conventions that predate opera (above all those of the *intermedio*), and many of which are cast in established musical forms and styles. Here again Monteverdi can be seen to be drawing both upon Mantuan traditions and on his own considerable experience as a madrigalist. Thus the opening toccata, strictly unnecessary in terms of the action, is played three times by all the instruments before the scene is revealed; the re-appearance of this music at the beginning of the 1610 Vespers suggests that it is no more than a formalisation of a set fanfare, perhaps announcing the arrival of the ducal family. The first chorus, 'Vieni Imeneo', is an entirely conventional homophonic madrigal which achieves its effect through sensitive declamation of the text allied to an adventurous harmonic palette capable of underscoring affective words by carefully calculated shifts in tension, a type of writing that Monteverdi had used before and was to develop almost as a hallmark. The second chorus, 'Lasciate i monti', described in the score as a 'balletto', is reminiscent of the general tone of any number of light canzonettas written in the 1580s and 1590s. And so we could go on. It would not be difficult to describe ways in which the structure of each act is articulated by similar traditional means, whether the duets and trios which are such a feature of the first two acts, or the instrumental sinfonias (also derived from the *intermedio* tradition) which assist the change in atmosphere from one act to another.

By bringing together styles that he had explored since his arrival in Mantua, Monteverdi rooted *Orfeo* firmly in Mantuan traditions. This is not to underestimate the highly original way in which these elements are welded together. Nor is it to understate the originality of some of Monteverdi's musical procedures, particularly in the use of ritornello or variation structures. This is true above all of Orpheus's prayer 'Possente spirto', the spiritual, dramatic and literal centre of the work. Both as a prayer and as an incantation aria, 'Possente spirto' is the forerunner of many early-seventeenth-century set pieces. Orpheus's song left more of a mark on history than any other part of the work, in a manner that is broadly analogous to the impact of Arianna's lament 'Lasciatemi morire', the only part of his next opera which has survived. They established a strongly characterised style of set piece (prayer, incantation, lament) which reappears time and again in early opera. And, in terms of Monteverdi's approach to solo song, 'Possente spirto' is an important landmark on the way towards the perfect fusion of words and music that was to be his preoccupation as a composer for the theatre.

Yet the most far-reaching of Monteverdi's innovations in *Orfeo* is his use of repeated musical material. Throughout the opera repetition is developed as a structural device, not only within recitative passages but elsewhere, as in the instrumental ritornellos in the Prologue. It is the key to the most significant novelty of *Orfeo* — the way in which larger structures are constructed — and indeed some parts of the opera seem to have been planned with large-scale symmetries in mind. The extent of these can be over-emphasised but the effect of balance in the first act, for example, can hardly be the result of coincidence, and has more to do with progress of text and action than with any supposed striving for abstract musical form. It is the repetition structure of Act One that marks it off from earlier Florentine opera, and it is in this that the novelty of Monteverdi's early operatic style really lies.

How that style developed is now difficult to reconstruct, since only the famous lament has survived from *Arianna*. This is particularly unfortunate

Music (Jennifer Smith) sings the Prologue at ENO in David Freeman's 1983 production for ENO, designed by Hayden Griffin and Peter Hartwell, and conducted by Peter Robinson (photo: Reg Wilson)

since it is clear from the composer's letters that he considered this opera (his last for the Mantuan court) to be crucial in his development as a composer for the stage. But, in fact, although we know that Monteverdi wrote a number of works in both old and new theatrical formats after his move to Venice in 1613, it is not until *Il ritorno d'Ulisse* (*The Return of Ulysses*) of 1640 that we have anything of substance. This work takes us away not only from the very different musical traditions of the early years of the century, but also out of the world of court opera and into the very different realm of the public theatres.

For the carnival season of 1637, a company of musicians rented the Teatro S. Cassiano (a Venetian theatre traditionally used for performances of the *commedia dell'arte*) and produced the first public opera. The next year they presented another, and then in 1639 their activities were transferred to another house, the Teatro SS. Giovanni e Paolo, which had been hurriedly renovated to accommodate operatic performances. Meanwhile, at the S. Cassiano, a competing group of musicians led by Monteverdi's pupil, Francesco Cavalli, set up a rival opera. The vogue for public opera, which was to sweep through the rest of Italy and then Europe, had started.

Why should the earliest opera house have been opened in Venice? It is sometimes said that the answer can be found in the republican nature of Venetian society; that since the audiences for Venetian opera were drawn from a reasonably wide spectrum of the population, the building of the first opera house was in some sense a response to popular taste, and so was commercially viable. This is a spurious argument. For all that Venetian writers and painters constantly emphasised the social cohesion and harmony of the Republic, Venetian society was as conscious of social class as any other part of Italy; the extent to which the opera could have been an entertainment for anyone other

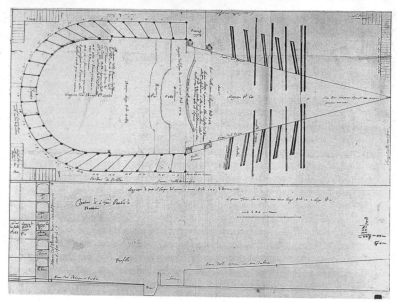

Ground plan of the Teatro SS. Giovanni e Paolo, Venice (The Trustees of Sir John Soane's Museum)

than patricians has been exaggerated. What is clear is that there was a long tradition of public spectacle in Venice. Visitors came from all parts of the continent and, as we know from their diaries and letters, many of them went to the opera, as did John Evelyn in 1646. The foundation of the opera houses took place in a buoyant economic atmosphere stimulated by the early-seventeenth-century version of mass tourism, and encouraged by the apparent stability of the city, unwalled yet unconquered for a thousand years.

The Teatro SS. Giovanni e Paolo, created or readapted for the opera in 1639, was the most sumptuous of all the early Venetian houses. In common with the other theatres of the period the building does not survive, but a late seventeenth-century drawing in the Soane Museum in London shows it with a long U-shaped floor plan and five tiers of boxes. Predictably, since the librettos of the first Venetian operas celebrate the beauty of the sets, the ingeniousness of the machines and the richness of the costumes, it also reveals that the house had an ample stage area. Although the Soane drawing reveals nothing about machines, trap doors or lights, it does indicate that there was plenty of room for them, including the space below the stage floor. There was an elaborate layout of grooves for sliding the backdrops and wings backwards and forwards, those for the backdrops being parallel to the proscenium and the five sets for the wings running slightly slantwise. This priority given to the problems of the stage is perfectly in line with the characteristic features of Venetian opera presentations, grandiose and composite spectacles in which the pathos of the earlier recitative has been somewhat overtaken by the notion of the pursuit of the marvellous and the importance of the idea of 'wonder' as an essential feature of the operatic experience.

It seems likely that Monteverdi would not have turned again to the composition of opera had it not been for the notable success of the new opera companies and the economic viability of the public theatres (some newly constructed, others adapted from existing buildings) in which they played.

That he did so at the age of seventy is remarkable. In purely social terms, the Venetian audience for opera was probably not much different from the Mantuan aristocrats and courtiers who had been present at the first performances of *Orfeo* and *Arianna*; that much at least we can tell from the seat prices. But, in a number of important ways, the Venetians had quite different musical and dramatic expectations. Firstly, the earlier court operas were devised for small-scale performance: *Orfeo*, for example, can be (and probably was) performed with a minimum of scenery which required changing only twice. In the Venetian theatre the emphasis was upon spectacle, much as it had been in the old sixteenth-century *intermedio* tradition; the audience required entertainment, and for this scenery and stage machines became important.

In this new atmosphere, the symbolic tales from classical antiquity which had been the staple fare of early court opera were replaced with historical dramas more concerned with human characters living in the real world. The earliest operas had dealt with the myths of Orpheus and Eurydice, or Apollo and Daphne, familiar legends which were eminently suitable for musical elaboration since the theme of the fabled power of Greek music and its ability to move the hearts and minds of men was central. Only gradually did librettists introduce comic elements and brisker plots, and for the first few seasons after the Venetian opera houses opened works were still mounted which adhered to this general format. But rapidly it became clear that audiences were primarily interested in recognisable human beings, recognisable both in their actions and emotional responses. Monteverdi had always been in sympathy with this idea; writing about a projected stage work for the Mantuan court in 1616 he said:

> I have noticed that the characters are winds, cupids, little zephyrs and sirens. How, dear sir, since winds do not speak, shall I be able to imitate their speech? And how, by such means, shall I be able to move the passions? Ariadne moved the audience because she was a woman, and Orpheus because he was a man and not a wind. And as to the story as a whole, I do not feel that it moves me at all . . . Ariadne inspired in me a true lament, and Orpheus a true prayer, but I do not know what this fable will inspire in me. So what does your Lordship want the music to do?

One important consequence of the changed nature of the libretto, as opera moved into the public realm, was to do with the number of characters. Whereas *Orfeo* involves only a handful of main characters, with other soloists drawn from the chorus, *Ulysses* has nineteen principal characters and *L'incoronazione di Poppea (The Coronation of Poppea)* twenty-one, while the role of chorus is negligible in both. For the most part, the music in these Venetian operas consists of recitative punctuated by self-contained closed forms such as arias and duets; indeed, in the course of the century the aria was to become the principal ingredient of Venetian opera, a development that is foreshadowed in *Ulysses* and *Poppea* where, nevertheless, it still remains subservient to recitative of a highly flexible and, at times, lyrical kind. In other words, Monteverdi's Venetian operas are designed to appeal to an audience brought up not on the recitative style of Peri and Caccini, nor upon the madrigal style of the late sixteenth century, but rather upon the arias and duets which fill the early-seventeenth-century song books which had poured from the Venetian presses. If one of the characteristic features of *Orfeo* is the way that Monteverdi pieced it together from so many of the different forms and styles which made up the early-seventeenth-century musical landscape, the same is true of the relationship of his Venetian operas to the musical world of their time. It was

'*The Return of Ulysses*', Kent Opera, 1978: Anne Pashley as Minerva, Neil Jenkins as Ulysses, Neil Mackie as Telemachus; production by Norman Platt, designed by Roger Butlin (photo: Mike Humphrey)

Monteverdi's accommodation to the social as well as to the technical and musical features of the 1630s that led him to evolve an approach to operatic writing which produced works that are quite different from the great efforts of 1607-8.

Ulysses and *Poppea* show this new style in rather different ways. The earlier of the two has come down to us anonymously in a single manuscript, now in Vienna, where it was perhaps taken by an Italian company performing at the Imperial court. This led some writers to claim that the work is not by Monteverdi at all, but his authorship is supported by contemporary literary comment and, more importantly, by the style of the music. It encompasses not only passages in the *genere concitato*, but also a large number of duets in a distinctly Monteverdian idiom and a number of arioso laments in direct line of descent from Arianna's lament. The story was taken by the librettist Giacomo Badoaro from the later books of Homer's epic, and it is characteristic of the new operatic fashions that this material allows the stage to be peopled with real human characters: Ulysses himself, his wife Penelope who has been waiting for his return, and his son Telemachus, all of whom are involved, at one level, in a story of depressing familiarity and ordinariness. Onto this skeleton are grafted a number of sequences involving classical deities, which are not an essential part of the story, but remnants of the traditions of court opera which afford an excuse for spectacle. Neptune's occasional appearances, for example, provide opportunities for sea-machines, and the opera opens with a prologue in which the the figures of Human Frailty, Fortune and Love point out the moral of the piece in the form of strophic variations, much like the personification of music at the beginning of *Orfeo*. The interventions of the gods, requiring much extra fussy stage business, may even seem to be a defect, a distraction from the simplicity of Homer's story, but they provide an essential part of the seventeenth-century theatrical experience.

For his last opera, *The Coronation of Poppea*, Monteverdi turned for a librettist to Busenello, who was, like Badoaro, a prominent figure in the principal mid-century Venetian academy (the Accademia degli Invaghiti). They chose, for the first time in the history of opera, a historical subject, taken from the *Annals* of Tacitus. It describes how the young and ambitious Poppea succeeds in infatuating the Roman emperor Nero; sexually obsessed by her, he abandons all reason, dignity and decorum, and finally crowns her as his empress. In doing so he causes the death of his counsellor Seneca and the exile of his wife, and legitimate empress, Octavia. The libretto shows signs that the tastes of the Venetian operatic public were moving away from the classic and the formal towards the more popular, earthy and even comic aspects of humanity. Both *Ulysses* and *Poppea* have happy endings, expressed in the form of an exultant love duet, but whereas in *Ulysses* the happy ending results from the triumph of love and patience over all adversity, that in *Poppea* apparently represents the defeat of reason by lust, passion and unrelenting ambition. As in *Ulysses*, Monteverdi constructs the work out of a wide range of different styles and forms including songs, duets, a trio (unusually for Venetian opera at this date), and recitative. The *genere concitato* makes a number of appearances, almost like a fingerprint, and one familiar enough to the musical *cognoscenti* after the publication of Monteverdi's eight madrigal book, the *Madrigali guerrieri, et amorosi* (Madrigals of War and Love), in Venice in 1638. Above all

Maria Ewing and Dennis Bailey as Poppea and Nero in Peter Hall's 1984 Glyndebourne production, designed by John Bury, and conducted by Raymond Leppard (photo: Guy Gravett)

there are laments, most notably Octavia's 'Addio Roma', sung as she prepares to leave Rome for ever. Made up of short phrases, making great use of dissonance, and deploying a flexible recitative style which ranges from rapid declamation at one extreme to lyrical arioso at the other, it too is distinctly reminiscent of Arianna's 'Lasciatemi morire'.

Taken together, *Ulysses* and *Poppea* illuminate almost every aspect of human emotional experience: laughter, weeping, raging, waking up and falling asleep. In this sense Monteverdi could be said finally to have achieved his ambition of discovering the 'via naturale all'immitatione' ('the true way of imitation'), that ultimate close bonding of word and note to which he often refers in his letters. But in addition to the portrayal of an unprecedented range of emotions, there is also in these last works an emerging idea of characterisation in music. In *Ulysses*, for example, the gods maintain their dignity in a style of arioso-recitative familiar from *Orfeo*: Neptune is easily recognisable as the natural successor to Charon and Pluto, a deep authoritative bass whose words are rather ponderously painted in conventional musical images. In both operas the most serious characters are provided with passages of dramatic monody, while the most light-hearted music is given to those whose function it is to provide contrast with the principals. Groups, suitors or mourners, are treated collectively with madrigal-like writing, and for the characters who at times have to provide pure comedy unrelated to the plot, there is another type of music — Irus and Arnalta are in fact the prototypes of a whole series of buffo types, those drunkards, idiots and unfortunates who vividly populate the pages of later Venetian opera. In writing for the Venetian stage Monteverdi effectively set standards and precedents which his pupils and successors (above all Cavalli) adopted and developed in the 1640s and 1650s, when the whole format of Venetian opera was tending towards standardization. On the one hand the increasing concentration of aria and closed forms was developed further and eventually dominated (even strangled) opera composition, as it gradually settled into a succession of set pieces. On the other hand the careful balance between serious and comic scenes, between reflection and action, ensembles and soliloquies, was much imitated in the works of Cavalli and Cesti. To conclude an opera with a love duet, as happens in both *Ulysses* and *Poppea*, also became common.

This leads us to an ironical conclusion very much in the spirit of seventeenth-century operatic experience. Two manuscript scores of *Poppea*, neither from Monteverdi's lifetime, have survived: one in Venice, the other in Naples; neither mention the composer's name, and both conclude with the highly sensual and erotic ecstasy of the love duet between Nero and Poppea, 'Pur ti miro, Pur ti godo, Pur ti stringo, Pur t'anodo'. Yet according to the *scenario* for the first Venetian performance, 'Nerone solemnly looks on at the coronation of Poppea who, in the name of the people and the Senate of Rome, is crowned by consuls and tribunes; Love, in similar fashion, descends from the skies (accompanied by Venus, the Graces and cupids) and crowns Poppea as goddess of beauty on earth; and the opera ends'. Whether the duet (and indeed some other parts of the surviving music) are by Monteverdi or not is open to serious question, and certainly it would be in keeping with contemporary practice for *Poppea* to have been a collective effort by a number of composers. Our ignorance over questions of authorship is also a sharp reminder not only of how little we know about opera of the period, but also of how little has come down to us. It is sobering to realise that while some of Monteverdi's operas have been lost, the performance of a masterpiece of the calibre of *Ulysses* is possible only because of the fortuitous survival of a single manuscript in an Austrian library.

On Translating Opera

Anne Ridler

Opera grows from the seed of the word. Renaissance theorists were in no doubt about that, and they based their arguments on Plato, who in a passage of his *Republic* says that song consists of word, harmony and rhythm, and that of these three, Word is the leader. Monteverdi, in a well-known letter to his Mantuan patron, explained that he could not use a libretto where the words did not inspire him. Objecting to a libretto he had been given where the characters were winds, he wrote:

> How, dear sir, since winds do not speak, shall I be able to imitate their speech? And how, by such means, shall I be able to move the passions? Ariadne moved the audience because she was a woman, and Orpheus because he was a man and not a wind. [. . .] Ariadne inspired in me a true lament, and Orpheus a true prayer, but I do not know what *this* will inspire in me.

A century later, we find the same point of view in Gluck, who wrote in the preface to his *Alceste*, that the music of opera should be secondary to the poetry and drama: it should be like the addition of colour to drawing, keeping the shape of the figures.

Nowadays, however, music has become so much the dominant partner that we are tempted to think of the libretto for an opera as more or less a necessary evil, and the plot a tiresome device that gets in the way of our enjoyment of the music. It is true that many of the great composers seem to have succeeded in spite of, rather than by means of, their collaborators. There is a curious paradox involved here: the words are nothing without the music (and the subtler the poetry, the more surely its own verbal music is distorted by the setting), yet the music must follow where the poetry leads — Plato was surely right in that.

These questions have a bearing on the subject of opera in translation, but because the translator is an interpreter and not a creator, the paradox no longer holds: the musical line here is always the leader, and he must strive to follow its twists and turns as though he were a shadow, tacked to its heels. His task is to match the emphasis and mood of the original, so that if the composer has coloured a certain phrase, even a certain word, with gravity or gaiety in his setting, an equivalent should be found in the translation. Yet giving certain words this importance may upset the natural word-order of the English sentence — a disadvantage which may have to be incurred for the sake of faithfulness to the original.

But, it could be argued, if the original text is so important, ought it ever to be transposed into another tongue — do we not lose something quite irreplaceable? We do, certainly; but then unless we are bilingual, we also lose much by not hearing the text in our native tongue. This raises the whole issue of communication which, as David Pountney has said (in an interview for *City Limits*), has to do with 'the innate understanding between singers singing in their own language to an audience in its own language. The sense of communication and the ease of nuance that singers have when they sing in their own language is completely different.'

A more obvious point is that audiences miss many of the jokes in a comedy in a foreign tongue — even in familiar Mozart. But the aim of the translator must be to accommodate the words so pliably to the needs of the voice, while

Sarah Walker (Octavia) and Ulrik Cold (Seneca) in Jonathan Hales' 1986 production of 'Poppea' for Kent Opera, designed by Roger Butlin (photo: Robert Workman)

keeping the natural speech-emphasis, that to the listener it will seem as though the work had been originally set to a text in his own language. (An impossible ideal, perhaps, but nonetheless to be striven for.) The text is above all a version for singing; a literal translation of the meaning comes second to this, though the essence must be kept — digested and then as it were re-created.

There is also the question of style and diction in modern versions of earlier operas. We cannot ignore our own contemporary literary tradition and habits of expression. Our ears are out of practice with rhetoric, and audiences react to it with disbelief. In some respects the problem for the translator is the same as for a playwright who is treating a story set in a past age: to create a timeless speech, one that will be credible as spoken in its period, yet free from the archaisms and clichés that would make it impossible for us to believe in the characters. Because of the distancing power of music, the librettist can take more risks than the playwright: there are, indeed, great attractions for a poet nowadays in this medium, which provides, as W.H. Auden has pointed out, almost his only remaining opportunity of attempting the high style. Moreover, it opens to a translator a variety of rhymes and metres which could no longer be used in lyrics where he speaks with his own voice. Here, however, he has to be warned against self-indulgence: if he rhymes, say, pleasure and treasure too often, the audience will be aware of it and feel bored. The seventeenth-century translator of Cavalli's *Erismena* could and did rhyme languish with anguish as often as he liked; in a modern work it should be rationed, if used at all, to one appearance.

Furthermore, full rhymes in English tend to draw attention to themselves in a way that may not suit the tone of the original. In the recitatives of the baroque composers, the rhymes are often unstressed, but used to knit the phrases together, and the music rises with no abrupt change of style to an aria or a lyrical passage. Here the dissonance and assonance of rhyme used in modern prosody is invaluable, to achieve an echo without over-emphasis.

A conscientious effort to reproduce the rhyme-scheme of the original has been the commonest cause of shipwreck for translators, plunged into seas of disastrous bathos or oddity. Bathos, such as this couplet from the Dies Irae in Dvořák's *Requiem*: 'In thy favourite sheep's position, Save me from the goat's condition.' Oddity, such as this for Leporello in *Don Giovanni*, speaking of the statue: 'Nothing I'll garble, That man of marble . . .' Keeping to the rhyme-scheme seems to be a point of honour for some translators but in my view, naturalness of speech comes first, and a translation that draws attention to itself, except in comedy, has failed.

The especial difficulty for the poet translating into English from German or Italian is, of course, our shortage of double rhymes, and the fact that too many feminine endings weaken the verse. If the disyllables are reproduced in English, there will be far too many present participles, ending in *ing*. Foreign translations *from* English are in the opposite difficulty: one notices it, for instance, with the German translation of *Messiah*, in 'How beautiful are the feet . . .', where the German gives two crochets, *Frieden*, for the emphatic final syllable *peace*. Music-directors vary in the latitude they allow to translators, but most will agree to a monosyllable, when the original disyllable is on a repeated note. *Addio* need not always be padded out to 'Farewell now'.

Certain metres, too, present problems in English. Dactyls for more than a line or two easily become broken-backed; the accent, instead of coming firmly on the first syllable of three, distributes itself between the others —

> Nymphs of the forest grove,
> Guardians and genii
> Of silent coppices,
> Of rocky precipice . . . (Pan, in Cavalli's *La Calisto*)

In English poems such as Nash's 'In Time of Pestilence' this produces a charming ambiguity which music has no place for.

There is a special language which translators fall into — translationese or operese — where, obsessed by the original text, the writer entirely forgets what his own language ought to sound like. Thus, in a twentieth-century translation of Monteverdi's *Orfeo*, Orpheus, told not to look back, is ponderously admonished: 'A single glance cause of a surety must be of loss eternal'; and Siegfried meeting the dragon (in a pre-Porter translation of the *Ring*) exclaims

'An extravagent frontage meets my gaze'. Clichés are moved into place whenever the button is pressed: dancers 'stir a wanton foot', and if a character is cheerful he is said to have 'doffed his sadness'. The Italian 'ohimé che odo?' translates all too easily into 'Alas, what do I hear?', but such stilted English will not do for Orpheus' agonized response to the Messenger's report of Euridice's death. The best solution I found at that point was to make Orfeo repeat her name, for it *was* the sound of her name spoken by the Messenger which struck right to his heart.

At moments of high emotion, some translators feel they must take liberties with the rhythm, for the sake of natural speech. Auden and Kallman single out one such moment in their translation of *The Magic Flute*, when Tamino in anguish demands of the invisible spirits 'Lebt sich Pamina noch?' Impossible to use the stilted phrase 'Lives then Pamina still?'; therefore nothing will do but the direct and simple 'Is Pamina still alive?', even though it alters the rhythm. At moments like this, the translator despairs of his task. For instance: Orfeo, remembering what Euridice was like, has a phrase of most poignant music to the words 'Tu bella fusti', and there is no way that the English 'You were beautiful' can match it, with the emphasis in the right place. My attempt — 'Great was your beauty' — inevitably loses the highlight on the word *bella*. Moreover, it is at such moments that I especially feel the need (impossible to realize fully) to match the actual vowel and consonant sounds of the original, for they are mysteriously involved with the emotion.

To give one example. The variants on the word *return* (*tornare* and *ritorno*) are charged with emotion for Monteverdi, as can be felt in the opening soliloquies of *The Return of Ulysses* and *The Coronation of Poppea*, in spite of the difference between the two characters and their situations. Not only does Penelope harp on the word *return*, as she admonishes the absent Ulysses, but the thought of returning elicits a wonderful lyrical passage about the impulse in nature of elements to return to their centre. And the forlorn Otho outside Poppea's window plays on the word with the same emotion: 'So I return here, I turn again to you, as lines to a centre, as flames to fire's source, or as a stream to ocean.' Happily the English word *return* does carry an emotional charge, even though the sound cannot be quite the same.

Not all adapters, I know, think this sound-matching important, but I have been told by singers who had come from *Orfeo* in Italian to my version that it made their task easier. And everyone will agree about the need to provide suitable vowel-sounds on very high or low notes. (Horrible sounds are produced by the choir at the end of the *St Matthew Passion* in English, trying to sing 'Sleep in Peace' on top F to A.)

I have said that the rhythm of the words must follow the music like a shadow, but in recitative, this does not mean that the time-values of crotchet and quaver must be kept exactly. The pitch-outline, or essential shape of the phrase, is to be followed, but the syllables can be redistributed to make the accents fall naturally in English — a need that would not be felt in French, where the stress can be varied at will. In arias, both the syllables and the strophic pattern are important, but not the literal meaning: one should digest sense, and then write a new lyric to fit the music.

Libretto-translating is a kind of verbal joinery — I use the word in no derogatory sense — where good craftsmanship is important. The reward for the translator of great operas is that he will have absorbed the music into his system while finding words to fit it; and hearing them sung, he has a brief illusion that he has originated the whole. And if the words are often missed by the audience, there is this consolation: it is important to the singer's own performance that he should have words he can believe in.

PART ONE

Mantua

The Stage Works

Two 'Entrate' for a ballet, Endimione (*lost*)	1605
De la bellezza le dovute lodi (*ballet*)	1607
Orfeo	1607
Arianna (*lost except for the lament*)	1608
Il ballo delle ingrate (*ballet*)	1608
A prologue to L'Idropica (*music lost*)	1608

Mantua in the sixteenth century.

'Orfeo': A Masterpiece for a Court

John Whenham

Monteverdi's *L'Orfeo, favola in musica* (a 'legend' or a 'play' in music), was prepared under the auspices of the 21-year-old Francesco Gonzaga, elder son of the Duke of Mantua, and first performed at the ducal palace in Mantua on February 24, 1607. Unlike Jacopo Peri's *Euridice* (first performed at Florence in 1600), on which it was in part modelled, *Orfeo* was not written to celebrate a wedding or other dynastic occasion: it was simply one of the entertainments customarily mounted during the carnival season to amuse the members of the Mantuan court. And though the opera is now widely regarded as a work of genius, and valued as the greatest of the early operas, its creation and its survival in print may have depended on little more than Francesco Gonzaga's wish to rival the activity of his music-loving and intellectually gifted younger brother Ferdinando.

Ferdinando had left Mantua in 1602 at the age of fifteen. He went first to study at Innsbruck, but returned to Italy three years later, and entered the University of Pisa to study law, theology and philosophy. Unlike many seventeenth-century patrons of music, he was genuinely interested in the art. He was himself both poet and composer, and he acted as 'protector' of the Florentine Accademia degli Elevati ('Academy of the Elevated Ones'), the membership of which included Jacopo Peri and Giulio Caccini, composers of the earliest Florentine operas. On February 7, 1606, a ballet for which Ferdinando had written both text and music was performed before the Florentine court, then resident at Pisa for carnival; and for carnival the following year he wrote another theatre-piece. This work (now lost) was performed at Pisa on February 26, 1607, and was described by the Florentine court diarist Cesare di Bastiano Tinghi as a 'comedia in musica' (a play in music), a term frequently used to describe opera in the early years of its history. Francesco was well aware of his brother's activities — Ferdinando had, indeed, sent him a copy of the music and text of his 1606 ballet — and it is surely more than mere coincidence that Francesco, not otherwise noted as an active patron of music, should suddenly have decided to commission an opera for performance at Mantua during carnival 1607 under the aegis of the Mantuan Accademia degli Invaghiti (the 'Charmed Ones'), of which he was a prominent member. When the score of *Orfeo* was first published in 1609, it was dedicated to Francesco, who had in all probability financed the publication.

In promoting his opera, Francesco was able to draw his resources almost entirely from the well-endowed establishment which his father maintained at the Mantuan court. The librettist, Alessandro Striggio, a court secretary, was himself a musician. The composer, Monteverdi, was the court choirmaster with overall responsibility for secular music at court, whether concerts of vocal and instrumental music, music to accompany meals, or theatrical entertainments such as ballets or the spectacular *intermedi* played between the acts of spoken drama. Under him worked a body of instrumentalists — players of string, wind and brass instruments, lutenists and keyboard players — well able to supply the rich variety of instrumental forces specified in the score of *Orfeo*. 38 instruments are listed at the beginning of the score, and others are called for during the course of the opera, but far fewer instrumentalists are required than these crude numbers would seem to imply. Several of the instruments listed, for example, are different varieties of keyboard instrument used by a single continuo player; and the two *violini piccoli alla francese*

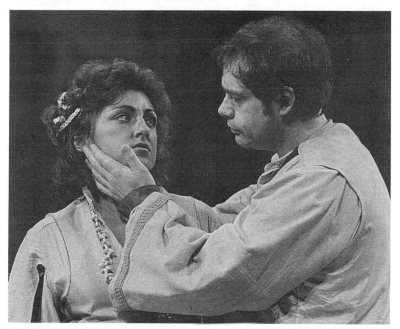

Patricia O'Neill and Anthony Rolfe Johnson (Eurydice and Orfeo) at ENO in 1981 (photo: Reg Wilson)

('French-style small violins') which are required for the ritornellos of Orpheus's three arias [8, 14 and 16] would probably have been played by two members of the main string group.[1] The court could also supply from its own resources engineers to construct staging and supervise lighting and scene changes during the performance, artists to paint the scenes, and a dancing master to direct the choreography. And the Gonzagas further maintained a group of highly trained solo singers who regularly performed songs and ensemble madrigals at court, as well as participating in larger-scale theatrical entertainments. According to one contemporary commentator, Vincenzo Giustiniani, by the end of the sixteenth century Mantuan singers were already cultivating an expressive, almost theatrical manner of performance even for songs and madrigals:

> they moderated or increased their voices, loud or soft, heavy or light, according to the demands of the piece they were singing; now slow, breaking off sometimes with a gentle sigh, now singing long passages legato or detached [...] They accompanied the music and the sentiment with appropriate facial expressions, glances and gestures, with no awkward movements of the mouth or hands or body which might not express the feeling of the song.[2]

The effect which this manner of performance had on Monteverdi's approach to madrigal writing can be detected as early as 1592 in the dramatic five-part setting of Armida's lament 'Vattene pur, crudel' which he included in his third book of madrigals; and the fourth and fifth books of madrigals (1603 and 1605 respectively) contain a number of settings of emotionally-charged texts whose declamatory settings and bold musical imagery were intended to be understood readily and appreciated by an audience. Although Monteverdi had not attempted an opera before 1607, therefore, he already had at his disposal a musical vocabulary which was easily transferred to the new medium, and singers not only capable of interpreting it, but also accustomed to working together.

Nevertheless, Francesco Gonzaga felt that the resources available to him at Mantua were inadequate, at least as far as singers were concerned, and on January 5, 1607, he wrote to Ferdinando, requesting the loan of a singer in the service of the Grand Duke of Tuscany. His letter also gave him the opportunity to announce his project to his brother:

> I have decided to have a play in music performed at carnival this year, but as we have very few sopranos here, and those few not good, I should be grateful if Your Excellency would be kind enough to tell me if those castrati I heard when I was in Tuscany are still there. I mean the ones in the Grand Duke's service, whom I so much enjoyed hearing during my visit. My intention is to borrow one of them [. . .] for a fortnight at most.[3]

The singer whom Ferdinando chose for his brother was the young castrato Giovanni Gualberto Magli, a pupil of Giulio Caccini. Magli was despatched to Mantua, but did not arrive there until February 15, only nine days before the first performance. The consternation that this caused was compounded by the fact that he had by then only been able to commit the Prologue to memory, the other (unspecified) part that he was to sing having proved too difficult; moreover, he was now required in addition to learn the part of Proserpine, since the singer who was to have taken this role was no longer able to do so. Fortunately, once installed at Mantua, Magli learned quickly, so that on February 23 Francesco was able to write to Ferdinando telling him that the young singer

> has done very well in the short time he has been here. Not only has he thoroughly learned the whole of his part, he delivers it with much grace and a most pleasing effect; I am delighted with him.

The letters from Francesco to Ferdinando, together with a small quantity of other surviving documentary evidence relating to the opera, give us important information about *Orfeo*. Perhaps the most surprising, given the importance of female singers at the courts of northern Italy during the late sixteenth century, is that four of the principal soprano roles were sung by castrati — the Prologue (Music), Proserpine and one other unspecified role by Magli, and the role of Euridice by a 'little priest'. The only other identifiable singer in the opera was the tenor Francesco Rasi, who also attained fame in his own right as a composer and poet, and who seems to have sung the title role. The surviving evidence confirms that *Orfeo* was the first opera performed at Mantua, but also suggests that it was not considered the main event of carnival 1607. A letter dated February 23 from a court official, Carlo Magno, reveals that a play had been performed the day before 'in the usual theatre and with all the customary splendour', that *Orfeo* was to be performed in an (apparently) smaller room in the apartments of Margherita Gonzaga, widow of the Duke of Ferrara, and that it was not only members of the Accademia degli Invaghiti who attended the performance:

> it should be most unusual, as all the actors are to sing their parts; it is said on all sides that it will be a great success. No doubt I shall be driven to attend out of sheer curiosity, unless I am prevented from getting in by lack of space . . .

The performance was, indeed, a success. Duke Vincenzo Gonzaga had shown considerable interest in the opera even during rehearsal. He ordered a further performance on March 1 and had in mind a third performance, perhaps for a projected visit of the Duke of Savoy, Francesco's prospective father-in-law. In the event, this third performance seems not to have taken place.

Francesco's letter of February 23 also reveals that the text of the opera was printed 'so that everyone in the audience can have a copy to follow while the performance is in progress'. Two printings of the text, presumably corresponding to the performances of February 24 and March 1, do survive, and present an intriguing problem, since they contain a different ending for the opera from that transmitted by the published score and thus heard in all subsequent performances of *Orfeo*. In the librettos, Striggio provided a conclusion approximating to that found in the main Latin sources for the story of Orpheus: Ovid's *Metamorphoses* (Books 10 and 11) and Virgil's *Georgics* (Book 4). In these sources Orpheus, having lost Eurydice for a second time, renounces the company of women and is torn limb from limb by the Bacchantes, whose advances he had spurned. In the 1607 librettos, after Orpheus has lamented the second loss of Eurydice he withdraws from the stage, giving way to a chorus of Bacchantes who vow vengeance upon him before concluding the opera with a finale of praise to Bacchus. For the published score, however, an ending based on a different Latin source, the *Astronomia* of Hyginus, was substituted. In this, Orpheus's father, Apollo, descends to bring comfort to his son and transports him to the heavens, from which he can look upon the 'fair semblance [of Eurydice] in the sun and stars'. Various hypotheses have been advanced for the difference in the endings of librettos and score. It has been suggested that the ending found in the score was the version first invented by Striggio and Monteverdi, but that this had to be abandoned when it became known that the opera was to be played in a room too small to accommodate the machinery for the ascent of Apollo and Orpheus to the heavens. On the whole, it seems more likely that the Bacchanalian finale was the original version. This being the case, opinions differ as to whether the more spectacular, but more perfunctory, ending was written in anticipation of the projected performance for the Duke of Savoy, or whether the original version was thought by Monteverdi or others to be too nearly tragic to provide a suitable ending for an opera.

To Striggio and Monteverdi the story of Orpheus, son of the muse Calliope and Apollo, god of music, a man imbued with human weaknesses, but a singer of supernatural powers, must have seemed a particularly apt choice for a play that was to be sung throughout. And it meant, too, that they were able to look to Florence, the birthplace of opera, for a model for their work: the published score of *Euridice* by Peri and Rinuccini. Indeed, they may have been encouraged by Francesco Gonzaga to choose the same subject in the spirit of rivalry which so often informed the cultural politics of Italian courts. Since Striggio was not writing for a court celebration he did not feel constrained, as Rinuccini had, to alter the story so that Orpheus and Eurydice were happily reunited at its end; nevertheless, as we have seen, the endings provided for both the 1607 (libretto) and the 1609 (score) versions of *Orfeo* are celebratory rather than violent in tone. He did, however, follow Rinuccini in shaping his libretto into a prologue and five acts, ending each act with a chorus. Within this division he adopted the procedure of elaborating one event of the story in each act: in Act One we are introduced to Orpheus and Eurydice on their wedding day; in Act Two Eurydice's death is announced and Orpheus resolves to descend to Hades to rescue her; in Act Three Orpheus overcomes Charon, boatman of the river Styx, and enters Pluto's domain; in Act Four Eurydice is released from the underworld, but Orpheus loses her for a second time through looking back upon her; and in Act Five, before the finale, we see Orpheus lamenting this second, irrevocable, loss.

The five-act shape and use of chorus are, of course, related to the structures of classical drama, though it is unlikely that either Rinuccini or Striggio laboured under the illusion that they were recreating Ancient Greek tragedy. Their relationship to classical drama was, in fact, mediated through a more recent Italian dramatic tradition — the pastoral tragicomedy, as represented in *Il Pastor fido* (The Faithful Shepherd) of Giovanni Battista Guarini, written in the early 1580s, which together with Guarini's theoretical writings on the subject of tragicomedy, formed the basis of much academic debate in late Renaissance circles. The play was performed at Mantua in 1598. The small group of unnamed nymphs and shepherds in Acts One and Two of *Orfeo* are close relatives of the Arcadian shepherds of Guarini's and other, similar, pastorals. Nevertheless, they, and the infernal spirits in Acts Three and Four, fulfil the choral functions which Renaissance theorists perceived in classical drama: that is, they participate in the action both as individuals and as an ensemble, reacting to the events of the drama at a personal level, but also standing aside, particularly at the ends of acts, to comment on the larger issues raised by the story. The choral ensembles at the ends of Acts Three and Four are particularly striking in this respect, and represent Alessandro Striggio's interpretation of the significance of the Orpheus myth: as Orpheus gains entrance to Hades, the chorus responds with a paean of Humanist praise for the achievements of man — 'Nulla impresa per huom si tenta in vano' ('Now sing praises to man and his endurance!') [15]; as Orpheus loses Eurydice for the second time, the chorus 'E la virtute un raggio' ('Virtue is beauty's radiance') [17] concludes with the moral that only the man who can control his passions is worthy of eternal glory.

The five-act structure provided the means by which Striggio shaped and articulated the action of *Orfeo*. It was not, however, intended as a prescription for performance with intervals between the acts. Renaissance theorists conceived the performance of classical drama as a single, unbroken action, and there are clear signals within the libretto and music of *Orfeo* which suggest that composer and poet conceived that their opera would be played without breaks from the raising of the curtain to the final chorus. The scene change from the Fields of Thrace to the Underworld between Acts Two and Three and back to Thrace between Acts Four and Five would have taken place before the eyes of the audience, perhaps using devices such as sliding flats and back-shutters. Moreover, it is only when one understands that the opera was conceived as a single action that it becomes clear that certain of the musical items in Act One are functional rather than decorative.

Acts One and Two are conceived as four paragraphs of action, prefaced by a 'toccata' or fanfare (the English equivalent is 'tucket') 'to be played three times before the curtain is raised' and by a prologue [2] sung by Music herself. Music introduces herself, and the theme of the opera, as the power which can soothe troubled hearts and inflame even the coldest minds; she sets the scene, too, by directing the audience's attention to the scenery set before them (there are several junctures in the libretto when the scenery is described — the only information which survives on the settings used for the 1607 performances). The stanzas of her song are introduced and punctuated by an instrumental ritornello [1] which Monteverdi brings back as an emblem of Music's power, at the end of Act Two and the beginning of Act Five, the two points at which Orpheus is most in need of her sustaining power.

The first main paragraph of Act One is a celebration of Orpheus and

Peter Knapp as Orfeo, with Rosalind Plowright as the Messenger, in Jonathan Miller's 1976 production for Kent Opera, designed by Bernard Culshaw, and conducted by Roger Norrington.

Eurydice's wedding day. A shepherd of the chorus tells us that this is the day on which Eurydice will put an end to Orpheus's 'amorous anguish' and urges his companions to sing in accents worthy of the great singer. They do so in a five-part choral invocation to Hymen, god of marriage [3], a chorus suggested no doubt by Ovid's description of Hymen's presence at the wedding, though 'the torch which he held kept sputtering and filled the eyes with smoke, nor would it catch fire for any brandishing':[4] an ill omen. A nymph calls on the Muses to tune their lyres to the chorus's song, and they do this in a five-part choral dance 'Lasciate i monti' ('Come from the mountains') [4], accompanied by a rich ensemble of strings, archlutes, harpsichords, double harp and sopranino recorder. Orpheus and Eurydice then pledge their love to each other, in a passage beginning with Orpheus's arioso 'Rosa del ciel' ('Rose of the heavens') [5], a reference to the sun — his father Apollo — and the first paragraph of the action is rounded off symmetrically by a shortened repeat of 'Lasciate i monti' and the invocation to Hymen.

The second paragraph is initiated by a shepherd, who states that the company should go to the temple to offer thanks to heaven. The shepherd's speech is clearly meant to be taken as a stage direction. In a continuous performance some reason has to be found for Eurydice to leave the stage so that her death can be reported in Act Two. This speech provides that reason, and Orpheus, Eurydice and some at least of their companions depart to the sound of a processional ritornello [6]. They leave on stage an ensemble who sing the first eight lines of the act-end chorus as a sequence of duet-trio-duet, beginning 'Alcun non sia che disperato in preda' ('Let none despair') [7], punctuated by the 'processional' ritornello, which is intended to suggest the passing of time while the wedding is being celebrated at the temple.

The final chorus of Act One as printed in the original librettos contained a total of 27 lines. Monteverdi did not set them all, but he allocated the next four to an ensemble of five voices, changing what was a reflective first line — 'Orfeo di cui pur dianzi' (*lit.* 'Orpheus, for whom not long ago sighs were food and tears drink') — into the active 'Ecco Orfeo, cui pur dianzi' ('Behold Orpheus, for whom . . .'), suggesting that Orpheus and his companions re-enter at this point. The change of tonality, and thus of dramatic direction, at the beginning of this section seems to confirm that this is, indeed, the beginning of the third paragraph of the action, which then runs smoothly into the instrumental introduction to Orpheus's words 'Ecco pur ch'a voi ritorno' (*lit.* 'Behold, indeed, I return to you'), words which form the nominal beginning of Act Two. Such reworking of the text, which blurs the division between the acts and brings Orpheus back on to the stage for a four-line chorus, would have been inconceivable if a break had been intended between the acts.

The third paragraph continues in a mood of rejoicing, though at a more personal level than the public celebrations with which Act One began. In six stanzas set to three different melodies and punctuated by the strings, recorders, lutes and harpsichords which characterize the accompaniments to the music of the pastoral scenes, Orpheus's companions express their pleasure in the countryside and call on him to sing to them. This he does in the aria 'Vi ricorda o bosch'ombrosi ('Shady woods, do you remember') [8] which forms the climax of the third paragraph of the action.

The final paragraph begins as if extending the third, with a shepherd urging Orpheus to continue his singing. In fact, we have reached the moment of *peripeteia*, the point at which a sudden reversal of fortune precipitates tragedy. The messenger enters [9], bearing the news of Eurydice's death. At first she refuses to give her news directly, but as realization gradually dawns upon Orpheus he finally persuades her to utter the fatal words 'La tua diletta sposa è morta' ('Your sweet Eurydice has perished'), at which he can only utter the word 'alas' before falling silent as the messenger proceeds to paint an emotional picture of the events surrounding the fatal accident. Only after the shepherds have reacted to the narrative, by taking up and echoing the messenger's initial phrase [9], does Orpheus rouse himself. In a brief lament [10] he conveys numbed disbelief in the finality of death before resolving to follow Eurydice to the Underworld. The messenger is left to express her self-disgust and the chorus to mourn [11] at the end of a scene which, for its sheer power, has caught the attention of commentators ever since the opera was first revived at the beginning of this century. Music's ritornello [1] is heard once more before the scene changes and the first of the Underworld *sinfonias* is heard, scored for the wind instruments traditionally associated with Underworld scenes in sixteenth-century *intermedi*.

The Underworld acts (Three and Four) presented Striggio with a potential problem. Both Ovid and Virgil mention Orpheus's journey to Pluto's kingdom, and Virgil, indeed, provided a vivid description of the dismal scene which confronted him, a description which Striggio took over into the lines which Speranza (Hope) utters at the beginning of Act Three. Neither author, however, mentions any obstacles which Orpheus had to overcome and which would have tested his powers as a singer. The vision of 'the demon Charon, with eyes of burning coal' whom Orpheus encounters in Act Three is, in fact, taken from Dante's account of his approach to the Inferno. The audience's attention is drawn to this by the allegorical figure of Hope, who abandons Orpheus at the gate to Pluto's kingdom, pointing to the words inscribed on it: 'Lasciate ogni speranza voi ch'entrate' ('All hope abandon, ye who enter'). This evocation of Dante served the dual function of explaining Charon's presence and evoking for a seventeenth-century Italian audience a vision of hell with Christian, as well as classical, resonances.

Orpheus sings the great central aria of the opera, 'Possente spirto' ('O mighty spirit') [14], in an attempt to impress Charon, and as a great singer he at first dresses his song in the virtuoso ornamented lines which were the early-seventeenth-century professional singer's stock-in-trade. Charon, though pleased by Orpheus's singing, still refuses to ferry him across the Styx, provoking Orpheus to a response in which he abandons the arts of the singer for a powerful direct appeal, but still to no avail. Frustrated, he tries the power of his lyre, represented by a sinfonia [13] which was also used as the introduction to 'Possente spirto'. The playing lulls Charon to sleep, allowing Orpheus to steal his boat and cross the Styx.

Although Orpheus's aria failed to move Charon, it has also been heard by Proserpine, and at the beginning of Act Four she intercedes with Pluto and persuades him to release Eurydice. This he agrees to do on condition that Orpheus does not look back at her as he leads her from the Underworld. Orpheus is now seen leading Eurydice, and singing an aria of praise to the power of his lyre [16]. After three stanzas, however, doubts assail him. How can he be sure that Eurydice is following him? Is it simply envy that makes Pluto forbid him to look at her? Why should he hesitate to turn, for what Pluto forbids Cupid demands? After each of these questions he pauses to listen, and on the last occasion there is a great noise offstage. Imagining that the furies are carrying off Eurydice, Orpheus turns, and for a few moments looks upon her before the vision is abruptly cut off and a spirit tells him that he has broken the law and is unworthy of grace. Eurydice is heard lamenting his losing her 'for too much love' before she is ordered back to the realms of the dead. Orpheus is drawn back to the upper world as the chorus reflect on his lack of self-control [17]. The Underworld sinfonia which began Act Three is heard again, and the scene changes back to the fields of Thrace to the sound of Music's ritornello [1]. In Act Five, Orpheus laments at length the second loss of Eurydice [18] until he is rescued from his self-pity by Apollo, with whom he ascends to the heavens [19], leaving the chorus to conclude the opera with a rather perfunctory ensemble [20] and a *Moresca*, a 'Moorish' dance which may be a leftover from the original Bacchic finale.

The musical fabric of *Orfeo* is a mixture of traditional and innovatory elements. Its rich instrumentation, with groups of 'pastoral' and 'underworld' instruments, was derived from the sixteenth-century *intermedio* tradition, as was its choral ensemble writing. The most striking new element was, of course, the one which made it possible to set a whole play to music: continuo-accompanied recitative. 'Recitative' is a difficult term, encrusted as it is by associations stemming from music of later periods, and inadequate as a description of the variety of styles that it comprehended in the early seventeenth century. In this respect, 'recitative' is best thought of as a technique rather than a style: a technique in which a solo voice was accompanied not by a complement of composed and fully written out instrumental parts, but by a simple, unobtrusive, chordal accompaniment improvised above a single bass line by one or more instruments (Monteverdi's favourite combination of continuo instruments was organ and chitarrone, a combination which he specifies, for example, for 'Possente spirto' [14]). One of the most important features of the new technique was that it allowed composers to write vocal lines which were free from the necessity to 'dance to the rhythm of the bass line'. That is, the voice could be allotted a number of notes against a sustained bass, freeing the singer to declaim the text in a rhetorical manner.

The new manner of singing was pioneered at Florence around the turn of the sixteenth century by Giulio Caccini, a professional singer, and announced in *Le nuove musiche*, the volume of solo madrigals and airs that he published in 1602. But it was in the hands of Jacopo Peri, Caccini's contemporary and rival at the Florentine court, that the new style acquired the expressive characteristics which interested Monteverdi. In the recitative style that Peri developed for his setting of *Euridice*, Peri allowed the vocal line not only to move more quickly than the bass, but also to be dissonant with it, a technique which allowed him more flexibility to match the stress patterns of the text and greater power to convey extreme emotion. In the hands of Peri and Monteverdi, 'recitative' became a medium capable of conveying a whole gamut of emotions. One of the most telling illustrations of this is the moment of the messenger's entrance in Act Two of *Orfeo*, where Monteverdi juxtaposes the tuneful style of the shepherd's 'Segui pur' with the declamatory style of the messenger's 'Ahi caso acerbo' ('Aï! Bitter Fortune!') [9]; the harsh dissonance of voice against bass for the syllable 'cer-' of 'acerbo' not only produces the correct stress pattern, but also conveys the notion of the 'bitterness' of fate.

The concept of 'recitative' also embraces that of 'aria' in early opera, for 'aria' here means not only 'tunefulness', but also, specifically, the setting of a strophic text. Some of the arias of *Orfeo* are, indeed, tuneful: 'Vi ricorda o bosch'ombrosi in Act Two [8] and 'Qual honor' in Act Four [16], for example. Other arias are not so easily recognisable as such. Music's prologue [2] and 'Possente spirto' [14] are both 'arias' in that they are settings of strophic texts, and both are set as variations over a bass which remains constant from stanza to stanza; but their style is more declamatory than tuneful in nature.

Technical explanation of the musical styles of *Orfeo* is, in a sense, unnecessary. Given a sympathetic performance, the power of Monteverdi's musical language speaks directly across the centuries without the need for apologists. It is for this reason that his first opera has enjoyed nearly a century of revivals and it also explains why, though the courtly society for which it was written has long since disappeared, *Orfeo* retains a place in the repertory.

1. See Glover, 'Solving the Musical Problems', *Claudio Monteverdi: 'Orfeo'*, ed. Whenham (Cambridge, 1986), 138-55.

2. *Discorso sopra la musica de' suoi tempi* (c. 1628). Translation by Iain Fenlon, *Music and Patronage in Sixteenth-Century Mantua* (Cambridge 1980-2), i. 126-7.

3. See Fenlon, 'The Mantuan "Orfeo"', *Orfeo*, ed. Whenham supra, 1-19 and Appendix 1. The translations of this letter, and the two excerpts following, are by Steven Botterill.

4. *Metamorphoses* (Loeb Classical Library), trans. Miller (London, 1916), ii. 65.

Music Examples

[1] RITORNELLO

[2] PROLOGUE: MUSIC

Dal mio __ Per-mes - so a - ma - to   a voi ne ve - gno
From my __ be-lo-ved Per-mes - sus   I come to greet you,

[3] CHORUS

Vie - ni I - me - neo, _____ deh, vie - ni,
Come Hy - men, come _____ with bles - sing,

[4] CHORUS

La - scia - te i mon - ti, la - scia - te i fon - - ti
Come from the moun-tains and from the foun - - tains

La - - scia - te i mon - ti, la - scia - te i
Come from the moun - tains and from the

[5] ORFEO

Ro - sa del ciel, vi - - ta del mon - do,
Rose of the heav'ns, light ____ of the li - ving,

29

[6] RITORNELLO

[7] CHORUS

Al - cun non sia che __ di - spe - ra - to in pre - da Si do - ni al duol
Let none des - pair though __ tides of grief in - va - ded his in - most soul,

[8] ORFEO

Vi ri - cor - da o bo - sch'om - bro - si, Vi ri - cor - da o bo - sch'om - bro - si
Sha - dy woods, do you re - mem - ber, sha - dy woods, do you re - mem - ber

[9] MESSENGER

Ahi ____ ca - so a - cer - bo! ahi fa - t'em - pio e cru - de - le!
Aï! ____ Bit - ter for - tune! Aï! Fate cal - lous and cru - el!

[10] ORFEO

Tu __ se' mor - ta, se' mor - ta mia vi - ta
You __ have left __ me, have left me, my dear - est

[11] CHORUS: TWO SHEPHERDS

Chi _____ ne con-so-la ahi las-si? O pur chi ne con-ce — de
Who _____ shall re-store our los-ses, or where may we dis-co — ver

[12] CHARON

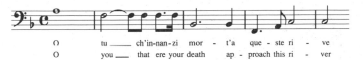

O tu _____ ch'in-nan-zi mor — t'a que-ste ri — ve
O you _____ that ere your death ap-proach this ri — ver

[13] SINFONIA

[14] ORFEO

Pos — sen — te spir — — — to _____
O migh — ty spi — — — rit, _____

[15] CHORUS OF SPIRITS

Nul — — la im-pre — sa per huom
Now _____ sing prai — ses to man

Nul — la im-pre — — sa per huom
Nul — — la im-pre — sa per huom _____

Nul — — la im — pre — — sa per huom
Now sing prai — — ses to man

[16] ORFEO

Qual ho-nor _____ di te sia de-gno Mia ce-tra on-ni-po — ten-te,
O my lyre, _____ who can be wor-thy to ce-le-brate your prai — ses?

31

[17] CHORUS OF SPIRITS

E, la vir - tu - te un rag - - - gio
Vir - tue is beau - ty's ra - - - diance,

E la vir - tu - [te]
Vir - tue is beau - [ty]

E la vir - tu - te un rag - gio
Vir - tue is beau - ty's ra - diance,

[18] ORFEO

Ques - sti i cam - pi di Trac - cia, e ques-t'è il lo - co
Once more, green fields of my coun - try, my steps have sought you.

[19] APOLLO AND ORFEO

Sa - liam, _____ sa - liam _____
We rise, _____ we rise _____

— can - tan - - - - [do]
— re - joi - - - - [cing]

[20] CHORUS

Van - ne Or - feo fe - li - ce a pie - no
Rise Or - feo our no - ble he - ro,

Van - ne Or - feo fe - li - ce a pie - no

Van - ne Or - feo fe - li - ce a pie - no
Rise Or - feo our no - ble he - ro,

32

Orfeo

Favola in Musica
A Legend in Music

Music by Claudio Monteverdi
Libretto by Alessandro Striggio the Younger
English singing version by Anne Ridler

Orfeo was first performed at the court of Vincenzo Gonzaga I in Mantua at the end of Carnival on February 24, 1607. The first performance in modern times was a concert on February 25, 1904, given by the Schola Cantorum in Paris, of a version arranged by Vincent d'Indy and this was first staged at the Théâtre Réjane, Paris, on May 2, 1911. This was the version heard at its first British performance, at the Institut Français (in concert) in 1924, and a stage version was given by the Oxford University Opera Club on December 7, 1925. The first North American performance was also in concert, at the Met on April 14, 1912; the first staging was at Smith College, Northampton on May 11, 1929, in an edition by Malipiero.

This translation was commissioned and first performed by Jane Glover and the Oxford University Opera Club in 1975, for the 50th anniversary of their pioneer performance.

Striggio's libretto was published twice in 1607, presumably to correspond with the two performances on February 24 and March 1, and the score was printed in 1609 after a revival in Mantua; it was reprinted in 1615 in Venice. The Italian text follows the librettos for punctuation, lay-out, accents and spelling, varying only where the words set to music in the score published in 1609 are different. Various inconsistencies and mistakes have been corrected. At the end of each act there are passages which do not appear in the 1609 score, and at the end of the fifth act there is the major point of divergence between the sources, the scene in which Orpheus is torn to pieces by the Bacchantes, for which no music by Monteverdi survives. These have been specially translated for this Opera Guide by Anne Ridler, and obviously do not form part of her performing version.

The scanty stage directions follow those in the librettos. By reference to the text we can say that Acts One, Two and Five take place in the Fields of Thrace, Acts Three and Four in the Underworld.

The numbers in square brackets refer to the musical examples. The musical sections ('toccata', 'ritornello', 'balletto', 'sinfonia') are interpolated from the score, from which it is evident that the drama played continuously (without intervals) and music joined the acts.

Music	La Musica	*soprano*
Orfeo	Orfeo	*tenor*
Euridice	Euridice	*soprano*
Messenger	Messagiera	*mezzo-soprano*
Hope	Speranza	*soprano*
Charon	Caronte	*bass*
Proserpina	Proserpina	*soprano*
Pluto	Plutone	*bass*
Echo	Eco	*soprano*
Apollo	Apollo	*counter-tenor*
Chorus of Nymphs and Shepherds, Spirits		*sopranos, mezzo-sopranos, tenors, baritones, basses*

Where the soloists from the chorus sing is not always identified in the librettos, and can then only be distinguished from the number of voices required in the score and the clef. Thus, following the librettos, we have not specified 'First' or 'Second' Shepherd, and so on, since the arrangements may differ according to each performance.

Philippe Huttenlocher in the title role of 'Orfeo' in Jean-Pierre Ponnelle's 1979 production in Zurich, conducted by Nikolaus Harnoncourt, designed by Pet Halmen (photo: Susan Schimert-Ramme)

Prologue

Ritornello [1]

MUSIC

From my beloved Permessus I come to greet you,
heroes renowned, born of the blood of monarchs,
whose deeds many a singer has celebrated,
yet missed the truth, too high for mortal vision.

[2] Dal mio Permesso amato à voi ne vegno
Incliti Eroi*, sangue gentil de Regi,
Di cui narra la fama eccelsi pregi,
Nè giunge al ver perch'è tropp'alto il segno.

Ritornello

Music am I, who with sweet accents
can charm and comfort the most despairing spirit:
now with noble anger's fire, and now with rage of desire
the coldest heart inflaming.

Io la Musica son ch'à i dolci accenti
Sò far tranquillo ogni turbato core,
Et hor di nobil ira, et hor d'amore
Poss' infiammar le più gelate menti.

Ritornello

I with my lyre of gold and with my singing
sometimes beguile men's mortal senses,
and by these charms I awaken desire
for the heavenly lyre's immortal music.

Io sù cetera d'or cantando soglio
Mortal orecchio lusingar talhora,
E in questa guisa a l'armonia sonora
De la lira del Ciel più l'alme invoglio.

Ritornello

Now I'll speak of Orfeo and his sad fortunes —
Orfeo, whose singing could draw wild beasts to follow,
great Pluto at his prayer subdued the demons:
matchless in verse and music, noble Orfeo.

Quinci à dirvi d'Orfeo desio mi sprona
D'Orfeo che trasse al suo cantar le fere,
E servo fè l'Inferno à sue preghiere
Gloria immortal di Pindo e d'Elicona.

Ritornello

So while my music changes, now gay now mournful, all be silent.
Let no bird among the branches be heard,
nor let the waves sound from the river,
and let the breezes attentive pause to hear me.

Hor mentre i canti alterno hor lieti, hor mesti
Non si mova augellin fra queste piante,
Ne s'oda in queste rive onda sonante,
Et ogni Auretta in suo camin s'arresti.

---

*i.e. the Gonzagas present at the performance.

35

Act One

SHEPHERD

On this most happy day when smiling Fortune
turns into joy the bitter pangs and sighing
of our sublime Orfeo, now sing, companions;
and with your sweetest music
offer here to Orfeo your celebrations.

In questo lieto e fortunato giorno
Ch'à posto fine à gl'amorosi affanni
Del nostro Semideo cantiam Pastori

In sì soavi accenti
Che sian degni d'Orfeo nostri concenti.

For this day he embraces
one who scorned his caresses —
his adored Euridice.
On her breast now her faithful Orfeo
may rest most welcome,
who once rejected in pain and sorrow
sighed, and with tears lamented.

Oggi fatta'è pietosa
L'alma già sì sdegnosa
De la bell' Euridice,
Oggi fatto è felice

Orfeo nel sen di lei, per cui già tanto
Per queste selve ha sospirato, e pianto.

So — on this most happy day when smiling Fortune
turns into joy the bitter pangs and sighing
of our sublime Orfeo, now sing, companions;
and with your sweetest music
offer here to Orfeo your celebrations.

Dunque in sì lieto e fortunato giorno

Ch'à posto fine à gl'amorosi affanni,
Del nostro Semideo cantiam Pastori

In sì soavi accenti
Che sian degni d'Orfeo nostri concenti.

CHORUS

Come Hymen, come with blessing,
be like a sun arising
and on these lovers shining,
that everlasting joy may smile serenely.
Now all their sorrows banish
even as before the dawn dark night must vanish.

[3] Vieni Imeneo, deh, vieni,
E la tua face ardente
Sia quasi un Sol nascente
Ch'apporti à questi amanti i dì sereni
E lunge homai disgombre
De gl'affanni e del duol gl'orrori e l'ombre.

NYMPH

Muses in lofty Parnassus, beloved of Heaven,
as you delight to comfort every wounded heart,
sound your melodious lyres:
chase cloudy night away and every shadow;
and while to Hymen we pray for our Orfeo
that his bright torch may bless him,
Oh let your heavenly singing
enrich our music, with truest sounds according.

Muse honor di Parnaso, amor del Cielo

Gentil conforto à sconsolato core

Vostre cetre sonore
Squarcino d'ogni nub' il fosco velo:
E mentre oggi propizio al nostro Orfeo

Invochiam Imeneo
Sù ben temprate corde
Sià il vostro canto al nostro suon concorde.

Balletto:

CHORUS

Come from the mountains
and from the fountains
nymphs in the dance delighting:
here each one traces
familiar mazes,
all in the chain uniting.

[4] Lasciate i monti
Lasciate i fonti
Ninfe vezzose e liete,
E in questi prati
A i balli usati
Vago il bel piè rendete.

The sun espying
these myriads flying

Quì miri il Sole
Vostre carole

delays to see this vision;	Più vaghe assai di quelle,
the Sisters Seven	Ond'à la Luna
stand still in heaven	La notte bruna
to watch our bright divisions.	Danzano in Ciel le stelle.

Ritornello

Like April showers	Poi di bei fiori
a thousand flowers	Per voi s'honori
bestrew these happy lovers,	Di questi amanti il crine,
the painful fires	C'hor de i martiri
of their desires	De i lor desiri
transformed in joy forever.	Godon beati al fine.

Ritornello

SHEPHERD

O noble singer who, with your lamenting,	Ma tu gentil cantor s'à' tuoi lamenti
made sympathetic tears flow from the valleys,	Già festi lagrimar queste campagne,
now let your lyre, its famous notes resounding,	Perc'hor al suon de la famosa cetra
make the valleys re-echo with your gladness	Non fai teco gioir le valli e i poggi?
and with the joy Love brought you;	Sia testimon del core
make them glad with the songs that Love has taught you.	Qualche lieta canzon che detti Amore.

ORFEO

Rose of the heavens, light of the living,	[5] Rosa del Ciel, vita del mondo, e degna
worthy son of the ruler who holds our world in harness!	Prole di lui che l'Universo affrena
Sun, O you on your daily course discerning	Sol che'l tutto circondi e'l tutto miri,
this globe in ceaseless turning,	Da gli stellanti giri
tell me, did ever you in all your journeys	Dimmi vedestù mai
see a happier lover?	Di me più lieto e fortunato amante?
How blessed was the moment	Fu ben felice il giorno
my love when first I saw you!	Mio ben che pria ti vidi,
More blessed still the moment	E più felice l'hora
when for you I was sighing.	Che per te sospirai.
For when you heard my sighs you sighed in pity.	Poich'al mio sospirar tù sospirasti:
Best of all was the moment	Felicissimo il punto
when you gave me your promise,	Che la candida mano
joining our hands together in faith eternal.	Pegno di pura fede à me porgesti,
Had I as many hearts	Se tanti Cori havessi
as the starry eyes of heaven,	Quant'occh' hà il Ciel eterno, e quante chiome
outnumbering even the leaves upon the wooded hills in Maytime,	Han questi colli ameni il verde maggio
every heart would be full and overflowing	Tutti colmi sarieno e traboccanti
because my dear lady is mine for ever.	Di quel piacer ch'oggi mi fà contento.

EURIDICE

I cannot tell, Orfeo,	Io non dirò qual sia
the joy that fills my heart at your rejoicing,	Nel tuo gioir Orfeo la gioia mia,
since my heart's mine no longer —	Che non hò meco il core,
for you it left me, and both by Love were stolen.	Ma teco stassi in compagnia d'Amore;
Go and enquire then of Love and he will tell you	Chiedilo dunque à lui s'intender brami
how my heart rejoices, how much I love you.	Quanto lieta gioisca, e quanto t'ami.

Come from the mountains
and from the fountains,
nymphs in the dance delighting:
here each one traces
familiar mazes,
all in the chain uniting.

[4] Lasciate i monti
Lasciate i fonti
Ninfe vezzose e liete,
E in questi prati
A i balli usati
Vago il bel piè rendete,

The sun espying
these myriads flying
delays to see this vision;
the Sisters Seven
stand still in heaven
to watch our bright divisions.

Quì miri il Sole
Vostre carole
Più vaghe assai di quelle,
Ond'à la Luna.
La notte bruna
Danzano in Ciel le stelle.

Ritornello

Come Hymen come with blessing
be like a sun arising
and on these lovers shining
that everlasting joy may smile serenely.
Now all their sorrows vanish
even as before the dawn dark night must
vanish.

[3] Vieni Imeneo, deh vieni,
E la tua face ardente
Sia quasi un Sol nascente
Ch'apporti à questi amanti i dì sereni.
E lunge homai disgombre
De gl'affanni e del duol gl'orrori e l'ombre.

Darkness turned into day and grief to gladness,

Ma s'il nostro gioir dal Ciel deriva

'tis heaven alone that can achieve such wonders,

Come dal Ciel ciò che quà giù n'incontra,

so to heaven we must offer
our grateful sacrifices.

Giusto è ben che devoti
Gli offriam incensi e voti.

To the temple then go with hymns and praises

Dunque al tempio ciascun rivolga i passi

offered to him who in his hand upholds us,

A pregar lui ne la cui destra è il Mondo.

and pray that he may evermore preserve us.

Che lungamente il nostro ben conservi.

Ritornello [6]

Let none despair
though tides of grief invaded his inmost soul,

[7] Alcun non sia che disperato in preda

though blackest doubts assailed him,
with such a force as should his life endanger.

Si doni al duol benche talhor n'assaglia
Possente si che nostra vita inforsa.

Ritornello [6]

＊

For though the tempest swells with grim foreboding,

Che poiche nembo rio gravido il seno

and brings the storm-clouds, shrouding the world in darkness,

D'atra tempesta inorridito hà il Mondo

dispersed they leave the sun to shine more brightly.

Dispiega il Sol più chiaro i rai lucenti.

Ritornello [6]

＊

When frost has pierced the bones of naked winter,

E dopo l'aspro gel del verno ignudo

festive with flowers the meadows welcome springtime.

Veste di fior la Primavera i campi.

---

* This chorus is broken up in the score into verses for two voices, three voices, and two voices.

See him come, see him come, brave Orfeo!
Who for bread tasted sighs, whose drink was weeping.
Now can he want for nothing: he thirsts no more whose wine is love unceasing.

But why so much rejoicing †
after such suffering? Eternal Powers,
mortal eye cannot see into your supreme works
for a dazzling mist obscures them.
However, if it is lawful to lay bare inward thought
in order to change it where error is revealed,
we shall say, that in this way Heaven
while it approves the vows of Orpheus
wishes to make more certain of his virtue.
For to endure miseries is but a small proof of worth,
but a favourable turn of fortune's wheel
is apt to distract the soul from the true path.
Now, tried in the fire, it is more precious.
Worth that has been tested
thus enjoys a loftier honour.

Ecco Orfeo cui pur dianzi

Furon cibo i sospir bevanda il pianto,

Oggi felice è tanto
Che nulla è più che da bramar gli avanzi.

[Ma perche tal gioire
Dopo tanto martire? Eterni Numi
Vostr'opre eccelse occhio mortal non vede
Che splendente caligine le adombra:
Pur se lece spiegar pensiero interno

Sol per cangiarlo ove l'error si scopra.

Direm, ch'in questa guisa
Mentre i voti d'Orfeo seconda il Cielo,
Prova vuol far di sua virtù più certa,
Ch'il soffrir le miserie è picciol pregio,

Ma'l cortese girar di sorte amica
Suol dal dritto camin traviar l'alme.

Oro cosi per foco è più pregiato.
Combattuto valore
Godrà così di più sublime honore.]

---

† This final passage is not in the score, although it appears in the 1607 librettos.

Della Jones as the Messenger, with Anthony Rolfe Johnson as Orfeo, at ENO, 1981.

Act Two

ORFEO

Happy woods, I'm now returning
blest by her whose eyes are sunshine.
Now my night is changed to daytime
and my heart with love is burning.

Ritornello

Ecco pur ch'à voi ritorno
Care selve e piagge amate,
Da quel Sol fatte beate
Per cui sol mie nott' han giorno.

SHEPHERD

These beeches in a shady grove Orfeo,
    offer shelter
from fierce and burning arrows
that Phoebus darts from heaven.

Ritornello

Mira ch'à se n'alletta
L'ombra Orfeo de que' faggi,
Hor che'nfocati raggi
Febo da Ciel saetta.

The waters of the river
whisper while we are dreaming,
our voices at our waking
are mingled with its murmur.

Ritornello

Sù quel'herbosa sponda
Posianci, e in varij modi
Ciascun sua voce snodi
Al mormorio de l'onde.

TWO SHEPHERDS

In our enchanting meadows
the gods and their companions
who love the flowery regions
will haunt the woods and hollows.

Ritornello

In questo prato adorno
Ogni selvaggio Nume
Sovente hà per costume
Di far lieto soggiorno.

And Pan, the god of shepherds
by all his loves rejected,
ill fortune recollected,
here wanders singing sadly.

Ritornello

Qui Pan Dio de' Pastori
S'udì talhor dolente
Rimembrar dolcemente
Suoi sventurati amori.

Here wood-nymphs tread their mazes,
garlands they make with flowers,
for their close-woven bowers,
they come to gather roses.

Ritornello

Qui le Napee vezzose
(Schiera sempre fiorita)
Con le candide dita
Fur viste à coglier rose.

CHORUS

Then come with us Orfeo,
sing to your lyre a blessing,
by your clear notes inspiring
each hill and vale and meadow.

Ritornello

Dunque fà degno Orfeo
Del suon de la tua lira
Questi campi ove spira
Aura d'odor Sabeo.

ORFEO

Shady woods, do you remember
how you heard my long lamenting,
and your grief for my tormenting
turned your spring to cold December?

Ritornello

[8] Vi ricorda ò bosch' ombrosi
De' miei lungh' aspri tormenti
Quando i sassi ai miei lamenti
Rispondean fatti pietosi?

With your winds you sighed in pity,
and made echo to my mourning.
Fortune now her wheel is turning,
and you whisper joy to greet me.

Dite, allhor non vi sembrai
Più d'ogn' altro sconsolato?
Hor fortuna hà stil cangiato
Et hà volto in festa i guai.

Ritornello

Though my life was dark and mournful,	Vissi già mesto e dolente,
yet I bless those days of sadness,	Hor gioisco, e quegli affanni
for when sorrow turns to gladness	Che sofferti hò per tant'anni
by that change is Love more joyful.	Fan più caro il ben presente.

Ritornello

You alone, dear Euridice,	Sol per tè bella Euridice
as you caused my bitter torment,	Benedico il mio tormento,
are the cause of my contentment	Dopò'l duol viè più contento,
and the source of every sweetness.	Dopò'l mal viè più felice.

SHEPHERD

See now, oh see, Orfeo, how wood and meadow	Mira, deh mira Orfeo, che d'ogni intorno
smile for joy at your good fortune!	Ride il bosco e ride il prato,
Sound once more a lover's blessing	Seguì pur co'l plettr' aurato
with golden music make more bright the sunshine.	D'addolcir l'aria in si beato giorno.

MESSENGER

Aï! Bitter Fortune! Aï! Fate callous and cruel!	[9]	Ahi caso acerbo, ahi fat' empio e crudele,
Aï! Jealous constellations! Aï! Death and sorrow!		Ahi Stelle ingiuriose, ahi Ciel avaro.

SHEPHERD

What dreadful message brings you to disturb us?	Qual suon dolente il lieto dì perturba?

MESSENGER

Sorrow fills my whole being.	Lassa, dunque debb'io
While Orfeo with his golden lyre charms Heaven,	Mentre Orfeo con sue note il Ciel consola
I with my fearful tale must pierce his heart's core.	Con le parole mie passargli il core?

SHEPHERD

This is Silvia, most gentle,	Questa è Silvia gentile
most precious of companions	Dolcissima compagna
to our dear Euridice. Oh with what torment she is shaken!	De la bell' Euridice: ò quanto è in vista
Why such sorrow? O mighty Heaven,	Dolorosa: hor che fia? deh sommi Dei
do not turn from our fate, be still our guardian!	Non torcete da noi benigno il guardo.

MESSENGER

No more! Now all be silent.	Pastor lasciate il canto.
Every joy that you cherished in death has perished.	Ch'ogni nostr' allegrezza in doglia è volta.

ORFEO

Who has sent you? With what news? Nymph, tell me quickly!	Donde vieni? ove vai? Ninfa che porti?

MESSENGER

To you I come Orfeo,	A te ne vengo Orfeo
as the bearer most hateful	Messaggiera infelice
of tidings still more hateful, still more cruel,	Di caso più infelice e più funesto.
that your dear Euridice . . .	La tua bella Euridice . . .

ORFEO

O Gods, have mercy!	Ohime che odo?

That your sweet Euridice has perished.   La tua diletta sposa è morta.

Alas!   Ohime.

She in a flowery meadow	In un fiorito prato
with all her young companions	Con l'altre sue compagne
wandered to gather blossoms,	Giva cogliendo fiori
and weave them into garlands for her tresses —	Per farne una ghirlanda à le sue* chiome,
when suddenly a viper	Quand' angue insidioso
lurking among the grasses	Ch'era frà l'erbe ascoso
upreared its head and pierced her foot with poison.	Le punse un piè con velenoso dente,
And straightway the colour vanished from her cheeks and she fainted.	Ed ecco immantinente Scolorissi il bel viso e ne'suoi lumi
And in her eyes was quenched that radiance which robbed the sun of brightness.	Sparir que' lampi, ond'ella al Sol fea scorno.
At once, in terror and in wild confusion we crowded round her:	Allhor noi tutte sbigottite e meste Le fummo intorno richiamar tentando
and with water dashed on her temples we tried	Gli spirti in lei smarriti
to summon her fleeting spirit, with loving spells to hold her.	Con l'onda fresca e co'possenti carmi;
But all in vain. Ah! Useless!	Ma nulla valse, ahi lassa,
She, but lifting a moment her closing eyelids,	Ch'ella i languidi lumi alquanto aprendo,
cried out your name — Orfeo! Orfeo!	E tè chiamando Orfeo,
Then sighed deeply and sadly	Dopò un grave sospiro
and in my arms she died; and I was left there with my heart full of anguish, my soul in terror.	Spirò frà queste braccia, ed io rimasi Piena il cor di pietade e di spavento.

Aï! Bitter Fortune! Aï! Fate callous and cruel!	Ahi caso acerbo, ahi fato empio e crudele,
Aï! Jealous constellations! Aï! Death and sorrow!	Ahi stell' ingiuriose, ahi Ciel avaro.

At this heart-rending story,	A l'amara novella
the poor unhappy lover, like a statue	Rassembra l'infelice un muto sasso,
and struck dumb by his grief, no grief can utter.	Che per troppo dolor non può dolersi.

Aï! Pitiless the heart, and fierce as tiger,	Ahi ben havrebbe un cor di Tigre o d'Orsa
that would not weep to see your sad misfortune,	Chi non sentisse del tuo mal pietate,
torn from your only joy, wretched lover.	Privo d'ogni tuo ben misero amante.

---

* The 1609 score has 'sue chiome', but both 1607 librettos have 'tue chiome'. John Whenham writes: 'The difference is that the librettos' version suggests that Eurydice lingers behind after thanksgiving at the temple in order to gather flowers to garland Orpheus's hair ('tue chiome'); the score has her lingering to gather flowers for her own hair ('sue chiome'). The former seems dramatically more plausible, and I suspect that 'sue' in the score is an error.'

You have left me, my dearest, and I still living?

You — gone from me for ever?

Gone from me for ever, and no more, no more may I see you. Yet I remain here?

No! If my singing still has power to help me

I shall descend into the deep abysses, there with my songs to melt the king of shadows,

and draw you with me to see again the starlight.

Or if Fate will deny me such a blessing, I will stay with you, your life to share, in darkness.

Farewell, meadows. Farewell, Heavens — and sunlight. I leave you.

[10] Tu se' morta mia vita, ed io respiro?

Tu se' da me partita

Per mai più non tornare, ed io rimango?

Nò, che se i versi alcuna cosa ponno

N'andrò sicuro à' più profondi abissi,
E intenerito il cor del Rè de l'Ombre

Meco trarròtti à riveder le stelle:

O se ciò negheràmmi empio destino
Rimarrò teco in compagnia di morte,

A dio terra, à dio Cielo, e Sole à dio.

CHORUS

Aï! Bitter Fortune! Aï! Fate callous and cruel!

Aï! Jealous constellations! Aï! Death and sorrow!

Joys are not won securely, nor faith contracted surely — we taste and lose them: and whoso ascends the mountain finds that a fall must follow.

Ahi caso acerbo, ahi fato empio e crudele,

Ahi stelle ingiuriose, ahi Cielo avaro.

Non si fidi huom mortale
Di ben caduco e frale
Che tosto fugge, e spesso
A gran salita il precipizio è presso.

MESSENGER

But I whose tongue is guilty,
I who thrust with my dagger to the heart of Orfeo,

draining his life-blood —
I am hateful to all my dear companions, to myself I am hateful. Where shall I hide now?

Bird of the night-time, the sunlight never shall find me.

Hid in some lonely cavern,
in its deep gloom I'll spend my days of mourning.

Ma io ch'in questa lingua
Hò portato il coltello

C'hà svenata d'Orfeo l'anima amante,
Odiosa à i Pastori et à le Ninfe,
Odiosa à me stessa, ove m'ascondo?

Nottola infausta il Sole

Fuggirò sempre e in solitario speco
Menerò vita al mio dolor conforme.

Sinfonia

CHORUS

Who shall restore our losses,
or where may we discover some healing?

Or find a fountain
for our tears as they flow that may relieve us?

O day that brought disaster,
how happy was the dawn, how sad the evening.

This day as in a whirlwind
died the two brightest planets
of all our constellations —
Euridice and Orfeo —
she by poison has perished,
he by sorrow was stricken; alas, both lifeless.

[11] Chi ne consola ahi lassi?
O pur chi ne concede
Ne gl'occhi un vivo fonte
Da poter lagrimar come conviensi

In questo mesto giorno
Quanto più lieto già tant'hor più mesto?

Oggi turbo crudele
I due lumi maggiori
Di queste nostre selve
Euridice, et Orfeo,
L'una punta da l'angue,
L'altro dal duol trafitto, ahi lassi ha spenti;

Aï! Bitter Fortune! Aï! Fate callous and cruel!
Aï! Jealous constellations! Aï! Death and sorrow!

But where now — Ah, where now—
what shelter have you found Euridice
what dwelling for your body?
Where does your spirit wander
that on this day of sorrow
sighing departed and in its flower of youth died?
Now come, companions, seek her,
in pity to discover where her cold body's lying,
and with tender lamenting
to pay our tribute,
with tears of pity to Euridice.

Aï! Bitter Fortune! Aï! Fate callous and cruel!
Aï! Jealous constellations! Aï! Death and sorrow!

But what funeral pomp could be worthy   †
of Euridice?
Let the Graces in black robes carry the great bier,
and let the disconsolate Muses with loosened hair accompany it,
singing with mournful voices her precious exequies.
Let Heaven girdle itself with clouds
and weep dark rain above the sepulchre;

and when it has mourned, let it shed a faint light,
and let the doleful sun be a gloomy lamp
for such a noble tomb.

Aï! Bitter Fortune! Aï! Fate callous and cruel!
Aï! Jealous constellations! Aï! Death and sorrow!

Ritornello [1]

Ahi caso acerbo, ahi fato empio e crudele,
Ahi stelle ingiuriose, ahi Cielo avaro.

Ma dove, ah dove hor sono
De la misera Ninfa
Le belle e fredde membra,
Dove suo degno albergo
Quella bell'alma elesse
Ch'oggi è partita in su'l fiorir de'giorni?

Andiam Pastori andiamo
Pietosi à ritrovarle,

E di lagrime amare
Il dovuto tributo
Per noi si paghi almeno al corpo esangue.

Ahi caso acerbo, ahi fat' empio e crudele,
Ahi stell' ingiuriose, ahi Ciel avaro.

[Ma qual funebre pompa
Degna fia d'Euridice?
Portino il gran feretro
Le Grazie in veste nera,
E con lor chiome sparse
Le Muse sconsolate
L'accompagnin cantando
Con flebil voce i suoi passati pregi.
Di Nubi il Ciel si cinga
E con oscura pioggia
Pianga sopra il sepolcro:
E poich'egli havrà pianto
Languida luce spieghi,
E lampada funesta
Sia di sì nobil tomba il Sol dolente.

Ahi caso acerbo, ahi fato empio e crudele,
Ahi Stelle ingiuriose, ahi Cielo avaro.]

Here the scene changes.

---

† This final passage is not in the score, although it appears in the 1607 librettos.

Act Three

ORFEO

Hope, you are still my escort,	Scorto da te mio Nume
kind goddess, I know you as a sure friend	Speranza unico bene
in the afflictions of mortals.	De gl'afflitti mortali, homai son giunto
With Hope to guide me,	
I now approach these dark and cheerless regions,	A questi mesti e tenebrosi regni
where no ray of the sun has penetrated.	Ove raggio di Sol giamai non giunse.
Still be my guide and comfort,	Tù mia compagna e duce
as I in perilous and secret pathways	In cosi strane e sconosciute vie
must journey on in doubtful fear and trembling.	Reggesti il passo debole e tremante,
Today, as you have told me,	Ond'oggi ancora spero
today once more those matchless eyes may bless me,	Di riveder quelle beate luci
and shine in darkest night, bringing the day-star.	Che sol' à gl'occhi miei portan' il giorno.

HOPE

Here are the desolate marshes, here is the oarsman	Ecco l'atra palude, ecco il nocchiero
who rows the naked spirits to that region,	Che trahe gl'ignudi spirti à l'altra riva.
that farther shore where Pluto has his kingdom.	Dove hà Pluton de l'ombr' il vasto impero.
Over this gloomy swamp, over this river,	Oltre quel nero stagn'oltre quel fiume,
in that country of wailing and of sorrow,	In quei campi di pianto e di dolore,
by Fate most cruel, all that you prize is hidden.	Destin crudele ogni tuo ben t'asconde.
Call now on all your courage, all your music:	Hor d'uopo è d'un gran core e d'un bel canto.
I no longer may guide you.	Io fin quì t'hò condotto, hor più non lice
Farther than this, a stern law decrees,	Teco venir, ch'amara legge il vieta.
I must not share your journey.	
Words inscribed in the stone with iron letters	Legge scritta co'l ferro in duro sasso
upon the entrance to Pluto's realm of shadows	De l'ima reggia in sù l'orribil soglia
proclaim this edict, with pitiless insistence:	Ch'in queste note il fiero senso esprime,
All hope abandon, ye who enter.	Lasciate ogni speranza voi ch'entrate.
Therefore if you've the heart still and the courage	Dunque se stabilito hai pur nel core
to cross the stream and enter that sad city,	Di porre il piè ne la Città dolente,
I say farewell now,	Da te me'n fuggo e torno
and turn back to the world of the living.	A l'usato soggiorno.

ORFEO

Do not, ah, do not desert me.	Dove, ah dove te'n vai
You that to my poor heart brought gentle comfort.	Unico del mio cor dolce conforto?
For now my weary journey	Poiche non lunge homai
to the land of the dead is almost over.	Del mio lungo camin si scopr' il porto,
Why do you go and leave me here deserted	Perche ti parti e m'abbandoni, ahi lasso,
to make the perilous crossing?	Su'l periglioso passo?
How shall I fare without you when you are gone,	Qual bene hor più m'avanza
O sweetest Hope, my saviour?	Se fuggi tù dolcissima Speranza?

45

O you that ere your death approach this river,	[12] O tu ch'innanzi mort' à queste rive
and would rashly demand my help to cross it,	Temerario te'n vieni, arresta i passi;
it is forbidden to any man still living,	Solcar quest'onde ad huom mortal non dassi,
nor may he find among the dead a lodging.	Nè può co'morti albergo haver chi vive.
Why? — it may be you plot against my master,	Che? voi forse nemico al mio Signore,
Cerberus decoying from the gates of Tartarus,	Cerbero trar da le tartaree porte?
or else, excited by passion unlawful,	O rapir brami sua cara consorte
you would steal from our lord his precious consort.	D'impudico desire acceso il core?
Your impudent designs you must abandon:	Pon freno al folle ardir, ch'entr'al mio legno
my boat is barred to you and every mortal.	Non accorrò più mai corporea salma,
My punishment, when once I disobeyed, still irks me	Sì de gli antichi oltragg' ancor ne l'alma
with fierce indignation and just resentment.	Serbo acerba memoria e giusto sdegno.

Sinfonia [13]

O mighty spirit, O valiant lord, all-powerful,	[14] Possente Spirto e formidabil Nume,
in whose power lies the path to the farther kingdom . . .	Senza cui far passaggio à l'altra riva
Without you, souls bereft of bodies in vain attempt it.	Alma da corpo sciolta in van presume.

Ritornello

No life have I, for since her life was taken,	Non vivo io nò, che poi di vita è priva
my dearest treasure, my heart has left my body.	Mia cara sposa il cor non è più meco,
When heart is gone, how can it be that I am living?	E senza cor com'esser può ch'io viva?

Ritornello

I go to join her, through cloud and darkness.	A lei volt' hò il camin per l'aër cieco,
But that place is not Hell: the realm enclosing beauty so wondrous	A l'inferno non già, ch'ovunque stassi
has paradise within it.	Tanta bellezza il paradiso hà seco.

Ritornello

Orfeo am I; I follow my Euridice,	Orfeo son io che d'Euridice i passi
follow among these gloomy labyrinths and caverns,	Segue per queste tenebrose arene,
where till this day no man has ever ventured.	Ove giamai per huom mortal non vassi.
Oh, from those brightest eyes, shining serenely,	O de le luci mie luci serene
one glance restores me in my mortal sickness:	S'un vostro sguardo può tornarmi in vita,
Ah, denying that dear hope, you would slay me.	Ahi chi niega il conforto à le mie pene?

But you, noble and wise, have power to help me.
Nor need you fear that I may harm your master,
only music I carry as my weapon;
yet those hearts hard and stony in vain resist it.

Sol tu nobile Dio puoi darmi aita,
Nè temer dei, che sopr' un'aurea Cetra
Sol di corde soavi armo le dita
Contra cui rigid'alma in van s'impetra.

CHARON

Much you delight and soothe me,
O melodious singer,
as you seek with such pleadings
and complainings to move me.
But no, ah no, I may not yield to pity.
Such weakness in a god would be unworthy.

Ben mi lusinga alquanto
Dilettandomi il core
Sconsolato Cantore
Il tuo piant' e'l tuo canto.
Ma lunge, ah lunge sia da questo petto
Pietà di mio valor non degno effetto.

ORFEO

Ah, miserable lover,
who so vainly had hoped
to move by my prayers you that dwell in Hades!
Am I to stray for ever like a dead man
all friendless and unburied?
Exiled from Heaven, must Hell be barred against me?
And does my fate compel me
through all these fearful regions
of death, my love, to wander,
calling your name so vainly,
and with sighing and crying sink in madness?
Oh give me back my love, you powers of darkness!

Ahi sventurato amante,
Sperar dunque non lice
Ch'odan miei priegh'i Cittadin d'averno?
Onde qual ombra errante
D'insepolto cadavero e infelice
Privo sarò del Cielo e de l'Inferno?
Così vuol empia sorte
Ch'in quest' orror di morte
Da te cor mio lontano
Chiami tuo nome in vano
E pregando, e piangendo io mi consumi?

Rendetemi il mio ben Tartarei Numi.

Sinfonia [13]

He sleeps now,
and though no pity in his hard heart awakened,
in spite of all my pleading,
a heavy slumber
is weighing down his eyes while I am singing.

Ei dorme, e la mia cetra
Se pietà non impetra

Ne l'indurato core, almen il sonno

Fuggir al mio cantar gl'occhi non ponno.

Noel Mangin as Charon in the 1965 production by Frank Hauser for Sadler's Wells, designed by Yolanda Sonnabend (photo: Reg Wilson)

Then hasten — why do I wait here?	Sù dunque, à che più tardo?
While he sleeps I may cross the silent river,	Tempo è ben d'approdar sù l'altra sponda,
and none shall now prevent me.	S'alcun non è ch'il nieghi
Valour shall win, though vain were all entreaties.	Vaglia l'ardir se foran vani i preghi.
For chance is like a flower,	E' vago fior del Tempo
and it will wither when the moment passes.	L'occasion, ch'esser dee colta à tempo.

Here he enters the boat, and crosses, singing.

I embark, shedding tears like bitter rivers:	Mentre versan questi occhi amari fiumi
Oh give me back my love, you powers of darkness!	Rendetemi il mio ben Tartarei Numi.

Sinfonia

CHORUS OF INFERNAL SPIRITS

Now sing praises to man and his endurance!	[15] Nulla impresa per huom si tenta in vano
He shall not fail who arms himself with patience.	Nè contr'a lui più sà natura armarse,
He makes the desert blossom,	Ei de l'instabil piano
he ploughs the arid pastures and makes them fruitful,	Arò gl'ondosi campi, e'l seme sparse
and from the barren height draws golden harvest.	Di sue fatiche, ond'aurea messe accolse.
Therefore acclaim his glory	Quinci perche memoria
with unremitting praises,	Vivesse di sua gloria,
and let his fame undying live in memory,	La Fama à dir di lui sua lingua sciolse,
who tamed the sea to hold his floating cities,	Ch'ei pose freno al Mar con fragil Legno,
and the winds harnessed to hasten his journeys.	Che sprezzò d'Austr' e d'Aquilon lo sdegno.

Through the airy countries of his journey	†	[Per l'aëree contrade à suo viaggio
craftsman Daedalus spread his light wings.		L'ali lievi spiegò Dedalo industre.
Neither the sun's hot rays nor marshy damps		Nè di Sol caldo raggio
damaged his feathers,		Ne distemprò sue penne humor palustre,
but seeming in his passage a new bird of the winged species,		Ma novo augel sembrando in suo sentiero A l'alata famiglia
his great enterprise approved by Fortune,		Fece per maraviglia
he marvellously achieves his flight,		Perch'arridea fortuna al gran pensiero
and both airs and winds pause		Fermar il volo, e starsi e l'aure e i venti
to admire such bold determination.		A rimirar cotanto ardire intenti.

Another stole living fire from the burning car,	Altri dal carro ardente e da la face
and from the torch that the day lights on earth when it	Ch'accende il giorno in terra al Ciel salito
has climbed to heaven.	Furò fiamma vivace.

But what heart was ever so ardent,	Ma qual cor fù giamai cotanto ardito
or equal to his, who today is seen	Che s'aguagli à costui ch'oggi si vede
in these dark cloisters,	Per questi oscuri chiostri
singing and boldly moving,	Fra larve e serpi e Mostri
among phantoms, snakes and monsters?	Mover cantando baldanzoso il piede?
In vain is Charon deaf to his prayers,	L'orrecchie in van Caronte à i preghi ha sorde,
in vain does Cerberus growl and bite.	E in vano homai Cerbero latra e morde.]

Sinfonia

---

† This passage appears in the 1607 librettos, but not in the score.

Act Four

My lord, here is a suppliant
to your kingdom of death sadly appealing
for his lost Euridice.
His sweet lyre and his singing
have sounded through our land in
   lamentation.
Such a burden of woe fills me with pity.
So once again I turn to ask a favour
of your great godhead
that you would show him mercy.
Oh if my eyes are lodestars with a
   loving attraction,
as you have told me,
if my brow is like the clear unclouded
   heaven
and serene as the daylight,
whence you have promised
that you would never envy Jove his
   kingdom —
now I pray by the flames of desire
that mighty Love has lit between us,
give Euridice freedom, that she may go
   rejoicing
where once she spent her days in songs
   and feasting,
and restored to Orfeo console his
   weeping.

Signor quell'infelice
Che per queste di morte ampie campagne
Và chiamand' Euridice,
Ch'udito hai tù pur dianzi
Così soavamente lamentarsi,

Moss'hà tanta pietà dentr' al mio core
Ch'un altra volta i' torno a porger preghi

Perch'il tuo Nume al suo pregar si pieghi
Deh se da queste luci
Amorosa dolcezza unqua trahesti,

Se ti piacqu' il seren di questa fronte

Che tù chiami tuo Cielo, onde mi giuri

Di non invidiar sua sorte à Giove:

Pregoti per quel foco
Con cui già la grand'alm' Amor t'accese,
Fa ch' Euridice torni a goder di quei giorni

Che trar solea vivend' in fest'e in canto

E del miser' Orfeo consola'l pianto.

Fate's laws unswerving
that rule our lives and actions
oppose, beloved mistress, your entreaties.
But when you lift your beautiful eyes to
   mine,
I can deny you nothing.

So his dear Euridice, though the Fates
   would deny it,
he shall recover.
But while they make their way from Hell's
   abysses,
no glance backward to her shall I allow
   him.
If he turn but a moment,
his dear wife will be lost to him for ever.

So I give my commandment.
Now through my kingdom make
   proclamation
that thus my will ordains it.
And so proclaim to Orfeo, and proclaim
   to Euridice,
that this my word is law, and none shall
   change it.

Benche severo et immutabil fato

Contrasti amata sposa i tuoi desiri,
Pur null' homai si nieghi

A tal beltà congionta à tanti prieghi.

La sua cara Euridice

Contra l'ordin fatale Orfeo ricovri.
Ma pria ch'i trag' il piè da questi abissi

Non mai volga ver lei gli avidi lumi.

Che di perdita eterna
Gli fia certa cagion un solo sguardo.

Io così stabilisco, hor nel mio Regno
Fate ò Ministri il mio voler palese

Sì che l'intenda Orfeo
E l'intenda Euridice,

Ne di cangiari altrui sperar più lice.

O ruler of the eternal realm of shadows,
most mighty King, all must obey your
   judgement.

O de gli habitator de l'ombre eterne
Possente Rè legge ne fia tuo cenno,

Your word is law, founded on truth unchanging:
'tis not for us, lesser in power, to doubt you.

Che ricercar altre cagione interne
Di tuo voler nostri pensier non denno,

To earth from these dark labyrinths and caverns
Orfeo may lead her.
But is his faith unswerving?
And can he conquer all his youthful longings,
Nor once by looking back, break the commandment?

Trarrà da quest' orribili caverne

Sua sposa Orfeo, s'adoprerà suo ingegno

Si che no'l vinca giovenil desio,

Ne i gravi imperi suoi sparga d'oblio.

Fervent thanks would I offer,
more than my tongue can utter,
that you have heard my prayer, my gracious master!
How blessed was the day when first I pleased you,
blest the day when you captured me by cunning.
Then, though I lost the sunlight,
Pluto made me his wife, and queen of Hades.

Quali grazie ti rendo
Hor che si nobil dono
Conced' à' preghi miei signor cortese?

Sia benedetto il dì che pria ti piacqui,

Benedetta la preda e'l dolc' inganno,

Poi che per mia ventura
Feci acquisto di tè perdendo il Sole.

Words so loving and tender,
once more inflame my senses
and fill my heart with longing.
Be true always to me,
and do not dwell upon the pleasures of heaven:
lest you abandon our wedded love and treasure.

Tue soavi parole
D'Amor l'antica piaga
Rinfrescan nel mio core,
Cosi l'anima tua non sia più vaga
Di celeste diletto,

Si ch'abbandoni il marital tuo letto.

Compassion, love and mercy
triumphant vanquish darkness.

Pietade oggi et Amore
Trionfan ne l'Inferno.

*

Here is the noble singer
to lead his Euridice to realms of daylight.

Ecco il gentil cantore
Che sua sposa conduce al Ciel superno.

Ritornello

O my lyre, who can be worthy
to celebrate your praises?
The hardest heart you melted, and charmed with your playing
the darkest places.

[16] Qual honor di te fia degno
Mia cetra onnipotente,
S'hai nel Tartareo Regno

Piegar potuto ogni indurata mente?

Ritornello

When you play, the stars fall silent
at music so celestial,
and all the constellations
dance in measure with swift or slow gyrations.

Luogo havrai fra le più belle
Imagini celesti,
Ond'al tuo suon le stelle
Danzeranno co' giri hor tardi hor presti.

---

* There is no indication in the librettos for the solo voice indicated in the score to announce Euridice.

I today through your sweet pleading
shall soon embrace my darling:
on the breast of my lady, so white and
    soft, lying
at last shall find rest.

But while I'm singing — Ah heavens —
how can I tell that she walks behind me?
Ah heavens, I may not turn to see her
    coming,
or show her where I'm leading.
What if the envious Pluto, the king of
    darkest Hades,
lest I should know a happiness denied
    him,
would steal again those eyes so lucid,
so clear and shining —
those eyes whose glances can make of
    Hell a Heaven?
Fear no longer, Orfeo,
that which Pluto forbids is Love's
    commandment.
So imperious a monarch
controls every other power,
I must obey his sentence.

But where is she? Euridice!
Would the Furies divide us?
In jealousy and anger they pursue me
and ravish you away, O my love? And am
    I helpless?

Io per te felice à pieno
Vedrò l'amato volto,
E nel candido seno

De la mia Donn' oggi sarò raccolto.

Ma mentre io canto (ohime) chi m'assicura
Ch'ella mi segua? ohime chi mi nasconde
De l'amate pupille il dolce lume?

Forse d'invidia punte
Le Dietà d'Averno
Perch'io non sia qua giù felice à pieno

Mi tolgono il mirarvi
Luci beate e liete
Che sol co'l sguardo altrui bear potete?

Ma che temi mio core?
Ciò che vieta Pluton comanda Amore.

A Nume più possente
Che vince huomini e Dei
Ben ubbidir dovrei.

A noise offstage.

Ma che odo ohime lasso?
S'arman forse à' miei danni
Con tal furor le furie innamorate
Per rapirmi il mio ben ed io 'l consento?

Marie Landis as Eurydice and John Wakefield as Orfeo in the 1965 production by Frank Hauser for Sadler's Wells, designed by Yolanda Sonnabend (photo: Reg Wilson)

Here he turns.

Eyes so tenderly shining, at last I see you,	O dolcissimi lumi io pur vi veggio,
at last . . . But all at once — Ah — you have vanished!	Io pur: ma qual Eclissi ohime v'oscura?

A SPIRIT

You broke the compact, and so the law condemns you.	Rott'hai la legge, e se' di grazia indegno.

EURIDICE

Ah! vision that I longed for — and yet so bitter!	Ahi vista troppo dolce e troppo amara:
And so through too much love our love must perish?	Così per troppo amor dunque mi perdi?
And I, wretchedly sighing	Et io misera perdo
never more shall I feel the warmth of earth or of sunlight,	Il poter più godere
and lost for ever, you, much more dear than life,	E di luce e di vita, e perdo insieme
O my companion!	Tè d'ogni ben più caro, ò mio Consorte.

CHORUS OF SPIRITS

Turn again to the darkness, most forlorn Euridice,	Torn' à l'ombre di morte Infelice Euridice,
nor ever hope to see again the starlight.	Nè più sperar di riveder le stelle
Our king from henceforth is deaf to all entreaty.	Ch'omai fia sordo a' preghi tuoi l'Inferno.

Laurence Dale as Orfeo in David Freeman's production at ENO, conducted by Peter Robinson, designed by Hayden Griffin and Peter Hartwell (photo: Andrew March)

Where have you gone, my life? Wait, I will follow.	Dove te'n vai mia vita? ecco io ti seguo.
Ah — someone holds me back — Phantom or demon?	Ma chi me'l nieg' ohime: sogn', o vaneggio?
Some mysterious power, from these dark terrors —	Qual occulto poter di questi orrori,
these dark yet precious terrors —	Da questi amati orrori
though I struggle, prevents me, and would drive me	Mal mio grado mi tragge, e mi conduce
towards the hateful daylight.	A l'odiosa luce?

Sinfonia

CHORUS OF SPIRITS

Virtue is beauty's radiance,	[17] È la virtute un raggio
like the herald of morning,	Di celeste bellezza
can pierce the darkness	Preggio de l'alma ond'ella sol s'apprezza;
and shining there console us.	
Though years may bring us sorrow,	Questa di Temp'oltraggio
where virtue is, no ageing can harm,	Non teme, anzi maggiore
in man she shows more brightly all her splendour.	Nel'huom rendono gl'anni il suo splendore.
But only the fog of human passions can darken her. †	[Nebbia l'adombra sol d'affetto humano, A cui talhor in vano
Against this, reason sometimes struggles in vain;	Tenta opporsi ragion, ch'ei la sua luce
so it extinguishes her light, and leads a man blindfold to the end.	Spegne, e l'huom cieco à cieco fin conduce.]
Orfeo first conquered Hades, then was defeated	Orfeo vinse l'Inferno e vinto poi
by his unruly passions:	Fù da gli affetti suoi.
who rules himself is worthy,	Degno d'eterna gloria
and he alone, to win eternal glory.	Fia sol colui c'havrà di sè vittoria.

Sinfonia

Here the scene changes again.

Costume design by Pet Halmen for Jean-Pierre Ponelle's Orfeo in Zurich.

---

† This passage in the 1607 librettos does not appear in the score.

53

Act Five

ORFEO

Once more, green fields of my country,   [18] Questi i campi di Tracia, e questo è il loco
my steps have sought you.
Here in one fearful moment, my rejoicing   Dove passomm' il core
was changed to tears and sorrow.   Per l'amara novella il mio dolore.

Lost, ever lost, my blessing,   Poiche non hò più spene
nor with my piteous crying,   Di ricovrar pregando
beseeching, and bitter sighing,   Piangendo e sospirando
can I ever restore her — what can I do?   il perduto mio bene,
So to you I return now, valleys so calm   Che posso io più? se non volgermi à voi
and peaceful.   Selve soavi un tempo
Consoling my despair, while heaven   Conforto a' miei martir, mentr'al ciel
allowed it,   piacque,
with your tears did you then share my   Per farvi per pietà meco languire
lamenting —
my wild lamenting.   Al mio languire.

You have been grieving, O mountains,   Voi vi dolesti ò Monti, e lagrimaste
and you lamented, O rocks,   Voi sassi al dipartir del nostro sole,
since she is gone, our shining day-star.
With you now I'll weep, and mourn her   Et io con voi lagrimerò mai sempre,
loss for ever,
and the hills shall re-echo my mourning,   E mai sempre dorròmmi, ahi doglia, ahi
my sorrow.   pianto.

ECHO

Thy sorrow.   Hai pianto.

ORFEO

O kind Echo, I hear you,   Cortese Eco amorosa
I know you mourn as I do,   Che sconsolata sei
and that with chiming voice you would   E consolar mi vuoi ne' dolor miei,
console me.
My tears, O gentle Echo,   Benche queste mie luci
spring fast and overflow like bitter   Sien già per lagrimar fatte due fonti,
fountains,
in floods of misery drowning the valleys: In così grave mia fiera sventura
still should sorrow have more, never to   Non ho pianto però tanto che basti.
cease now.

ECHO

Cease now!   Basti.

ORFEO

The hundred eyes of Argus,   Se gli occhi d'Argo havessi
if there flowed from each eye a sea of   E spandessero tutti un Mar di pianto,
weeping,
could not convey such mourning, such   Non fora il duol conforme à tanti guai.
lamentations.

ECHO

Patience!   Ahi.

ORFEO

Since you have shown your pity, I truly   S'hai del mio mal pietade, io ti ringrazio
thank you,
your sympathy I welcome.   Di tua benignitade.
But while I speak my sorrow,   Ma mentre io mi querelo

why — why do you respond with just the last of my sentence? Give me my whole complaint, O faithful Echo.	Deh perchè mi rispondi Sol con gl' ultimi accenti? Rendimi tutti integri i miei lamenti.
But you, soul of my soul, if you revisit from gloomy Hades, this land that once you cherished, take once again fervent and lasting praises, I consecrate here all my faithful music; as I once made for you my heart an altar, and laid my soul there in sacrificial offering.	Ma tu anima mia se mai ritorna La tua fredd'ombra à queste amiche piagge, Prendi da me queste tue lodi estreme C'hor à te sacro la mia cetra e'l canto Come à te già sopra l'altar del core Lo spirto acceso in sacrifizio offersi.
Great was your beauty, and wisdom: on you from Heaven every perfection fell that graces mortals. Therefore every other by your wealth is poorer. Every tongue, every nation to you pays tribute, where such beauty is a temple for such goodness: so meek a mind — so great a praise we bring you. All other women full of lies and perfidy betray their lovers with their heartless wantoning; their foolish heads contain no thought of noble deeds. I give no praise to such as these, nor think of them. Therefore I'll never look for love in womankind, nor with golden dart shall Cupid pierce my heart.	Tu bella fusti e saggia, e in te ripose Tutte le grazie sue cortese il Cielo, Mentre ad ogn'altra de suoi don fù scarso, D'ogni lingua ogni lode à te conviensi Ch'albergasti in bel corpo alma più bella, Fastosa men quanto d'honor più degna. Hor l'altre Donne son superbe e perfide Ver chi le adora dispietate instabili, Prive di senno e d'ogni pensier nobile Ond'à ragion opra di lor non lodansi, Quinci non fia giamai che per vil femina Amor con aureo stral il cor trafiggami.

Sinfonia

*

Apollo descends in a cloud, singing.

APOLLO

My son Orfeo, why make your soul a captive to black despair and torment? No more, no more let passion destroy your noble spirit, nor pine in useless longing. By such shameful enslavement I see your life endangered. Therefore, parting the clouds I come to save you. If you obey me you shall have life and glory.	Perch'a lo sdegno et al dolor impreda Così ti doni ò figlio? Non è, non è consiglio Di generoso petto Servir al proprio affetto. Quinci biasmo e periglio Già sovrastar ti veggio, Onde movo dal Ciel per darti aita; Hor tu m'ascolta e n'havrai lode e vita.

ORFEO

Most gentle Father, in direst need you find me, for since I lost my treasure	Padre cortese, al maggior uopo arrivi, Ch'a disperato fine

---

* The 1607 librettos do not include the next scene but have another ending (which appears
on page 57).

55

in my grieving and sadness	Con estremo dolore
the agonies of love drive me to madness.	M'havean condotto già sdegn' et Amore.
Therefore I wait attentive while you chide me,	Eccomi dunque attento a tue ragioni,
celestial Father, what will you now command me?	Celeste padre, hor ciò che vuoi m'imponi.

APOLLO

Rashly, rashly rejoicing	Troppo troppo gioisti
in your transient good-fortune,	Di tua lieta ventura
too rashly weeping you now the Fates importune.	Hor troppo piagni
Do you not know yet	Tua sorte acerba e dura. Ancor non sai
that to mortals on earth all joy's uncertain?	Come nulla qua giù diletta è dura?
Come then, if life immortal can still delight you,	Dunque se goder brami immortal vita
mount to the skies with me,	Vientene meco al Ciel ch'a se t'invita.
for Heaven invites you.	

ORFEO

And shall I never see her?	Si non vedrò più mai
Is my dear Euridice lost for ever?	De l'amata Euridice i dolci rai?

APOLLO

With joy and adoration	Nel Sole e nelle stelle
perceive her form among the constellations.	Vagheggerai le sue sembianze belle.

ORFEO

I would be no unworthy son of great Apollo.	Ben di cotanto Padre Sarei non degno figlio
Lead on my Father, and fearless I will follow.	Se non seguisci il tuo fedel consiglio.

APOLLO AND ORFEO
rise to the heavens, singing

We rise rejoicing to Heaven above.	[19] Saliam cantand'al Cielo
True virtue there abounding	Dove ha virtù verace
gains eternal reward, delight unending.	Degno premio di se, diletto e pace.

Ritornello

CHORUS

Rise Orfeo our noble hero,	[20] Vanne Orfeo felice a pieno
to enjoy your celestial glory,	A goder celeste honore,
where the blest know endless pleasure,	La ve ben non mai vien meno,
Death can never steal their treasure.	La ve mai non fù dolore,
Our devotion to your altar	Mentr'altari, incensi e voti
with our faithful prayers we offer.	Noi t'offriam lieti e devoti.

Ritornello

Thus he goes without delaying	Così và chi non s'arretra
great Apollo's call obeying.	Al chiamar di Nume eterno,
In the skies he'll live contented	Cosi gratia in ciel impetra
who was here by Hell tormented.	Che qua giù provò l'inferno
Though today he sowed in sorrow,	E chi semina fra doglie
he shall reap in joy tomorrow.	D'ogni gratia il frutto coglie.

Moresca

The end of the opera.

The original ending to Act Five.

According to the 1607 librettos, but not to the 1609 score, there is a different ending to the opera, in which the followers of Bacchus (or Bassareus, or Lyæus, or Lenæus) the god of wine, turn upon Orpheus.

ORPHEUS

But here is the hostile troop	Ma ecco stuol nemico.
of women, friends of the tipsy god.	Di Donne amiche à l'ubbriaco Nume,
I must escape from the hateful sight	Sottrar mi voglio à l'odiosa vista
which my eyes shun, my soul abhors.	Che fuggon gli occhi ciò che l'alma aborre.

CHORUS OF BACCHANTES

Hail, Father Lyaeus,	Evohe padre Lieo
we Bassarids acclaim you with clear voices.	Bassareo Te chiamiam con chiari accenti,
Hail, joyful and laughing	Evohe liete e ridenti
we praise you, god of the wine-feast.	Te lodiam padre Leneo
Now we feel the height of your divine fury.	Hor c'habbiam colmo il core Del tuo divin furore.

A BACCHANTE

Now Thracian Orpheus, our wicked enemy,	Fuggito è pur da questa destra ultrice L'empio nostro avversario il Trace Orfeo
who scorned our noble worth,	
has fled from this avenging right hand.	Disprezzator de' nostri pregi alteri.

ANOTHER BACCHANTE

He shall not escape, for the later it comes	Non fuggirà, che grave
the heavier shall fall divine wrath on the guilty head.	Suol esser più quanto più tarda scende Sovra nocente capo ira celeste.

TWO BACCHANTES

Meanwhile we sing to Bacchus,	Cantiam di Bacco intanto, e in varij modi
in various modes we bless and praise his Deity.	Sua Deità si benedica e lodi.

CHORUS OF BACCHANTES

Hail, Father Lyaeus,	Evohe padre Lieo
we Bassarids acclaim you with clear voices.	Bassareo Te chiamiam con chiari accenti,
Hail, joyful and laughing	Evohe liete e ridenti
we praise you, god of the wine-feast.	Te lodiam padre Leneo
Now we feel the height of your divine fury.	Hor c'habbiam colmo il core Del tuo divin furore.

A BACCHANTE

You first discovered the beneficent plant	Tu pria trovasti la felice pianta
whence sprang that liquor which cures all sorrow,	Onde nasce il licore Che sgombra ogni dolore,
and is the father of sleep, and the sweet forgetting	Et à gli egri mortali Del sonno è padre e dolce oblio de i mali.
of mortal pain and sickness.	

CHORUS

Hail, Father Lyaeus,	Evohe padre Lieo
we Bassarids acclaim you with clear voices.	Bassareo Te chiamiam con chiari accenti,
Hail, joyful and laughing	Evohe liete e ridenti
we praise you, god of the wine-feast.	Te lodiam padre Leneo,
Now we feel the height of your divine fury.	Hor c'habbiam colmo il core Del tuo divin furore.

The bringer of day sees you, tamer of the shining East,	Te domator del lucido Oriente
on your golden car, nobly laden with spoils.	Vide di spoglie alteramente adorno
	Sopr'aureo carro il portator del giorno.

A BACCHANTE

You like a powerful lion	Tu qual Leon possente
with strong right hand and invincible heart	Con forte destra e con invitto core
	Spargesti et abbattesti
scattered and brought low the phalanxes of the Giants:	Le Gigantee falangi, et al furore
	De le lor braccia ferreo fren ponesti.
you bound their arms with iron chains	Allhor che l'empia guerra
when the earth fought against Heaven in a wicked war.	Mosse co' suoi gran figli al Ciel la Terra.

CHORUS

Hail, Father Lyaeus,	Evohe padre Lieo
we Bassarids acclaim you with clear voices.	Bassareo
	Te chiamiam con chiari accenti,
Hail, joyful and laughing	Evohe liete e ridente
we praise you, god of the wine-feast.	Te lodiam padre Leneo,
Now we feel the height of your divine fury.	Hor c'habbiam colmo il core
	Del tuo divin furore.

A BACCHANTE

Without you the holy goddess whom Cyprus honours	Senza te l'alma Dea che Cipro honora
would be cold and spiritless.	Fredda e insipida fora
O you, the spice of every human pleasure	O d'ogni human piacer gran condimento
and the comfort of every afflicted heart.	E d'ogni afflitto cor dolce contento.

CHORUS

Hail, Father Lyaeus,	Evohe padre Lieo
we Bassarids acclaim you with clear voices.	Bassareo
	Te chiamiam con chiari accenti,
Hail, joyful and laughing	Evohe liete e ridente
we praise you, god of the wine-feast.	Te lodiam padre Leneo,
Now we feel the height of your divine fury.	Hor c'habbiam colmo il core
	Del tuo divin furore.

The end of Act Five.

PART TWO

Venice

The Stage Works

Tirsi e Clori (*ballet, for Mantua*)	1616
Le nozze di Tetide (*unfinished, lost*)	1616
Andromeda (*unfinished, lost*)	1618-20
Apollo (*unfinished, lost*)	1620
Combattimento di Tancredi e Clorinda	1624
La finta pazza Licori (*for Mantua, unfinished, lost*)	1627
Gli amori di Diana e di Endimione (*for Parma, lost*)	1628
Mercurio e Marte (*for Parma, lost*)	1628
Proserpina rapita (*lost, except for a trio*)	1630
Volgendo il ciel (*ballet, for Vienna*)	1636?
Il ritorno d'Ulisse in patria	1640
Le nozze d'Enea con Lavinia (*lost*)	1641
La vittoria d'Amore (*for Piacenza, lost*)	1641
L'incoronazione di Poppea	1642

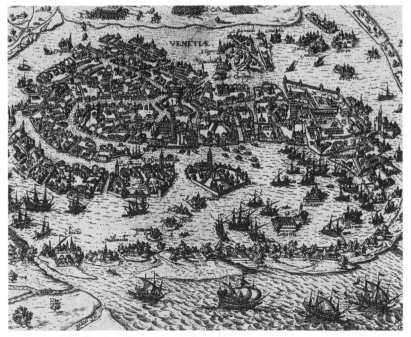

Venice and the lagoon, by Keller, 1607.

Musical Theatre in Venice

Paolo Fabbri

References to Venice are strikingly absent from the landscape of Italian opera during the first half of the seventeenth century. Although it was a thriving centre for conventional spoken theatre, the city was comparatively slow to embrace the novelty of plays that were sung throughout. It may even be that it was because of this highly developed theatrical tradition that the new genre failed to take root.

It is tempting to explain this reluctance in terms of the Republic's peculiar social structure and of the differences between a princely state and a republic. There is a clear connection between the beginnings of opera and the princely courts in Florence, Mantua and even Rome. On the other hand Bologna, which — like Venice — was an oligarchy without a princely court, was one of the first cities to cultivate opera. More to the point is the fact that there was no official indoor theatre in Venice where the cultural and political events of state could be held. During his period as Doge (1595-1605), Marino Grimani made some moves towards the creation of a state theatre by officially promoting several spoken plays with musical interludes but it is a perfect illustration of the workings of an oligarchy that most of Venice's many theatres were private and belonged to aristocratic families. The public and ceremonial aspects of government were performed out of doors, and took place at different locations throughout the city in front of spectators from every class of society.

Musical performances on the scale of those staged in Florence, Rome and Mantua started in Venice only after 1637, the year in which *L'Andromeda* (with music by Francesco Manelli and text by Benedetto Ferrari) was performed in the Teatro S. Cassiano. Before this, as far as we know, there were a few experimental productions, which were all in one way or another linked to Monteverdi, who had been Director of Music at St Mark's since 1613. We learn from his correspondence that a performance was planned for the 'distinguished company of ladies and gentlemen' at a celebration in the Bembo household during the 1620 carnival season. As well as the customary 'hour of instrumental music', an 'Apollo's lament' on the sad fate of Daphne was to be sung (with text by Striggio, music by Monteverdi). The performance was to be 'on a senetta', or small stage. A production of the *Combattimento di Tancredi e Clorinda (The duel of Tancredi and Clorinda)* was given at the Palazzo Mocenigo in 1624, again 'as part of the entertainment at a carnival ball, in the presence of all the nobility'. On this occasion Monteverdi set some verses of Tasso's *Gerusalemme Liberata*, slightly altered and with some borrowings from *Gerusalemme Conquistata*. He included the resulting composition in his *Madrigali Guerrieri, et Amorosi (Madrigals of War and Love)*, published in 1638. This version is accompanied by stage directions indicating details of the first performance: 'After a few madrigals have been sung without movements, Clorinda, armed and on foot, enters suddenly from that part of the room where the music is to be played. She is followed by Tancredi, armed and astride a [theatrical] horse. At that moment the singing begins.' Monteverdi began setting another episode of *Gerusalemme*, starting from Armida's words: 'O tu che porte teco di me, parte ne lassi', and continuing through her lament and fury at Ruggiero's answers (recte Rinaldo). In a letter of May 1, 1627, he suggested this as a theatrical spectacle for the Mantuan Court. Then, in the spring of 1630, Strozzi's pastoral tale of *Proserpina Rapita (The abduction of Proserpine)* was staged at a wedding at the Palazzo Mocenigo. Music was commissioned from Monteverdi but it is not certain whether it was sung throughout.

Thus, until 1637, Venice had not experienced much purely musical theatre. A small circle of people had occasionally witnessed dialogues which were sung and partly acted, or plays that were sung throughout but relatively short, or other hybrid dramas. The 'revelation' of *Andromeda* must therefore have been considerable — all the more because it was not a private entertainment for an invited audience, as had always been the case in Florence, Rome, Mantua and Bologna, but for a paying public. Indoor venues open to all on payment of an admission fee had existed for Italian spoken theatre since the mid-sixteenth century, generally for performances by professional comedians (the *commedia dell'arte*). Such halls existed at various times between 1540 and 1570 in Modena, Bologna, Piacenza, Genoa, Udine, Mantua and Reggio Emilia. As for Venice, in 1580 Francesco Sansovino observed in his description of the city (*Venezia Nobilissima*): 'Near this church [S. Cassiano] there are two very beautiful theatres — one oval, one circular — built at great expense. They can hold large numbers of people for the city's traditional carnival plays.' Sansovino is referring here to two halls which were permanently equipped to receive paying audiences for the *commedia dell'arte*. The Teatro Vecchio belonged to the Michiel family, and the Teatro Nuovo to the Tron family. In the first half of the seventeenth century there were performances in the Teatro S. Moisè (which belonged to the Giustinian family), the Teatro S. Salvador (which belonged to the Vendramin and opened in 1622), and the Teatro Nuovo. When this was destroyed by fire in 1629, it was rebuilt in brick and renamed the Teatro S. Cassiano. Tommaso Garzoni also records that, until 1616, comedies were given 'at the Pellegrino Inn' before paying audiences.

The enormous success of *Andromeda* at the S. Cassiano may be easily judged from a few eloquent facts. During carnival in the following years the S. Cassiano confirmed the fashion by programming musical theatre instead of spoken comedy. Other theatres immediately copied this: the S. Moisè may have staged a revival of Monteverdi's *Arianna* as early as 1639-40, and certainly went over to a musical drama in 1640 with two Ferrari premières: *Il pastor regio* (*The shepherd king*) and *La ninfa avara* (*The avaricous nymph*). Academies which offered musical entertainments, such as the Accademia degli Unisoni, founded by Strozzi in 1637, gave public performances. During the 1638 carnival this academy gave an opera season that included a revival of *La Favola di Giasone e di Medea* (*Jason and Medea*), composed by Monteverdi ten years previously for the court in Parma. Conclusive proof of public enthusiasm for the new genre is that purpose-built opera houses were soon being built in addition to the existing theatres. The SS. Giovanni e Paolo (belonging to the Grimani) was constructed out of wood in 1638 and inaugurated the following year with *La Delia* by Giulio Strozzi (music by Manelli and Francesco Sacrati). The Novissimo was built in 1641 and inaugurated with *La finta pazza* (*The feigned madwoman*) by Strozzi and Sacrati; it closed down in 1647. The SS. Apostoli opened in 1649 with *Orontea* by Giacinto Andrea Cicognini and Marcantonio Cesti, and was active until 1688. The Novissimo di S. Aponal (the property of the Duodo and Correr) opened in 1651 with works by Cavalli (*L'Oristeo*, *La Rosinda*, *La Calisto*) but stopped musical performances in 1657.

So although theatre which was entirely sung came late to Venice, it met with immediate and unprecedented success: it effectively replaced spoken drama not just in the favour of the public, but literally in the theatres where spoken drama had previously been given. The genre quickly acquired features of the Venetian theatrical milieu it had so successfully penetrated: the need to make

Ethna Robinson (Melanto) and Jean Rigby (Penelope) in David Freeman's production of 'Ulysses' at ENO in 1989 (photo: Laurie Lewis)

financial profit, a public character (a 'democratic' opportunity for everyone to become a member of the audience by buying a ticket), the repetition of performances and regular seasons. Whereas before productions had been infrequent and staged only for special events, musical drama now became a seasonal custom, usually during carnival between December 26 and Shrove Tuesday. No longer an extravagant expression of political supremacy in the guise of an artistic statement, it became a profit-making exercise, ruled by the laws of financial enterprise. It ceased to be the prerogative of an aristocratic élite and became instead a 'temporary' privilege which was on sale to all for quite a long time. The change is clear if we compare the four performances of *Chi soffre speri* (*He who suffers should hope*) at the Palazzo Barberini in Rome during February and March 1639 with the twenty-four of *Antioco* by Minato and Cavalli in Venice (January 25 to February 24) in 1659.

After 1637, apart from a few interruptions because of wars, there were extremely regular performances of opera in Venice, and a number of theatres were open at the same time. The consequences were extremely important. Firstly a class of professional musicians with theatrical connections emerged — composers and librettists, singers and dancers, not to mention the impresarios, scenographers and costume-designers. Musical drama had previously appeared intermittently (if at all) in the work lists of most composers — depending on whether they had come into contact with a court, academy or aristocratic group that wished to stage a performance. Even in that case the work would be squeezed between books of songs, madrigals and sacred music. But of the composers writing for the Venetian stage until around 1650, the majority (Francesco Manelli, Benedetto Ferrari, Francesco Sacrati, Francesco Cavalli) had a large number of operas to their names. Only Nicolò

Anonymous-Monteverdi, 1641; *Sidonio e Dorisbe*, Melosio-Cavalli, 1642; *L'Ulisse errante*, Badoaro-Sacrati, 1644).

Seeing the success of comic roles in Roman operas, Venetian musical dramatists started writing similar parts, and these roles eventually became an established feature of Venetian opera. These are the flirtatious old governesses (Scarabea in *Maga fulminata*; Grimora in *Sidonio e Dorisbe*, Cirenia in *Alcate* by Tirabosco-Manelli, 1642), or the satyrs and country nymphs (Tamburla and the Satyr in *L' Armida*, Tritone in the *Nozze di Teti e di Peleo*, the Satyrs in *L'Adone* and *Torilda*, both by Bissari-?Cavalli, 1648); the yokels (Tacco in *Pastor regio*, Ghiandone in *Ninfa avara*, Erbosco in *Sidonio e Dorisbe*, Giamba in *Finta savia* by Strozzi and various authors, 1643) and the foolish servants (Trulla in *Venere gelosa* by Bartolini-Sacrati, 1643, Corbacchio in *Finta savia*, Nuto in *Torilda* by Bissari-?Cavalli, 1648); the canny page-boys (Sinone in *Didone*, Vafrinio in *Sidonio e Dorisbe*, Lesbino in *Amori di Giasone e d'Isifile*), the vainglorious parasites (Iro in *Ritorno d'Ulisse in patria*, Numano in *Nozze d'Enea in Lavinia*, Giroldo in *Amori di Giasone e d'Isifile*), the pedants (Rodante in *Finta savia*, the Pedant in *Sidonio e Dorisbe*), and the amorous old men (Minocle in *Bellerofonte*, Prospino in *Alcate*). On the other hand, the Venetians never took to religious history as a source for opera, chiefly because musical theatre was linked with carnival entertainment. How different from Rome, with its different political and cultural situation, and narrower aims of musical theatre! Even Venetian dramatists, however, saw that history in general, apart from religious matters, was a promising source of material. The earliest writers to use historical subjects (which were often more legend than history) were Marcantonio Tirabosco in *L'Alcate*, Scipione Errico in *La Deidamia* (1644), Giulio Strozzi in *Il Romolo e'l Remo* (1645), Giovanni Faustini in *La Doriclea* (1645), Pietro Paolo Bissari in *La Torilda* (1648), Maiolino Bisaccioni in *La Semiramide* (1648) and Giacinto Andrea Cicognini in *L'Orontea* (1649). Above all, it was Gian Francesco Busenello who dealt with historical themes assiduously and successfully, tackling through them the polemics of the debate over absolute monarchy: *L'Incoronazione di Poppea* (1643, for Monteverdi) and *La prosperità infelice di Giulio Cesare dittatore* (1646, for Cavalli).

The practice of dividing operas into three acts became the custom in Venice. Authors had previously chosen between three and five acts — the division which recalled classical tragedy and Aristotle's rules. Venetians showed a marked preference for three acts: in the preface to *Delia*, Giulio Strozzi called it the 'general division of everything' on the grounds that everything has its 'beginning, middle, end'. Nevertheless, a few works (*Adone* by Vendramin, *Amore innamorato* by Fusconi, *La prosperità infelice di Giulio Cesare dittatore* by Busenello) had the classical five acts. As for the prologue, it was customary at first to allocate it to single character; but after a few had been written in dialogue, following the latest Roman fashion — which had more potential for spectacle — this captured the imagination of the Venetians, and for several decades after 1642 all prologues were in dialogue.

Plots increasingly became comedies of intrigue, with complicated and interwoven events, and all the devices of that variety of drama (misunderstandings, changes of identity, disguises, confessions and so on). The popular taste for songs encouraged composers to include more of them. In pre-Venetian opera, arias had punctuated the drama only occasionally and for very specific dramatic purposes. In Venice the number of arias multiplied rapidly, and their potential for lyrical and expressive communication, which had been previously unexplored, was exploited. It was this development, of course, which was destined to have the greatest influence of all on the future of opera.

Fontei and Giovanni Rovetta composed a single opera apiece. Monteverdi completed three operas between 1640 and 1643 — and we should never forget how inappropriate it was for the Director of Music at St Mark's to be involved with public theatres (death cut short his career in musical theatre, and that of Rovetta, his successor, was abortive, while Cavalli gave it up as soon as he took up the post at St Mark's). The same development occurred among singers. Although some regarded opera as temporary work — a supplement to their employment at St Mark's (as had previously been the case at princely courts, or in Rome) — others started to become famous specifically because of it, and eventually to make their careers exclusively through their dramatic work. Furthermore, public musical theatre did not only encourage professional musicians; the need for more and more texts bred an army of specialised writers, who were often noblemen and lawyers turned theatre poets.

The explosion of the musical theatre business in Venice prompted a second fundamental development — in the conventions which applied to drama, music, literature and stage-design. The regular turnover of productions led inevitably, on the one hand, to standardisation and clichés of every kind, and on the other it stimulated a need to revitalise and refresh them because they were overworked and worn out. It was a matter of mass production — even in this highly skilled field. The pieces were conceived to be very ephemeral. It was most unusual for the same musico-dramatic text to be produced in more than one season in the same place, and generally alterations were essential before it could be revived elsewhere. Variations in taste mostly concerned the music: a libretto might be unearthed decades later and subjected to radical revisions, but it was unimaginable to recreate, even in part, the original musical setting.

At the end of the 1630s the traditions of musical theatre which had developed in Rome were undoubtedly the strongest and liveliest in Italy — because of the sheer number of productions, and the enormous influence they consequently exerted. The core of the troupe who wrote, performed and promoted *Andromeda* and *La maga fulminata* in Venice in 1637 were Roman in origin and training: Francesco Manelli the composer and actor, Maddalena his wife and prima donna, and Ferrari the librettist and theorbo-player.The seasons at the Palazzo Barberini in Rome thus deserve our attention because they provide many of the *topoi* later developed in Venetian opera.

For instance, when choosing subjects for Venice, librettists and composers most often selected plots which involved the element of the fantastic which was very much part of the Roman tradition. They might either be settings of famous myths (*L'Andromeda* by Ferrari-Manelli; *Le nozze di Teti e di Peleo* by Persiani-Cavalli, 1639; *La Delia* by Strozzi-Sacrati, 1639; *Ercole in Lidia* by Bisaccioni-Rovetta, 1645); or mythological tales with pastoral backgrounds (*L'Adone* by Vendramin-Manelli, 1639; *Gli amori d'Apollo e di Dafne* by Busenello-Cavalli, 1640; *Amore innamorato* by Fusconi-Cavalli, 1642; *La virtu de' strali d'Amore* by Faustini-Cavalli, 1642; *Il Bellerofonte* by Nolfi-Sacrati, 1642; *Narciso et Eco immortalati* and *Gli amori di Giasone e d'Isifile* by Persiani and perhaps Cavalli and Marazzoli respectively, 1642), or simply pastorals (*Il pastor regio* and *La ninfa avara* by Ferrari, 1640 and 1642; *L'Egisto* by Faustini-Cavalli, 1643). There were also operas inspired by the Roman taste for epics and novels (even modern ones), or which were straightforward comedies of intrigue. They might mix gods and mortals, and introduce magical and fantastic developments (*La maga fulminata* by Ferrari-Manelli, 1638); or they might concern famous heroes from literature (*L'Armida*, Ferrari, 1639; *Il ritorno di Ulisse in patria*, Badoaro-Monteverdi, 1640; *La Didone*, Busenello-Cavalli, 1641; *La finta pazza*, Strozzi-Sacrati, 1641; *Le nozze d'Enea in Lavinia*,

The Spanish Contribution
to the Birth of Opera

Jack Sage

In a foreword to his play *Il trionfo di David*, written in Florence in 1633, the poet and playwright Jacopo Cicognini (1577-1633), told his readers that he was 'imitating' Spanish drama, especially that of the famous Lope de Vega, who 'recommended and beseeched him to come to terms with plays which exceed the twenty-four-hour unity-of-time rule and to seek to give pleasure by representing actions which extend beyond not only one day but also many months or years. The purpose,' he continued, was 'that we may delight in the accidents of history, not just by relating what has gone before but by representing these diverse actions in sequence. If the author heeds the advice of Lope de Vega [. . .] and thus weaves the grave with the ridiculous, pleasure with profit, history with invention, [. . .] intelligent audiences will admit to having experienced exceptional delight. In short, one sees that the practice of these modern writers [the Spanish dramatists such as Lope], concerned to please the listener, has broadened the narrow and severe rules of art.' These words suggest a vital link between Spanish and Italian dramatic aesthetics during the seventeenth century, and in particular that Italian opera librettists, and hence Italian opera composers, explored new paths signposted by Spanish dramatists of the Golden Age.

The Spanish Golden Age in the arts was a remarkable one not only because of the astonishing achievements of masters such as Góngora, Quevedo and Cervantes in poetry and prose, Velázquez, Ribera and Zurburán in painting, Lope de Vega, Tirso de Molina and Calderón in drama, or Victoria, Guerrero and Comes in music, but also because it flourished for two centuries, the sixteenth and seventeenth, while Spain swelled only to decline drastically as an imperial power. In the course of those two centuries, Spanish artistic life changed radically, reflecting a sea-change in the nation's mood from self-confidence to disillusion and ironical self-questioning. Not that this ironical reappraisal meant running away from the issues of everday life. As the attentive reader of *Don Quixote* will know, part of the ironical humour of Quixote's folly is that his idealistic ventures lead us, with a helping hand from the (initially) pragmatic Sancho Panza, to have a healthy respect for those who see windmills as windmills and convicts as convicts rather than those who see what they want to see. A decade or so before 1600, the Spanish guitar burst on to the street and into the tavern to stake its claim through the seventeenth century and beyond as the instrument anyone could teach himself to strum accompanying popular songs and dances. For all the horrified protests of established moralists, within a couple of decades the humble guitar and its swinging dance rhythms had injected new vitality into the works of cultured poets and musicians. It was not a fortuitous coincidence that a sense of commitment to mass entertainment brought new vitality to works written for the popular Spanish stage at about the same time. All over Europe, and in all the arts, the influence of the Spanish artistic achievement was felt more or less directly. On the other hand, Italy was the country where opera was pioneered and cultivated, at least until the middle of the century; the first faltering steps in wholly sung opera (aside from the relatively different genre of the court spectacle-play) were not taken until 1627 in Spain and Germany, and later still in France and England. Nevertheless Spain's contribution to the development of the new genre in Naples (still a Spanish colony), Florence and Venice was greater than that of any other country outside Italy.

The main reason was a Spanish dramatist: Lope de Vega (1562-1635), 'the monster of Nature' as Cervantes and others dubbed him. Of comparable significance was a (qualified) follower of Lope: Calderón de la Barca (1600-1681), perhaps the most cogent Christian dramatist of all time. Lope, in his *New Art for Writing Plays in our Time* (1609) and in 800 or more plays he somehow managed to write and get performed in his lifetime, set out guidelines for playwrights that proved more compelling for contemporary dramatists in France and Italy than those of any other writer in any other country. No doubt this was because Lope demonstrated pragmatically and with prudent, self-effacing irony that a new kind of tragicomedy was the answer to many of the demands of the new, commercial theatre, not simply because of the need (as history manuals are fond of saying) to free the playwright from the shackles of the Aristotelian 'Rules' but because he justified tragicomedy as a true representation of the actual comic-serious nature of life itself, buttressed by a revalued principle salvaged from classical theory: the writer's duty to entertain and teach, or, more precisely, to instruct through pleasure.

Of course, not all of Lope's plays were tragicomedies along these new 'true-to-life' lines; not a few are better described as comedies of intrigue — and pretty frivolous ones at that; but these were mostly written before 1600. Much more characteristic of Lope's maturity are comedies such as *La dama boba*, with its ironic, socially focused approach to nobles trying to mask their cunning self-centredness behind a parade of honourable, Platonic ideals; or tragicomedies such as *El caballero de Olmedo*, with its painful exposition of the Quixotic absurdity of a nobleman behaving with sublime heroism in an unheroic world. A handful were published in Lope's day as tragedies, such as *El castigo sin venganza*, with its pathetic revelation of the ambivalent motives of a ruler of Ferrara seeking to restore both his rightful authority in the eyes of his subjects and his own self-esteem through questionable vengeance.

These were not 'pure' tragedies according to classical canons, however, but 'tragedies in the Spanish style', concerned far more with the catastrophes of everyday life than with what Spaniards came increasingly to see as the remoteness and indeed wrongheadedness of sublime myths. And of course Lope turned his hand from time to time to conventional court command-plays, including the libretto for Spain's nominal first opera, a one-act 'pastoral eclogue', *La selva sin amor* (1627), set to music by two little-known Italians, Filippo Piccinini and Bernardo Monanni. It is tempting to explain the apparent failure of this venture partly by Lope's addiction in his text to the kind of old-style sublimity he normally eschewed in his plays for the popular stage. This view is reinforced, turning to Calderón, by recent interpretations of his court spectacle-plays such as *Fortunas de Andrómeda y Perseo* (1653) or *La estatua de Prometeo* (c.1670), including his two opera librettos, *La púrpura de la rosa* and *Celos aun del aire matan* (1659/1660), as thoughtful studies of the conjunction of mythic and human levels of reality. Likewise, his 'cloak and dagger' type of intrigue play now tends to be seen as a comic-serious genre pointing an ironic or even satiric finger at posturing nobles rather than as a mere frolic.

Lope de Vega and his followers, notably Tirso de Molina and Calderón, set up dramatic models offering a range of ideas, topics, sentiments, characters and styles which certainly enthused Rotrou, Racine and Corneille in France, certainly impressed Rospigliosi, Cicognini, Busenello and Badoaro in Italy, and almost certainly therefore affected the kind of librettos and hence the musical settings these librettists and their composers wrote for operas in Naples, Rome and Venice.

To talk simply in terms of 'influences' would obscure most of the real issues, primarily because sixteenth-and seventeenth-century Europe enjoyed an exceptional degree of reciprocal cultural exchange between individuals, courts and nations. Wealthy Spanish parents, as Cervantes often notes in his novels, took it for granted that their children should be sent to Italy as a sort of mature 'finishing school'. Italian scene-designers and engineers, notably Monara, Cosimo Lotti and Baccio del Bianco, as well as musicians, came to the Spanish court to set up spectacular command plays written by esteemed Spanish dramatists such as the Count of Villamediana (1622), Hurtado de Mendoza (1623), Lope de Vega (1627) or Calderón (from 1635). A monarch or other dignitary en route from one country to another would be regaled with the most impressive show of artistry the host state could muster, as when Mariana of Austria, on her way from Vienna to Madrid to marry Philip IV, was entertained in Milan with Ziani's *Teseo*, and in Venice with Cavalli's *Giasone*, libretto by the Hispanophile Cicognini, as well as a 'most striking [bizarrissima] Spanish play in three acts' together with its 'charming and tender entracte [vago e gentile intermedio]'. (In all probability an entracte would have been performed between each of the three acts of the main play.) In the first half of the *Seicento*, while Italian music-drama on the one hand was lighting a beacon for the rest of Europe, and Italian spoken drama on the other was at a low ebb, what could be more natural in this European common market of political and artistic give-and-take than that Spanish dramatists should provide a vital spark when their Italian counterparts did not? And what more persuasive a champion could they expect than the leading librettist in Count Barberini's circle in Rome, Giulio Rospigliosi, who had been papal nunzio to Philip IV in Madrid from 1646 to 1653, following an earlier stay in Madrid from 1625 to 1629 in Lope's lifetime, and who was himself elected Pope Clement IX in 1667? Even in the case of an epic opera such as Cavalli's *Didone* (1641), Busenello, in the preface to his libretto, wrote: 'This work reflects modern opinions. It is constructed not in accordance with the Rules of Antiquity but according to Spanish methods, which permit the years, not just the hours, to be represented.' That such remarks by Italian librettists about 'Spanish modern methods' were not narrowly focused just on the 'Rules' of time, place and action, may be gauged by reading in the context of his *New Art* Lope's advice to Jacopo Cicognini, cited in the opening paragraph, advocating natural variety over artificial unity. Or the plea of Jacopo's more famous son, the playwright and librettist G.A. Cicognini, for dramatic pragmatism (in the 'Foreword to Readers and Spectators' of his libretto for Cavalli's *Giasone* Venice, 1649). Or the careful points made by Badoaro in his letter to Michelangelo Torrigliani (printed in the preliminaries to Sacrati's *Ulisse errante*, Venice, 1644): '[Aristotelian precepts] are not like the proportions of mathematics, certain and permanent [. . .] no one cares in present times [. . .] so long as the path of inventiveness is seen to open up [. . .] leading the spirits [of the audience] in whatever way appropriate to things marvellous and delightful by virtue of the greatest effort of art [. . .] For the true rule is to satisfy the listener.' Such remarks by Jacopo Cicognini, G.A. Cicognini and Badoaro clearly stem from four basic points: that art is not an immutable, sacrosanct gift handed down only to the select few; that creative imagination matters more than strict notions of verisimilitude; and that the audience should feel both pleased and astonished. These points are those, among others (including some mentioned in the opening two paragraphs above), made by Lope de Vega in his *New Art* of 1609.

Against the view that Italian librettists owed a great deal to Spanish drama, it has been argued that Rospigliosi and Cicognini, for instance, drew more upon the *commedia dell'arte* and melodramatic reinterpretations of classical myths within the traditions of Italy itself. While it is prudent to emphasize again that much more research needs to be done in this supranational area before safe conclusions can be drawn, it is surely necessary to argue further that any notion of one-way influence in this period is a nebulous one, that these *commedia dell'arte* and mythic traditions were common bases of dramatic art in both Spain and Italy, as indeed was also the comic-serious tradition ironically signalled by Ariosto in *Orlando Furioso*. After all, an essential part of Lope's contributon was to move from the one-dimensional masked figures of the *commedia dell'arte* towards more complex characters who expressed inner thoughts at odds with their outward intentions, and these were often given an ironical twist by the more earthy sentiments of the characters in the subplot. Furthermore, an essential part of Calderón's contribution was his development of an intricate and integrated technique for marrying ancient myths with contemporary issues in lavish allegorical dramas both secular (as indicated above) and religious in his *autos sacramentales*. These were performed annually at Corpus Christi in Madrid, with such approval from the religious and governmental establishment that Philip IV's papal nunzio, Rospigliosi, could hardly have failed to attend them — and to report favourably on them to authorities, including Barberini and his opera circle, back in Italy.

In sum, there are obvious parallels between the developments fostered by Lope in the Madrid *corral* from c.1600 and those in the commercial theatre of Venice towards 1650, and between the developments espoused by Calderón from the 1620s in Madrid's court and squares and those of the lavish operas staged in Rome from the 1630s. Some degree of cultural interchange between the two countries is undeniable.

Though these parallels remain to be properly explored in the Spanish and Italian texts themselves, here are some for a start. Rospigliosi's Roman spectacle-opera, *Sant'Alessio* (1632) is a religious work wherein the formal way the homophonic choruses are counterpoised against each other recalls Calderón's symbolical 'contraponiendo' technique in his allegorical dramas and *autos sacramentales*. The work is comic-serious: the saintly sentiments of the hero are set against the pedestrian, at times witty, at times farcical, comments of the three wholly comic figures. More particularly there is a tragicomic quality in the contrast of Saint Alessio's sublime sentiments with the high-minded but ironically impractical quest of his family to find their beloved son (who in fact, unrecognized behind his disguise, has already returned). In short, the libretto is much more in tune with Lope de Vega's subtle reappraisal of tragicomedy than with *commedia dell'arte* tradition. So too is the way the disguised saint's return to the bosom of his family links the divine with the worldly. Something of this tragicomic mixture is surely woven into Badoaro's and Monteverdi's *Il ritorno d'Ulisse in patria* (Venice, 1641), again not just because of the presence of comic figures like Eumæus and Irus alongside the celebrated hero but rather because of the interplay of the sublime with the worldly in the disguised Minerva and Ulysses and, even more ironically, in the contrast between Penelope's staunch loyalty and the absurd aspirations of her noble suitors. There are comparable tragicomic qualities even in the comic intrigue ingredients of Cicognini's and Cavalli's *Giasone* and Cicognini's and Vesti's *Orontea* (both Venice, 1649). The allegedly frivolous comedies given in Venice in the 1640s and 1650s, of which Strozzi's and Sacrati's *La finta pazza* (1641) is an early example, might seem more weighty if the heroic characters' behaviour is seen in the ironically absurd light of

Spanish tragicomedy. Such an interpretation is all but certainly valid of the plays Rospigliosi specifically based upon Spanish models, usually Calderón's 'cloak-and-dagger' or allegorical dramas, such as Mazzocchi's (and Marazolli's?) *Il falcone/Chi soffre speri* (Rome, 1637), Giulio and Giacomo Rospigliosi's *Dal male il bene* (Florence, 1654, modelled in this instance partly upon a work ascribed to Calderón's rival, Sigler de Huerta, *No hay bien sin ajeno daño*, 1652), or Giulio Rospigliosi's *L'armi e gli amore* (Florence, 1656, based on Calderón's *Los empeños de un acaso*, 1651).

Spain itself had to wait until 1659/1660 before it could savour wholly-sung operas in Spanish with music by a Spanish composer. These were *La púrpura de la rosa*, text by Calderón, music probably by Juan Hidalgo, and *Celos aun del aire matan*, libretto again by Calderón, music certainly by Hidalgo, and certainly Italianate for the most part, after Cavalli. Wholly-sung opera was a novelty for the Spanish court which proved not to their taste. At about the same time, Cardinal Mazarin, partly out of love of opera and partly from political expediency, brought opera to Paris; this too proved not to the court's taste, perhaps for comparable reasons. In any case, Calderón's fears (expressed in the prologue to *La púrpura de la rosa*) that the Spanish temperament ('cólera') would prove impatient of opera's vocal 'monotony' were thereby vindicated. For the next three decades the Madrid court reverted almost always to the kind of partly-sung opera known as *zarzuela* which it had been enjoying from the hand of Calderón and his collaborators for some twenty years. Yet, since *zarzuela* librettos fed on the ingredients of Spanish tragicomedy rather as Italian opera librettos did, Madrid had managed after all not to turn its back on a musical form no European court could now afford to ignore.

Further Reading

Lope de Vega, *Arte nuevo de hacer comedias en este tiempo*, ed. Juana de José Prades (Madrid, 1971).

Shirley B. Whitaker, 'Florentine opera comes to Spain: Lope de Vega's *La selva sin amor*', *Journal of Hispanic Philology*, ix (1984), pp. 43-66.

Juan Vélez de Guevara, '*Los celos hacen estrellas*' ed. por *J.E. Varey & N.D. Shergold, con una edición y estudio de la música por Jack Sage* (London, 1970).

Jack Sage, 'The function of music in the theatre of Calderón', *Critical Studies of Calderón's Comedias*, ed. J.E. Varey (London, 1973), pp. 209-230.

Jack Sage, 'Music as an *instrumentum regni* in Spanish seventeenth-century drama', *Bulletin of Hispanic Studies*, lxi (1984), pp. 384-390.

Margaret Rich Greer & Louise Stein, *Pedro Calderón de la Barca, 'La estatua de Prometeo'. A Critical Edition by M.R.G. With a Study of the Music by L.S.* (Kassel, 1986).

Angeles Cardona, Don Cruikshank & Martin Cunningham, *Pedro Calderón de la Barca, Tomás de Torrejón y Velasco, 'La púrpura de la rosa'* (Kassel, 1990).

B. and C.L. Brancaforte, *La primera tradución del 'Lazarillo de Tormes' por Giulio Strozzi* (Ravenna, 1977).

Sally Burgess as Minerva in David Freeman's 1989 production for ENO, conducted by Paul Daniel and designed by David Roger (photo: Laurie Lewis)

Monteverdi Returns to his Homeland

Tim Carter

In a sense, Monteverdi's home had always been the theatre: his dramatic madrigals, and his *Orfeo*, by common consent the first great opera, reveal his fascination for the stage and its potential for displaying music's power. But he came late to the new Venetian opera. Now in his seventies, he was the 'grand old man' of music in Venice — he had been Director of Music at the Basilica of St Mark since 1613. Perhaps he wanted to keep his distance from the rather sordid world of the public opera house, where time and money were at a premium (no less than five new operas were performed in the three seasons following the opening of the Teatro S. Cassiano in 1637). However, Monteverdi was also anxious to guard his reputation — younger men were fast making their mark — and his powers of invention had scarcely diminished with age: indeed, he published his Eighth Book of Madrigals (the *Madrigali guerrieri, et amorosi*, 'Madrigals of War and Love') in 1638 and the massive collection of sacred music, the *Selva morale e spirituale*, in 1640-41. As for opera, he bided his time — as contemporaries noted — before reviving his *Arianna* in 1639-40 (it was first staged in Mantua in 1608). This served to remind Venetians of his considerable musical presence: although never published in full — and the work is almost entirely lost today — *Arianna* had somehow gained an extraordinary reputation in opera's brief history. The revival also allowed Monteverdi to test the water: opera was now very different from what the composer had known in his Mantuan years.

Just how much things had changed is clear from the differences between *Arianna* (even with cuts and adaptations) and Monteverdi's first new opera for Venice, *Il ritorno d'Ulisse in patria* (The Return of Ulysses to his Homeland), also produced in 1640. The classical context is the same, but we move from the rather rarefied world of Ovid — and the refined literary world of the tragedy (so *Arianna* was styled on the title-page of its libretto) — towards the rough-hewn terrain of Homer (*Odyssey*, XIII-XXIII), with his swashbuckling characters and their rumbustious deeds. The Trojan War and its aftermath provided ideal material for the new epic opera: Monteverdi returned there in his next (now lost) opera, *Le nozze d'Enea e Lavinia* (The Wedding of Aeneas and Lavinia) of 1641. Moreover, contemporary audiences gladly recognized the well established connection between Troy, classical Rome and the new Rome, Venice. In this and other ways, and like all the arts, opera served to articulate the so-called 'myth of Venice', extolling the greatness of the Most Serene Republic:

> Venice, always and on every occasion extraordinary, and never tired of displaying her greatness, has discovered the remarkable also in virtuoso entertainment, having introduced a few years ago the presentation in music of grand drama with such sets and stage-machines that they surpass all belief; and what the richest treasuries can produce only with difficulty (and only rarely) in royal halls here we see easily achieved with private resources, not only in one, but in three theatres at once; and competing with each other for the greatest perfections, they each draw spectators from the most remote parts of Italy. (Maiolino Bisaccioni, *Apparati scenici per lo Teatro Novissimo* (1644), trans. Ellen Rosand)

Scenes from 'The Return of Ulysses' at ENO in 1989: the return of Telemachus with Minerva (Laurence Dale and Sally Burgess), and Neptune (Clive Bayley) about to turn the Phaeacians' ship into a rock (photos: Laurie Lewis)

There are problems with the sources for *Ulysses*. The libretto (in five acts) was not published for the performance: we have only a number of manuscript copies. The score (in three acts) survives in manuscript in Vienna (Österreichische Nationalbibliothek, MS 18763). By the mid-1630s, Monteverdi had close connections with the Habsburg court in Vienna, and he dedicated his *Madrigali guerrieri, et amorosi* and the *Selva morale e spirituale* respectively to Emperor Ferdinand III and his wife, Eleonora Gonzaga. But there is as yet no evidence to associate this copy of the score directly with Monteverdi, and the idea that he himself sent it to Vienna for a possible performance remains pure (and perhaps idle) speculation. Similarly, the relation of the Vienna score to the Venetian première of *Ulysses* is unclear, and it has a number of omissions (one section, at least, because it was 'melancholic', referring to Act Three, scene two).

Monteverdi's librettist was the Venetian nobleman and amateur poet Giacomo Badoaro (1602-1654). Like Giovanni Francesco Busenello (the librettist of *L'incoronazione di Poppea*), Badoaro was a member of the Accademia degli Incogniti, a rather libertine group of literati who as ideologues and entrepreneurs had a significant influence on early Venetian opera. He told Monteverdi that he had written his text precisely 'to excite Your Lordship's skill to make known to this city that in the warmth of the emotions there is a big difference between a real sun and a painted one', and both the libretto and the composer's response to it suggest an effort to make an impression. A synopsis reveals the kinds of subject matter and scenic and musical effects required of opera in its new public context.

Prologue: After the opening sinfonia, Human Frailty, lamenting her mortality in a recurring refrain [1], acknowledges her submission to Time, Fortune and Love. They, in turn, proclaim their dominion over men [2].

Act One: In her palace in Ithaca, Penelope awaits the return of her husband Ulysses, twenty years absent after the Trojan War. She cannot be consoled by her nurse, Ericlea — her two heartfelt refrains [3,4] provide a powerful statement of the pains of separation. In contrast, the love-pains of Melanto [5] and Eurimachus are but fleeting. Neptune — long opposed to Ulysses — complains to Jove about his rescue by the Phæacians: they have brought Ulysses back to Ithaca [6], leaving him sleeping on the beach. In punishment, Neptune turns their ship into a rock. Ulysses awakes [7] and believes himself to have been abandoned. But Minerva enters disguised as a shepherd — a jolly song makes the point [8] — and tells Ulysses that the island is his home. She reveals herself to his amazement: his 'O fortunato Ulisse' ('O blest and happy Ulysses') will recur as a refrain [9]. Ulysses is told to bathe his forehead in a nearby fountain, which changes him into an old man. He is to enter his palace unrecognized and outwit Antinous, Peisander and Amphinomous, the suitors who are squandering the wealth of the state while wooing his chaste wife; meanwhile, Minerva will bring Ulysses' son, Telemachus, from Sparta. Ulysses again rejoices (a new version of 'O blest and happy Ulysses'). Melanto urges Penelope to forget Ulysses and love another [10]. Eumæus, a shepherd faithful to Ulysses, tends his flock and argues with the social parasite Irus. Ulysses, disguised, enters and tells Eumæus of the imminent return of his sovereign.

Act Two: Telemachus arrives with Minerva on her chariot [11]. Eumæus welcomes the prince and presents the old man who, he says, has news of his father's return. A fire-bolt descends from heaven to reveal Ulysses in his true form. Father and son are joyfully reunited [12], and they plan their return to the palace. Melanto and Eurimachus discuss Penelope's continued devotion to her husband. The suitors enter to pursue their advances, but Penelope staunchly resists [13]. Eumæus announces the imminent return of Telemachus and Ulysses, and the suitors are disconcerted. They plot to kill Telemachus, but the sight of Jove's eagle flying overhead warns them against the plan, and they decide instead to redouble their wooing of Penelope with songs and (musically imitated) sighs [14]. Minerva outlines to Ulysses a plan to remove the suitors, and Eumæus recounts Penelope's lasting fidelity, while Telemachus discusses his recent travels with Penelope. Antinous and Irus meet Eumæus and Ulysses, dressed as a beggar. Antinous treats them badly and Irus provokes Ulysses into a fight [15]: he is roundly thrashed. Penelope orders that the beggar be made welcome. The suitors redouble their efforts to gain her favour with gifts, and she proclaims that she will marry whoever manages to string Ulysses' great bow. The suitors agree willingly, but all three fail the test. The beggar asks to enter the competition, while renouncing the prize, and succeeds in stringing the bow. Invoking Minerva's protection, Ulysses lets fly his arrows at the suitors, killing them all [16].

Act Three: Irus grieves for his colleagues, and himself [17], in a splendid take-off of the typical lament-scene (a following scene for Mercury and the ghosts of the suitors is missing). Penelope refuses to believe Eumæus' claim that the beggar who bent the bow was indeed Ulysses [18], and even Telemachus cannot convince her. Minerva and Juno decide to plead with Jove on Ulysses' behalf [19]. Neptune is pacified, and choruses of celestial and maritime spirits praise the new accord. Ericlea ponders whether or not to tell of Ulysses' return [20]; and Penelope still refuses the assurances of Eumæus and Telemachus. Even when Ulysses enters in his true form, she fears a trick, proclaiming her constancy [21]. Ericlea insists that it is indeed Ulysses [22]: she saw him in his bath and recognized a hunting scar. But only when Ulysses correctly describes the embroidered quilt on their nuptial bed is Penelope convinced, finally recognizing her husband [23]. They are united in a blissful love-duet.

Only three sets are specified ('reggia', a palace; 'marittima', the sea; 'boscareccia', a grove; we do not know the setting for the Prologue): perhaps significantly, another set (a desert opening to reveal the inferno in the second scene of Act Three) is omitted in the score. Thus *Ulysses* was scarcely as spectacular as some contemporary operas, particularly those staged at the Teatro Novissimo (1641-5) under the influence of the prominent stage designer Giacomo Torelli. Badoaro seems to have been sensitive to the criticism: in the preface to *L'Ulisse errante* (Ulysses the Wanderer), a 'prequel' to *Il ritorno d'Ulisse in patria* set to music by Francesco Sacrati in 1644, he responds to the accusation of poverty of invention. Yet there is a fair amount of stage business designed to amaze the audience: gods emerging from the sea and seated in the heavens, the Phæacian ship turned into a rock, Telemachus and Minerva on a chariot flying through the air, Ulysses struck by heavenly fire and disappearing beneath the earth, and the eagle flying over the head of the suitors, not to mention the blood-bath (with Minerva in a machine) at the end of Act Two. Badoaro also exploits other devices now standard in Venetian opera: the sententious prologue, scurrilous (Irus) and comic characters (Ericlea, compare Arnalta in *Poppea*), dallying lovers (Melanto and Eurimachus, compare Damigella and Valletto in *Poppea*) and disguises (Minerva, Ulysses). Not suprisingly, the opera seems to have been a success: it was staged in Bologna in 1640 and revived in Venice in 1641; one commentator noted that 'it was described poetically and represented

Penelope (Janet Baker) and her three suitors (John Fryatt, Ugo Trama, Bernard Dickerson) in Peter Hall's 1972 production for Glyndebourne, conducted by Raymond Leppard, and designed by John Bury (photo: Guy Gravett)

musically with that splendour that will make it remembered in every century'; and there are allusions to *Ulysses* in later operas, including Francesco Sacrati's *La finta pazza* (The Feigned Madwoman) of 1641 and Badoaro and Sacrati's *L'Ulisse errante*.

Monteverdi would have been familiar with most of these scenic devices from his earlier experience of writing music for operas, *intermedi* and tournaments for Mantua and Parma. But the musical garb in which the action was now to be clothed was very different. In *Orfeo* and (as far as we can tell) *Arianna*, the musical focus lay in the recitative, the flexible, declamatory speech-song devised by Jacopo Peri and Giulio Caccini for the first operas in Florence ([7,21] provide straightforward examples in *Ulysses*). This recitative, halfway between speech and song according to Peri, was authenticated by (more than inspired by) precedents drawn from Classical Antiquity, and it carried the torch for 'naturalism' in musical discourse (witness the term *recitar cantando* —to recite in song — commonly used for this musical speech). Certainly other forms and styles appear in early operas, not least *Orfeo*: strophic songs, polyphonic choruses, instrumental sinfonias and ritornellos all have their part to play. But typically, the set-piece climax of *Arianna* (and the one section to survive) is a recitative lament, where, for all Monteverdi's intense melody and searing dissonances, it is the speech-like flow of the music that fixes the expression of Ariadne's grief.

In one sense, Venetian opera of the late 1630s and 1640s marks a reduction in musical possibilities for the composer. The commercial exigencies of the public opera house prohibited the extensive choruses and large-scale instrumental participation characteristic of *Orfeo*: witness the near total absence of choruses in *Ulysses*, and the use of only a small-scale string ensemble (sometimes simply improvising on a bass) and a few continuo instruments. Nevertheless, the expressive potential of operatic music was vastly expanded. By the 1630s, more structured — and more tuneful — musical styles and forms were coming to the fore, in the manner popularised by the arias in contemporary song-books. These arias are strophic settings of strophic poems (one with regularly structured stanzas): the regular poetic structure also establishes standard musical characteristics — clear-cut melodies, strong harmonic support and rhythmic drive. Arias are often in triple time (compare [5,10]), although duple time (for example, [8,11]) starts to make a significant appearance from the 1610s. Also, by the 1620s and '30s, Venetian composers were developing sensuous new kinds of triple-time writing, both in their song-books and (later) in their operas. More to the point, such structured melodies were increasingly usurping the place of recitative as the sign of serious musico-dramatic statement. This is not necessarily to say that composers pandered to the less sophisticated tastes of audiences outside the intellectual and court circles associated with early Florentine opera and solo song. Rather, composers seem to have realised that the formal distancing of the aria engages — perhaps paradoxically — far more closely with the emotions in hand. Monteverdi argued the point, as it were, in a number of crucial settings in his Eighth Book of Madrigals: 'Non havea Febo ancora' — the so-called *Lament of the Nymph* — constructed over a repeating ground bass is the best example. Here the composer seems to be reclaiming the ground for music as music, rather than as some spurious form of speech.

One of the striking features of early Venetian opera, particularly Monteverdi's, is that the music seems able to shift flexibly between recitative- and aria-styles, sometimes within the space of only two or three bars. Such shifts will generally be prompted by one or more textual cues. For example, the composer can move into patterned triple- or duple-time writing to imitate (in the literal sense) a specific word: 'singing' or 'song' is the obvious example. Here the use of aria-styles stands in the category of stereotyped imitative gestures: other examples are Irus' stuttering — and indeed other humorous features of his mock lament opening Act Three [17] — and also the so-called *stile concitato*, the 'aroused' style, coined by Monteverdi in the 1620s. The *stile concitato*, with its triadic fanfares and fast repeating rhythms, appears in the Eighth Book whenever 'war' or the like is mentioned (see the *Combattimento di Tancredi e Clorinda*, first performed in 1624), and there are a number of examples in *Ulysses*, particularly as Ulysses attacks Irus and then the suitors [15,16].

Other cues for aria are less to do with the content of the text (although that remains important) than its structure. Even in the earliest operas, texts for arias and related forms were differentiated from those for recitative by their poetic structure. Recitative verse is in free-rhyming seven- and eleven-syllable lines: the loose structure well suits its musical and dramatic function as the main carrier of the action. 'Aria' texts, however, exploit more regular rhyme-schemes, and often other line-lengths (say, five-, six- or eight-syllable lines) — contemporary writers justified this non-classical use of varied verse forms by the fact that, to quote the anonymous librettist of *Le nozze d'Enea e Lavinia*, 'tragedies in music are permitted that freedom which those simply recited do not have'. Monteverdi was certainly able to construct arias from recitative-type verse: this is one of his trademarks, developed to the full in his Eighth Book of Madrigals (witness the duet 'O sia tranquillo il mare, o pien d'orgoglio'). But in opera, and at least in the first instance, it is the responsibility of the librettist to indicate to the composer the musical style to be used at any given moment in the work. Thus seven- and eleven-syllable lines with little or no rhyme prompt recitative, and more structured verse, often using other line-lengths, prompt some kind of aria writing, with or without strophic structures: this establishes structural paradigms for text-music relationships in Italian opera that last through the nineteenth century and beyond.

As a result, within any libretto changes of line-length, and of metrical accentuation and rhyming structure, have clear implications for the composer. He may accept or reject such implications — of course, rejection is the more interesting possibility — but we are dealing here with a true, if often difficult, partnership between verse and music. The issues can best be explored by looking at the beginning of Act Two of *Ulysses*, where Telemachus is brought to Ithaca by Minerva and is greeted by the shepherd Eumæus and

Minerva presides over the destruction of the Suitors in Pierre Audi's production of 'Ulysses' for the Netherlands Opera, 1990, designed by Michael Simon and Jorge Jara, lit by Jean Kalman, and conducted by Glen Wilson (photo: Jaap Pieper)

the disguised Ulysses. Here is the Italian text, with indications of rhyme and metre, and of the musical style chosen for each section (a straight line indicates an aria-style in duple time; a wavy line an aria-style in triple time; and a dotted line, recitative):

Line		Rhyme-scheme	Metre	Musical style
	TELEMACHUS			
1	Lieto cammino,	A	5	
	dolce viaggio,	B	5	*duple*
	passa il carro divino	A	7	*time*
	come che fosse un raggio.	B	7	
	MINERVA/TELEMACHUS			
5	Gli Dei possenti	C	5	
	navigan l'aure,	D	5	*triple*
	solcano i venti.	C	5	*time*
	MINERVA			
	Eccoti giunto alle paterne ville,	E	11	
	Telemaco prudente.	F	7	
10	Non ti scordar già mai de' miei consigli,	G	11	*recitative*
	che se dal buon sentier travia la mente	F	11	
	incontrerai perigli.	G	7	
	TELEMACHUS			
	Periglio invan mi guida,	H	7	
	se tua bontà m'affida.	H	7	*recitative*
	EUMÆUS			
15	O gran figlio d'Ulisse,	I	7	
	è pur ver che tu torni	J	7	
	a serenar della tua madre i giorni,	J	11	
	e pur sei giunto al fine	K	7	
	di tua casa cadente	L	7	*triple*
20	a riparar l'altissime ruine?	K	11	*time*
	Fugga, fugga il cordoglio e cessi il pianto;	M	11	
	facciam, o pelegrino,	N	7	
	all'allegrezze nostre honor col canto.	M	11	
	EUMÆUS/ULYSSES			
	Verdi spiagge, al lieto giorno	O	8	
25	rabellite herbette e fiori,	P	8	*triple*
	scherzin l'aure con gli amori,	P	8	*time*
	ride il ciel al bel ritorno.	O	8	
	TELEMACHUS			
	Vostri cortesi auspici a me son grati ...	Q	11	

Telemachus' quatrain of five-, then seven-syllable lines (lines 1-4) — praising his 'happy journeying' — is followed by three five-syllable lines (5-7) for him and Minerva — invoking the power of the gods — and then a group of seven- and eleven-syllable lines (8-14) as Minerva tells Telemachus that he is in his homeland. The loosely rhyming seven- and eleven-syllable lines continue as Eumæus greets Telemachus (15-23); then the text shifts to rhymed eight-syllable lines (24-27) for Eumæus and Ulysses noting the 'Woods and meadows freshly springing' as happiness returns to Ithaca. Finally, Telemachus responds (28 *et seq.*) in eleven-syllable lines. These changes in metre (and in the use of rhyme) reflect the dramatic function of the various sections of the text: the free rhymed seven- and eleven-syllable lines (8-23) represent action-dialogue — one character speaks to another — while the sections in other line-lengths (1-4, 5-7, 24-27) involve more passive statement or commentary.

No less straightforward, with one notable exception, is the correlation between these verse structures and the music. Telemachus' first quatrain becomes a duple-time aria [11] extended, by repetition of the first two lines at the end, into a rounded ABA structure. The duet for Minerva and Telemachus (5-7) adopts a suave triple time, a style also used in the duet for Eumæus and Ulysses (24-27). But when the text first shifts to dialogue in seven- and eleven-syllable lines (at line 8, as Minerva tells Telemachus 'Safely I've brought you to your father's kingdom'), the music changes to free recitative.

The exception is Eumæus' speech in lines 15-23 greeting Telemachus ('O great son of Ulysses'). The structure of the verse — and its status as speech directed to another character — prompts recitative: only the last line ('all'allegrezze nostre . . .' — 'in joyful celebration raise our voices'), with its reference to 'canto' (song), suggests imitation in a brief aria — Monteverdi acts accordingly, preceding it with one line in recitative to make the point. But the decision to begin Eumæus' speech as a triple-time aria overrules the text. It is certainly an appropriate gesture — the shepherd's joy at seeing Telemachus bursts the bounds of controlled speech — but it is one produced solely by the composer, as a result of what Ellen Rosand has called 'Monteverdi's powerful brand of editing'. Not for the first time, and most certainly not for the last in the history of opera, a composer exerts his right to prevail over his librettist in producing drama through music. Yet Monteverdi thereby causes himself problems: in constructing an aria from verse that the librettist has devised for recitative (with long lines and a lack of patterning), he has to manhandle the text, repeating words for melody's sake ('O gran figlio, gran figlio d'Ulisse, o, o, o, o gran figlio d'Ulisse . . . e pur sei giunto, sei giunto al fine, al fine . . .'). Not for nothing did Badoaro claim that 'I no longer know how to recognise this work as mine'.

Apart from their dramatic impact, the arias provide relief from the recitative and also give a sense of shape to a scene. There is always a tension in opera between the need to present a forward-moving drama and the fact that music (we assume) requires some sense of structure, which normally involves repetition of some kind. Monteverdi took the point in *Orfeo*, and likewise in *Ulysses* we find him exploiting repetition, refrain and ritornello —often in spite of the verse — to give cohesion. Two of many possible examples are revealing in their different ways. As Ericlea considers telling Penelope of Ulysses' return (Act Three, scene eight), Monteverdi manipulates Badoaro's 24 lines (largely of *versi tronchi* — foreshortened lines with the accent unusually on the final syllable) into four sections linked by similar melodic ideas and musical refrains [20], with three statements of an instrumental ritornello further binding things together. Another instance is Penelope's recitative lament which opens Act One, in the heightened speech-song of *Orfeo* and *Arianna*. It has two striking ideas — 'Tu sol del tuo tornar perdesti il giorno' ('But you alone make no returning') [3] and 'Torna, deh torna Ulisse' ('Homeward turn, Ulysses') [4] — each recurring at key points in the scene.

Penelope's recitative echoes (in parts, literally) the great laments of Orpheus and Ariadne. But the choice of style here is significant. Triple- and duple-time arias, for all their virtues, are problematic in opera on the grounds of verisimilitude. In a period when the theatre was continually subject to Humanist strictures on realism — that art should somehow imitate life — opera could scarcely avoid the criticism that it was entirely illogical and implausible. In real life, social intercourse is carried out through speech, not song. Yet in opera, singing is the normal condition: the paradox has both buttressed and undermined the genre throughout its long history. The first opera composers tried to sweep the problem under the carpet, choosing

Neptune rises from the waves in Hans Werner Henze's 'Ulysses' at Salzburg in 1985 (photo: Linares)

mythological or pastoral subjects — music was the language of the gods, and of the shepherds and shepherdesses of Arcadia — preferably with heroes renowned for their musical prowess (Orpheus is the obvious example). But as the anonymous author of *Il corago*, a Florentine treatise on opera written around 1630, said: 'If we take as characters people close to our times, and of manners more obviously similar to ours, all too clearly this manner of sung speech soon presents itself to us as improbable and not lifelike [*inverisimile*]'. Even as opera gained slow and painful acceptance on the Italian stage — and as musical recitative became accepted as a plausible representation of speech — the question of verisimilitude continued to worry librettists and composers. Just how far could they go?

Their insecurity is apparent in many prefaces and treatises. Badoaro himself was sensitive to the complaint that, as Penelope says (in Act Three, scene nine), 'le favole fan riso, e non dan vita' (the singing translation is 'your tales may bring us laughter, not consolation', but there is another reading: 'stage-actions cause laughter, and do not present life'). He also raised the problems in his preface to *L'Ulisse errante*:

> Today, no one worries, to increase the delight of the spectators, about giving way to something not lifelike, which does not damage the action. Thus we see that to give more time for the changes of scene, we have introduced music, in which we cannot avoid something not lifelike — that men should carry out their most important business in song. Moreover, so as to enjoy all kinds of music in the theatre, we are accustomed to hearing pieces for two, three and more voices: this produces something else not lifelike — that talking together men should without thinking happen to say the same things. Therefore it is no wonder that, devoting ourselves to pleasing modern taste, we have rightly moved away from the ancient rules.

But the problem would not go away: hence the further attempts to establish reasonable principles whereby song (aria), not just 'speech' (recitative), could be allowed in opera without impropriety. Gods and allegorical figures —

Neptune, Jove, Minerva, Juno, Human Frailty, Time, Fortune, Love — can sing rather than speak by virtue of their superhuman powers. Indeed, it is song that distinguishes them from normal human beings, especially when that song contains virtuoso ornamentation (witness Minerva), establishing a connection between supernatural powers and vocal virtuosity lasting through Mozart's Queen of the Night and beyond. Shepherds, too, can sing (Eumæus) — by virtue of the pastoral convention   as can 'low' characters such as nurses (Ericlea) and servants such as Melanto and Irus: their social status is not at issue, and for that matter, such characters were often heard singing in contemporary comic theatre (for example, the *commedia dell'arte*). Noble characters, however, cause problems. We may be able to accept Ulysses singing rather than speaking: he is superhuman, if not half-god, and anyway he spends a good deal of the opera in disguise, which loosens the constraints (indeed, the fact that he sings enhances the disguise). But Penelope is in an entirely different position. What, other than the genre itself, will permit her to 'sing' aria, rather than 'speak' recitative?

Just as Penelope shuts herself away in her palace, just as she uses her chastity as a defence against the world, so does she effectively imprison herself in the world of recitative: she will not allow herself — or cannot be allowed — to sing. Certainly she can speak — indeed at great length in Acts Two and Three — and with profound emotion, as in her opening lament. But song is foreign to her: significantly, even when Badoaro provides textual cues for aria, Monteverdi rejects the possibility (Penelope's speech at the end of Act Two, scene five — from the second appearance of 'Non voglio amar', 'I will not love' — is an intriguing example). The composer's decision is all the more striking in the light of his evident commitment to aria seen at the beginning of Act Two. More than her palace, or even her chastity, it is Penelope's refusal to express herself in and through song that protects her from the outside world.

But Penelope eventually learns to sing — she escapes her self-constructed prison — and wonderfully so. When she finally acknowledges Ulysses, the barriers come down, and Penelope can take up her song. At first, she does so hesitantly ('Hor si ti riconosco', 'Yes now I can believe you'), but as her confidence grows, she revels in a ravishing triple-time aria ('Illustratevi, o cieli', 'Shine in glory, o heavens' [23]). Here, for the first time in the opera (the brief passage for Ulysses in Act Two, scene twelve [16] is a different case), the instruments join the voice in celebratory refrains. And once again, the decision is chiefly Monteverdi's, not Badoaro's. It is a stunning moment of emotional, even sexual, release: Ulysses' return to his homeland is nothing in comparison with Penelope emerging from twenty years of doubt, despair and self-repression to sing the language of love, a language described earlier by the three suitors in a very different context [14]:

In Love's harmonious consort   Amor è un' armonia,
sweetest singing is deep sighing . . .   sono canti i sospiri . . .
                                                (*lit.* Love is harmony, sighs are songs . . .)

Monteverdi has indeed returned home, and with the insight to exploit the essential paradox of opera to make profound emotional and dramatic points both about his characters and about sung drama as a whole. By learning to sing again, Penelope becomes emotionally whole: this is a timeless message not only, perhaps not even, about the power of love — it is the power of song, indeed a matter of life, not laughter. But power corrupts when placed in the wrong hands. Nero and Poppea, for example, need no lessons in song: they know the words and music of love right from the start of Monteverdi's last opera. Where that leads them, however, is quite another matter.

Music Examples

[1] HUMAN FRAILTY

Mor - tal co - - sa son i - - o
A frail mor - tal you see me,

[2]

TIME   FORTUNE   LOVE

Per me fra - gi - le   Per me mi - se - ro   Per me tor - bi - do
Time's harsh ban-ish-ment   For-tune's pun-ish-ment   Love's fierce chas-tise-ment

[3] PENELOPE

Tu sol_____ del tuo tor - nar   del tuo tor - nar   tu
but you,_____ but you a - lone,   but you a - lone,   but

sol_____ del tuo tor - nar   per - des-ti il gior - no.
you,_____ but you a - lone   make no re - turn - ing.

[4] PENELOPE

tor - na tor - na   tor - na   deh _ tor - na   tor - na U-lis - se _
Home-ward, home-ward,   home - ward,   ah, _ home-ward   turn, U - lys - ses. _

[5] MELANTO

Du - ri e pe - no - si son gli a - mo - ro - si fie - ri de - sir
La - dies, take warn-ing lest thought - less scorn - ing quen-ches love's fire;

[6] PHÆACIANS

In ques - to bas - so mon-do l'huo-mo puol quan - to vuol
We hap-py bold Phæ - a - cians sail the seas as we please;

[7] ULYSSES, *waking*

Dor-mo an - co - ra? Dor-mo an - co - ra o son des - to
Am I sleep - ing? Am I sleep - ing or a - wake?

[8] MINERVA, *dressed as a shepherd boy*

Ca-ra ca-ra e lie-ta ca-ra e lie-ta ca-ra e lie - ta gio-ven - tù
Mer-ry, gay and joy-ful, gay and joy-ful, gay and joy - ful days of youth!

[9] ULYSSES

O for - tu - na - to, O for - tu - na - to U-lis - se.
O blest and hap-py, O blest and hap - py U - lys - ses!

[10] MELANTO

A - ma dun - que che d'A - mo - re
There - fore love, since Love and Beau - ty

[11] TELEMACHUS

Lie - to lie - to lie - to cam-mi - no
Hap - py, hap - py, hap - py our jour - neying,

[12]

TELEMACHUS   ULYSSES

Oh pa - dre so-spi - ra - to Oh fi - glio de-si - a - to
O fa - ther I have sighed for, O son whom I have longed for,

[13] PENELOPE

Non vo - glio a-mar no no ch'a-man - do pe - ne - rò
I will not love, no no, for love brings bit - ter woe,

A - mor è un ar - mo - ni - a   so - no   can - ti   i   so - spi - ri
In Love's har - mo - nious con - sort sweet - est   sing - ing   is   deep sigh - ing.

[15] IRUS, *preparing to fight*

Su su dun - que su su   al - la ciuf - fa al - la   ciuf - fa
Now then, cow - ard, come on!   We'll fight to the   fin - ish,

[16] ULYSSES, *killing the Suitors with his arrows*

[plus strings]

Al - le mor - ti al - le stra - gi al - le mor - ti al - le stra - gi al - le ru - i - ne
We bring fear, we bring death, we bring fear, we bring death, we bring des - truc - tion,

[17] IRUS, *making a ridiculous entrance*

Basso continuo

do - lor   o   mar - tir
what pain,   O dis - tress

[18] EUMÆUS

U - lis - se U - lis - se è vi - vo è vi - vo è qui è qui.
U - lys - ses, U - lys - ses is liv - ing, is liv - ing, is here, is here.

U - lis - se trop-po er - rò
U - lys - ses waits too long,

[20] ERICLEA

non si de' sem - pre dir ciò che si sa
To keep si - lent is best, is ho - nes - ty,

[21] PENELOPE

Con-sor-te io so - no con - sor-te io so - no ma del per - du - to U-lis - se
True wife am I, true wife am I, but to the lost U - lys-ses.

[22] ERICLEA

è que-sto è que-sto U-lis - se ca-sta e gran don - na
This man is in - deed U - lys - ses, no - ble La - dy:

[23] PENELOPE

Il - lu - stra - te-vi o cie - li rin - fio - ra - te-vi o pra - ti
Shine in glo - ry, O hea-vens, bloom with flow - ers, O mea-dows.

85

Janet Baker and Benjamin Luxon (Penelope and Ulysses) in Peter Hall's production at Glyndebourne, 1972 (photo: Guy Gravett)

The Return of Ulysses
Il ritorno d'Ulisse in patria

Dramma in musica

Opera in Three Acts and a Prologue
by Giacomo Badoaro

English version by Anne Ridler

Music by Claudio Monteverdi

Il ritorno d'Ulisse in patria was first performed at the Teatro SS. Giovanni e Paolo, Venice in 1640. The first performance in Britain was in a broadcast on January 16, 1928. The first staged performance in Britain was at the St Pancras Town Hall, London on March 16, 1965. The first performance of this version was by English National Opera at the London Coliseum on November 8, 1989.

Hans Franzen as Neptune in Jean-Pierre Ponnelle's 1979 production in Zurich, conducted by Nikolaus Harnoncourt, designed by Pet Halmen (photo: Susan Schimert-Ramme)

CHARACTERS

Human Frailty	L'Humana fragilità		*mezzo-soprano*
Time	Il Tempo		*bass*
Fortune	La Fortuna		*mezzo-soprano*
Love	Amore		*mezzo-soprano*
Jove	Giove		*tenor*
Neptune	Nettuno		*bass*
Minerva	Minerva		*soprano/ mezzo-soprano*
Juno	Giunone		*soprano/ mezzo-soprano*
Ulysses	Ulisse		*tenor*
Penelope	Penelope	*wife to Ulysses*	*mezzo-soprano*
Telemachus	Telemaco	*their son*	*tenor*
Eumæus	Eumete	*faithful servant of Ulysses and a swineherd*	*tenor*
Antinous	Antinoo		*bass*
Peisander	Pisandro	*suitors to Penelope*	*tenor*
Amphinomous	Anfinomo		*tenor or counter-tenor*
Eurimachus	Eurimaco	*Melanto's lover*	*tenor*
Melanto	Melanto	*Penelope's maid*	*mezzo-soprano*
Irus	Iro	*a glutton*	*tenor*
Ericlea	Ericlea	*Ulysses's old nurse*	*mezzo-soprano/ counter-tenor*

Chorus of Phæacians, Chorus from Heaven, Chorus from the Sea

The drama takes place on the island of Ithaca.

There are several manuscript copies of the libretto in Venice, and a single manuscript score in Vienna. These sources diverge in many ways: the libretto is in five acts while the score is divided into three, and the composer restructured or cut passages, and added interjections and repetitions. Our Italian text follows the score, with the words laid out according to the general principles of a libretto. Footnotes indicate important discrepancies, and musical numbers ('ritornello', 'sinfonia') have been taken from the score.

The numbers in square brackets refer to the musical examples.

Prologue

Human Frailty, Time, Fortune, Love.

HUMAN FRAILTY

A frail mortal you see me, my life's uncertain;
every tremor disturbs me, a breeze can overthrow me.
As Time was my creator, he shall destroy me.

[1] Mortal cosa son io, fattura humana:
tutto mi turba, un soffio sol m'abbatte;
il Tempo, che mi crea, quel mi combatte.

TIME

Time's tooth is sharper
than a dagger;
more fiercely
it pierces.
You will feel it, foolish creatures,
for though my step is lame and halting
    I've wings for flying.

Salvo è niente
dal mio dente:
ei rode,
ei gode.
Non fuggite, o mortali,
che se ben zoppo ho l'ali.

Sinfonia

HUMAN FRAILTY

A frail mortal you see me, my life's uncertain,
seeking a refuge where I may dwell in safety.
But cruel Fortune makes game of mortal frailty.

[1] Mortal cosa son io, fattura humana:
senza periglio invan ricerco loco,
che frale vita è di Fortuna un gioco.

FORTUNE

Blind Fortune now blesses,
now sorely distresses.
I'm deaf to all pleading,
I'm blind and unheeding,
delight or displeasure
I deal in due measure.

Mia vita son voglie,
le gioie, le doglie.
Son cieca, son sorda,
non vedo, non odo;
ricchezze, grandezze
dispenso a mio modo.

HUMAN FRAILTY

I am frail, I am wretched, my life's uncertain.
I must suffer this pain through Love's ill-treating;
he steals my precious youth, so fair, so fleeting.

[1] Mortal cosa son io, fattura humana:
al tiranno d'Amor serva sen pace
la mia fiorita età verde e fugace.

Ritornello

LOVE

All the gods fear my darts,
and I can wound all hearts.
Blindly my arrows fly, the sport commences:
naked archer am I, against my arrows
    all vain are your defences.

Dio de' Dei feritor
mi dice il mondo Amor.
Cieco saettator, alato, ignudo,
contro il mio stral non val difesa
o scudo.

HUMAN FRAILTY

I am frail, I am wretched, my life's uncertain.
Tricked by a blind god, a lame god,
and cheated by fickle Fortune.

[1] Misera son ben io, fattura humana:
creder a ciechi e zoppi è cosa vana.

Time's harsh banishment —	[2] Per me fragile —

FORTUNE

Fortune's punishment —	Per me misero —

LOVE

Love's fierce chastisement —	Per me torbido —

TIME, FORTUNE, LOVE

This man shall know.   Quest'huom sarà.

TIME

I hasten, I threaten,	Il Tempo ch' affretta,

FORTUNE

By peril he's stricken,	Fortuna ch' alletta,

LOVE

False hopes I can quicken,	Amor che saetta,

TIME, FORTUNE, LOVE

No pity we'll show.   Pietate non ha.

Penury, agony, misery, this man shall know.

[Fragile, misero, torbido quest' huom sarà.]

The prologue in Pierre Audi's production for the Netherlands Opera in 1990 (photo: Jaap Pieper)

Act One

Sinfonia

PENELOPE

Poor wretched queen	Di misera Regina
condemned to never-ending grief and bitter crying.	non terminati mai dolenti affanni.
He is absent whom I long for,	L'aspettato non giunge,
yet the years are flying.	e pur fuggono gli anni;
The sequence of my days is weary and endless,	la serie del penar è lunga ahi troppo,
Time is halting and lame to one who's friendless.	a chi vive in angoscie il tempo è zoppo.
Lying hopes, you deceived me,	Fallacissima speme,
and now you are no longer green and youthful	speranze non più verdi ma canute,
you cannot bring me healing,	all'invecchiato male
For to your tender promise you were unfaithful.	non promettete più pace o salute.
Twenty years have vanished	Scorsero quattro lustri
since that unforgettable day	dal memorabil giorno
on which that Trojan,	in cui con sue rapine
disdainful and reckless,	il superbo Trojano
brought war upon his country and final ruin.	chiamò l'alta sua patria alle rovine.
So did Troy perish justly,	A ragion arse Troja,
for an unchaste desire	poichè l'amore impuro,
that burns in sinful longing	ch'è un delitto di foco,
by fire should be punished.	si purga con le fiamme;
But I suffer unjustly, though I am innocent,	ma ben contro ragione per l'altrui fallo
endure condemnation,	condannata innocente
and through another's fault	dall'altrui colpe io sono
I must suffer retribution.	l'afflitta penitente.
Ulysses, wise and bold Ulysses,	Ulisse accorto e saggio,
you may boast of punishing adultery,	tu che punir gli adulteri ti vanti,
sharpening weapons, fanning the flames	aguzzi l'armi e susciti le fiamme
to avenge the errors	per vendicar gli errori
of Helen the faithless! And yet you left me,	d'una profuga Greca, e intanto lasci
your chaste wife, forsaken	la tua casta consorte
among enemies and rivals	fra nemici rivali
by whom my honour, my life, may be taken.	in dubbio dell' honore, in forse a morte.
Every farewell looks homeward	Ogni partenza attende
with a hope ever-burning,	desiato ritorno,
but you alone make no returning.	[3] tu sol del tuo tornar perdesti il giorno.

ERICLEA

I, unhappy Ericlea,	Infelice Ericlea,
your nurse and your companion,	nutrice sconsolata,
would share your grief, O my beloved sovereign.	compiangi il duol della Regina amata.

PENELOPE

Is it only for me Fate is unchanging?	Non è dunque per me varia la sorte?
And has Fortune exchanged	Cangiò forse Fortuna
her ever-changing wheel for one immovable?	la volubile ruota in stabil seggio?
And must her sails hang lifeless	E la sua pronta vela

that should bear every mortal	ch'ogni human caso porta
over life's ocean flying,	fra l'incostanza a volo,
yet for me no breath of wind supplying?	sol per me non raccoglie un fiato solo.
Is there no hope for me, when for other mortals	Cangia per altri pur aspetto in cielo
the planets can change their courses?	le stelle erranti e fisse.
Homeward, ah, homeward turn Ulysses!	Torna, deh torna Ulisse!
Homeward Ulysses, Penelope awaits you.	Penelope t'aspetta,
Innocent, she sighs for you;	l'innocente sospira,
injured, she suffers;	piange l'offesa e contro
but in spite of your great offence	il tenace offensor nè pur s'adira
she will not blame you.	all'anima affannata;
Before my afflicted soul I will plead your pardon,	porto le sue discolpe acciò non resti
because I find in you no taint of cruelty.	di crudeltà macchiato,
Fate contrived my sorrows and Fate is guilty.	ma falso de' miei danni incolpo il Fato.
And so as your defender	Così per tua difesa
I'll do battle. To Destiny, to highest heaven,	col déstino, col Cielo
my fearless challenge rises.	fomento guerre e stabilisco risse.
Homeward, ah, homeward turn Ulysses! [4]	Torna, deh torna Ulisse!

ERICLEA

Parting that knows no returning	Partir senza ritorno
is not in heaven's decree.	non può stella influir.
It cannot be,	non è partir, non è
ah no, it cannot be.	ahi, che non è partir.

PENELOPE

Quiet returns to the waters,	Torna il tranquillo al mare,
zephyrs return to the meadow,	torna il zeffiro al prato,
Aurora now the sun has sweetly invited	l'aurora mentre al sol fa dolce invito
to return with the day that had departed.	a un ritorno del dì che è pria partito.
Melting, the snows turn earthward,	Tornan le brine in terra,
rocks must return to the centre,	tornano al centro i sassi,
and with gliding passage	e con lubrici passi
rivers return to the ocean.	torna all'oceano il rivo.
Man in his lonely dwelling,	L'huomo qua giù ch'è vivo
far from his high beginning,	lunge da suoi principi
bears his heavenly spirit in a fragile body;	porta un'alma celeste e un corpo frale;
death will come to it swiftly,	tosto more il mortale
and the soul returns to heaven,	e torna l'alma in Cielo
the body returns to dust	e torna il corpo in polve
after life's short journey.	dopo breve soggiorno;
But you, but you alone make no returning.	tu sol del tuo tornar perdesti il giorno.
Hasten, for while you stretch my bitter sorrow	Torna, che mentre porti empie dimore
to an endless tomorrow,	al mio fiero dolore,
see how the hour of death swiftly approaches.	veggio del mio morir l'hore prefisse.
Homeward, ah, homeward turn Ulysses. [4]	Torna, deh torna Ulisse.

Sinfonia

Scene Two. *Melanto, Eurimachus.*

MELANTO

Ladies, take warning	[5] Duri e penosi
lest thoughtless scorning	son gli amorosi
quenches love's fire.	fieri desir;

Kind looks are better
and smiles much fitter
to strengthen desire.
Love is a game to be enjoyed in losing,
let no lover complain of smarts and
bruising.

If looks inflame him,
ah, do not blame him
but grant him ease.
If he seeks harbour,
your breast gives shelter
from stormy seas.
Love is an appetite that grows with
using,
let no lover complain of smarts and
bruising.

Sinfonia

ma alfin son cari,
se prima amari,
gli aspri martir.
Chè s'arde un cor è d'allegrezza un foco,
nè mai perde in amor chi compie il
gioco.

[5] Chi pria s'accende
procelle attende
da un bianco sen,
ma corseggiando
trova in amando
porto seren.
Si piange pria, ma alfin la gioia ha loco,

nè mai perde in amor chi compie il
gioco.

EURIMACHUS

Lovely Melanto, dearest,
O delightful Melanto,
your sweet singing is an incantation,
your fair features, inspiration.
You captivate the heart and man is
helpless;
if he slips from the snare, his life is
worthless.

Bella Melanto mia,
graziosa Melanto,
il tuo canto è un incanto,
il tuo volto è magia.
È tutto laccio in te ciò ch'altri ammaga;

ciò che laccio non è fa tutto piaga.

MELANTO

Your honeyed speech deceives me,
oh, what a cunning poet!
Well you know how to flatter and
bestow
pretty words to your own profit.
Gaily then play your part with lies so
pleasing,
and beguile me with teasing.

Vezzoso garruletto,
o come ben tu sai
ingemmar le bellezze,

illustrar a tuo pro d'un volto i rai,
lieto vezzeggia pur le glorie mie

con tue dolci bugie.

EURIMACHUS

A lie would it be if I
in praising did not love you;
'tis a lie to deny
adoration to a god,
as an honest lover should.

Bugia sarebbe s'io
lodando non t'amassi;
chè il negar d'adorar
confessata deità
è bugia d'empietà.

MELANTO AND EURIMACHUS

Now with a pure devotion
may both our hearts be blended,
for he who will not love has love
offended.

De' nostri amor concordi
sia pur la fiamma accesa,
ch'amato il non amar arreca offesa.

EURIMACHUS

And what a foolish lover is he
who when rejected his love would offer.

Nè con ragion s'offende
colui che per offese amor ti rende.

MELANTO

If I'm faithless, my dearest, then let the
heart
that beats in my breast be turned to ice
and perish.

S'io non t'amo, cor mio, che sia di gelo
l'alma ch'ho in seno a tuoi begli occhi
avante.

And if my heart forgets your love to cherish,
then let no world give refuge, no skies give shelter.

Se in adorarti cor non ho costante,
non mi sia stanza il mondo, o tetto il cielo.

MELANTO AND EURIMACHUS

Gently, my dearest, your love I'll treasure.
Truly, my blessing, I'm yours for ever.
Compact so fair, none shall dissolve or sever.

Dolce mia vita sei,
lieto mio ben sarai,
nodo si bel non si disciolga mai.

MELANTO

How the desire takes me,
Eurimachus my best,
without check, without remorse,
as I lie on your breast, to taste my joys in freedom.

Come il desio m' invoglia,
Eurimaco, mia vita,
senza fren, senza morso
dar nel tuo sen alle mie gioie il corso.

EURIMACHUS

How gladly
would I change this kingdom for a desert,
where the eyes of curious men
could not spy on our tender and sweet caresses.

O come volentieri
cangerei questa Reggia in un deserto
ove occhio curioso
a veder non giungesse i nostri errori.

MELANTO AND EURIMACHUS

For Love in hot ambition
knows no caution or contrition.

Che ad un focoso petto
il rispetto è dispetto.

EURIMACHUS

[If beautiful Penelope
is not on her guard against
the claims of rival loves,
our secret love
will be in danger.]
You then the glorious flame
in her must strive to enkindle.

[Se Penelope bella
non si piega alle voglie
de rivali amatori,
mal sicuri starrano
i nostri occulti amori.]*
Tu dunque t'affatica,
suscita in lei la fiamma.

MELANTO

I will attempt that spirit
so persistent and stubborn,
who keeps her honour fastened
in a casket of diamond.

Ritenterò quell' alma
pertinace ostinata,
ritoccherò quel core
ch'indiamante l'honore.

MELANTO AND EURIMACHUS

Gently, my dearest, your love I'll treasure.
Truly, my blessing, I'm yours for ever.
Compact so fair, none shall dissolve or sever.

Dolce mia vita sei,
lieto mio ben sarai,
nodo si bel non si disciolga mai.

Scene Three (The seashore: chorus of Nereids and Sirens) is missing from the score.

Scene Four. *The Phœacians cross the sea in their ship, disembark with the sleeping Ulysses and leave him at the entrance to the Naiads' cave with his treasure. This scene is in dumbshow, accompanied by a sinfonia. In the score there is only a repeated bass note and the instruction: 'Here the Phœacians' boat appears carrying the sleeping Ulysses, and, so as not to wake him, the following sinfonia is played softly and always on one chord'.*

---

* These lines, taken from the libretto, do not appear in the score. Without them it is hard to understand that Eurimachus has started talking about Penelope.

Scene Five. *Neptune, rising from the sea, and Jove.*

NEPTUNE

All men are proud, and though they try to hide their offence	Superbo è l'huom cd è del suo peccato
Yet they are guilty. But courteous heaven ever is ready to grant the offender pardon.	cagion, benchè lontana; il Ciel cortese facile ahi troppo in perdonar l'offese.
He battles with his fate, struggles with destiny;	Fa guerra col Destin, pugna col Fato,
all-daring, all-defiant,	tutt'osa, tutt'ardisce
he claims his right to freedom,	l'humana libertate,
his reckless deeds defending,	indomita si rende,
the frail judgement of man with heaven contending.	a l'arbitrio de l'huom col Ciel contende.
But if Jove in his mercy	Ma se Giove benigno
leaves the offence of man ever unpunished,	i trascorsi de l'huom troppo perdona,
the power of his right hand, his noble weapon,	tenga egli a voglia sua nella gran destra
the lightning then hangs idle	il fulmine ozioso.
that should chastise the sinner,	Tengalo invendicato,
but great Neptune will punish	ma non soffra Nettuno
that mortal who has sinned and wronged his honour.	col proprio dishonor l'human peccato.

Sinfonia

JOVE

Great master of the salty billows,	Gran Dio de' salsi flutti,
how foolishly you murmur	che mormori e vaneggi
against the wisdom of Jove, your sovereign ruler.	contro l'alta bontà del Dio sovrano?
For it becomes my godhead	Mi stabilì per Giove
to govern men by mercy	la mente mia pietosa
much more than warlike power.	più ch'armata la mano.
Jove's dread thunderbolt strikes earthward,	Questo fulmine atterra,
but his love and persuasion	la pietà persuade,
bring men to adoring submission;	fa adorar la pietade,
how can a man give praise whom death has smitten?	ma non adora più che cade a terra.
But what lawful complaints, calling for vengeance,	Ma qual giusto desio d'aspra vendetta
so embitter your judgement	furioso ti move
that you accuse us and demand atonement?	ad accusar l'alta bontà di Giove?

NEPTUNE

Neptune's decree is thwarted,	Hanno i Feaci arditi
and by cunning his just revenge is cheated,	contro l'alto voler del mio decreto
for Ulysses has landed	han Ulisse condotto
in Ithaca his country, ferried in safety	in Itaca sua patria, onde rimane
by the impious Phaeacians,	de l'humano ardimento
and my absolute decree	de l'offesa deitade
they have held in derision.	ingannato l'intento.
'Tis weakness and not compassion	Vergogna e non pietade
such crimes to set aside and pardon the sinner.	comanda il perdonar fatti sì rei.
Does Jove compete with man	Così di nome solo
and pronounce him the winner?	son divini gli Dei.

JOVE

The gods will not despise a just vendetta,	Non sien discare al Ciel le tue vendette,
for by reason we rule and are united.	che comune ragion ci tiene uniti,
Neptune himself may castigate the wicked.	puoi da te stesso castigar gli arditi.

Since Jove who rules the heavens
accords divine permission,
I will take vengeance upon the rash
  offender:
that ship returning homeward
I'll fix as a rock for ever.

Hor già che non dissente
il tuo divin volcre,
darò castigo al temerario orgoglio;

la nave loro andante
farò immobile scoglio.

JOVE

Act in your righteous anger,
punish the evil-doer;
waves obey their ruler;
those whose sin was to move shall
  move no further.

Facciasi il tuo comando,
veggansi l'alte prove
abbian l'onde il suo Giove;
e chi andando peccò pera restando.

Scene Six. *Chorus of Phœacians in their ship, then Neptune.*

PHÆACIANS

We happy bold Phæacians
sail the seas
as we please.
What you fancy, freely do,
the gods don't notice you, don't think of
  you.

[6] In questo basso mondo
l'huomo puol
quanto vuol.
Tutto fa, tutto fa,
che 'l Ciel del nostro oprar pensier non ha.

NEPTUNE
turning the ship to stone

Changeable waves be still now,
this new rock is your fetter.
In sorrow, bold Phæacians, you now are
  learning
that if mortal voyage
crosses the will of heaven there's no
  returning.

Ricche d'un nuovo scoglio
sien quest'onde fugaci.
Imparino i Feaci in questo giorno

che l'humano viaggio
quand' ha contrario il Ciel non ha
  ritorno.

Scene Seven. *Ulysses, awaking.*

ULYSSES

Am I sleeping or awake?
And what country surrounds me?
What strange land lies beneath me,
what is the air I'm breathing?
But sleep for me, but sleep
with its sweet deception is now become an
  enemy
and minister of torments.
Who has changed to unrest my peaceful
  slumbers?
What heavenly power has care of helpless
  sleepers?
O, sleep, O mortal sleep,
whom men have often called death's brother,
now homeless and deserted,
deluded and bewildered,
I have known you, yes indeed I have known
  you, father of errors.
Yet I myself of my own errors am guilty.
For a phantom is the sister
of sleep, or sleep's companion,
and he who trusts in phantoms
and then is lost cannot complain to
  heaven.
O gods ever unfriendly,
powers that know no mercy,

[7] Dormo ancora o son desto?
Che contrade rimiro?
Qual aria vi respiro?
E che terren calpesto?
Chi fece in me, chi fece
il sempre dolce e lusinghevol sonno

ministro de' tormenti,
chi cangiò il mio riposo in ria sventura?

Qual Deità de' dormienti ha cura?

O sonno, o mortal sonno!
Fratello della morte altri ti chiama.
Solingo trasportato,
deluso et ingannato,
ti conosco ben io, padre d'errori.

Pur degli errori miei son io la colpa.
Chè se l'ombra è del sonno
sorella o pur compagna,
chi si confida all'ombra
perduto alfin contro ragion si lagna.

O Dei sempre sdegnati,
Numi non mai placati,

even in sleep Ulysses must feel your rancour.	contro Ulisse che dorme anco severi,
Let your divine decrees rule over human wills with force redoubled, but the dead allow, alas, to rest untroubled.	vostri divini imperi contro l'human voler sien fermi e forti, ma non tolgano ahimè la pace ai morti.
O treacherous Phæacians, you swore, and I believed you, to bring me safely homeward to Ithaca my country. And all my treasures too, my prized possessions.	Feaci ingannatori, voi pur mi prometteste di ricondurmi salvo in Itaca mia patria con le ricchezze mie, co' miei tesori.
O traitorous Phæacians, ah, how could you betray me, could you bring me to this lonely seashore, this desert where you leave me, desolate and quite forsaken, while the breezes convey you, the guilty, safe homeward by no storms overtaken! If so monstrous a crime should go unpunished,	Feaci mancatori, hor non so com'ingrati mi lasciaste in questa riva aperta, su spiaggia erma e deserta, misero, abbandonato; e vi porta fastosi e per l'aure e per l'onde così enorme peccato! Se puniti non son sì gravi errori,
Jove no longer make ready your lightning-flash of vengeance, for the judgement of Chance gives more assurance.	lascia, Giove, deh lascia de fulmini la cura, chè la legge del caso è più sicura.
Treacherous and false Phæacians, as you sail upon your journey, may the winds be hostile, and may your ship be blown before	Sia delle vostre vele, falsissimi Feaci, sempre Borea inimico, e sian qual piuma al vento o scoglio in mare
the tempest as lightly as a feather, yet heavy as a rock in fairer weather.	le vostre infide navi: leggiere agli aquiloni, all'aure gravi.

Scene Eight. *Minerva, in the form of a shepherd, and Ulysses.*

Sinfonia

MINERVA

Merry, gay and joyful days of youth! Though we know you cannot last, what's to come or what is past does not trouble us in truth.	[8] Cara e lieta gioventù che disprezza empio desir, non dà a lei noia o martir ciò che viene e ciò che fu.

Ritornello

ULYSSES
speaking to himself

Heaven is always mindful of man's distresses. This beardless stripling surely is too youthful to cheat or prove untruthful, therefore I'll hear his answers to my questions. Till a boy's beard has sprouted he is uncorrupted.	Sempre l'human bisogno il Ciel soccorre. Quel giovinetto tenero negli anni, mal pratico d'inganni, forse che 'l mio pensier farà contento: chè non ha frode in seno chi non ha pelo al mento.

Ritornello

MINERVA

Happy springtime of Life's delight! Endless time before us lies,	[8] Giovanezza è un bel tesor che fa ricco in gioia un sen.

yet on wings young Cupid flies	Per lei zoppo il tempo vien,
to entrance us day and night.	per lei vola alato Amor.

ULYSSES

I greet you, handsome shepherd,	Vezzoso pastorello,
ah, take pity on a stranger,	deh sovvieni un perduto
be my helper and adviser, and tell me first,	di consiglio e d'aiuto, e dimmi pria
what is this harbour, this rocky coast and country?	di questa spiaggia e questo porto il nome.

MINERVA

This is Ithaca, an island cradled in these waters,	Itaca è questa in sen di questo mare,
great in renown, a welcoming harbour,	porto famoso e spiaggia
a land of blessing.	felice avventurata.
What I have said must please you,	Faccia gioconda e grata
for you look smiling and joyful.	a sì bel nome fai.
But you — what is your country and what your journey?	Ma tu come venisti e dove vai?

ULYSSES

inventing

A Greek am I, and here from Crete I've travelled	Io Greco sono et hor di Creta io vengo
to escape from punishment	per fuggir il castigo
for a murder I committed.	d'omicidio eseguito;
The Phæcians received me, and they had promised	m'accolsero i Feaci e m'han promesso
to bring me safe to Elis,	in Elide condurmi,
but by the faithless winds and furious billows	ma dal cruccioso mar dal vento infido
we were driven all helpless to this harbour.	fummo a forza cacciati in questo lido.
And so till now Fate was unfriendly, Fate was my enemy.	Sin qui, pastor, hebbi nemico il caso.
I came ashore to rest here	Ma sbarcato al riposo,
till the winds should be still,	per veder quieto il mar secondo i venti,
and then as I was drowsy, I slept so soundly	colà m'addormentai sì dolcemente,
I neither heard nor saw	ch'io non udii nè vidi
that the cruel Phæcians	de' Feaci crudeli
stole away with their vessel. I sleeping remained here	la furtiva partenza, ond'io rimasi
with all my treasure upon the lonely shore,	con le mie spoglie in su l'arena ignuda
where I am lost and friendless,	isconosciuto e solo,
and waking I perceive my sorrow is endless.	e 'l sonno che partì lasciommi il duolo.

MINERVA

Deep were your slumbers, nor are you yet awakened:	Ben lungamente addormentato fosti
you still tell me of phantoms, of dreams and shadows.	ch'ancor ombra racconti e sogni narri.
Though cunning is Ulysses,	È ben accorto Ulisse,
yet much wiser is Minerva.	ma più saggia è Minerva.
Therefore Ulysses must yield and offer obedience.	Tu dunque, Ulisse, i miei precetti osserva.

ULYSSES

Who would believe it, whoever would believe it?	Che crederebbe mai!
The goddess here, disguised and dressed up like a man!	Le Dietà vestite in human velo!
And do they really play such tricks in heaven?	Si fanno queste mascherate in Cielo?

Thanks do I offer, O goddess, my
   protectress.
I know that it is only through your love
that my falsehoods may go unpunished.
Now, well directed, I'll obey
your heavenly counsels.

Grazie ti rendo, o protettrice Dea:

ben so che per tuo amore
furon senza periglio i miei pensieri.
Hor consigliato seguo
i tuoi saggi consigli.

MINERVA

Your person I'll disguise,
until your angry eyes see how your rivals
with impudent abandon
live in riotous luxury.

Incognito sarai,
non conosciuto andrai sinchè tu vegga
dei Proci tuoi rivali
la sfacciata baldanza.

ULYSSES

O blest and happy Ulysses!

[9] O fortunato Ulisse!

MINERVA

And Penelope's chaste
and still-unchanging constancy.

Di Penelope casta
l'immutabil costanza.

ULYSSES

O blest and happy Ulysses!

[9] O fortunato Ulisse!

MINERVA

Bathe your forehead with water
from the spring that's yonder,
so that no one shall know you
in the shape I shall give you.

Hor t'adacqua la fronte
nella vicina fonte,
ch'anderai sconosciuto
in sembiante canuto.

ULYSSES

I go at once and will obey you, quickly
   returning.

Ad obbedirti vado, indi ritorno.

MINERVA

I saw my lawful vengeance
when sinful Troy was burning.
Shortly Ulysses shall see his home again,
   his foes shall perish.
For those who flout my wishes, swiftly I
   punish.
Henceforth remember this, foolish mortal
   creatures,
at your peril you join with meddling finger
in the disputes of the gods and heavenly
   anger,
for you are earthbound, with finite human
   natures.

Io vidi per vendetta
incenerirsi Troja, hora mi resta
Ulisse ricondur in patria in regno;

d'un'oltraggiata Dea questo è lo sdegno.

Quinci imparate voi stolti mortali,

al litigio divin non poner bocca;
il giudizio del Ciel a voi non tocca,

chè son di terra i vostri tribunali.

ULYSSES
as an old man

Wonderful transformation!
These white hairs, gracious lady,
emblems of bent old age,
are a perfect deception.

Eccomi, saggia Dea,
questi peli che guardi
sono di mia vecchiaia
testimoni bugiardi.

MINERVA

First to hide all the treasure
with which your ship was loaded.
Here in this cave we'll entrust them
to the Naiads who dwell here, to heaven
   devoted.

Hor poniamo in sicuro
queste tue spoglie amate
dentro quell'antro oscuro
delle Najadi, Ninfe al Ciel sacrate.

ULYSSES AND MINERVA

while the nymphs take the treasure into the cave

Naiads devoted	Ninfe serbate
to heaven's pleasure,	le gemme e gl' ori,
guard well the treasure,	spoglie e tesori,
safely protected,	tutto serbate,
Naiads devoted.	ninfe sacrate.

Scene Nine. The chorus of Naiads is missing from the score.

MINERVA

Go to Arethusa's fountain and there await me.	Tu d'Aretusa a fonte intanto vanne
There you will find the swineherd Eumæus,	ove il pastor Eumete,
your faithful servant,	tuo fido antico servo,
who is guarding the herd. Meanwhile I leave you	custodisce la gregge: ivi m'attendi
and make my journey to Sparta, from where your dear son	in sin che pria di Sparta io ti conduca
Telemachus I'll bring you.	Telemaco tuo figlio.
What you must do thereafter I shall instruct you.	Poi d'eseguir t'appresta il mio consiglio.

Ritornello

ULYSSES

O blest and happy Ulysses!	[9] O fortunato Ulisse!
Banish your doubt and care, all gloom forswear,	Fuggi del tuo dolor l'antico error.
leaving sadness,	Lascia il pianto,
while a song of gladness	dolce canto
from your heart gaily arises.	del tuo cor lieto disserra.
So nevermore despair, whom heaven advises.	Non si disperi più mortale in terra.
O blest and happy Ulysses!	O fortunato Ulisse!
Trusting to conquer,	Cara vicenda
we can endure	si può soffrir,
tribulations less or more, now peace, now battles.	hor diletto, hor martir, hor pace, hor guerra.
So nevermore despair on earth, you mortals.	Non si disperi più mortale in terra.

*

Scene Ten. *The Palace. Penelope, Melanto.*

PENELOPE

O heaven, I pray imploring,	Donate un giorno, o Dei
have pity on my suffering!	contento a' desir miei.

MELANTO

Dear and beloved lady,	Cara amata Regina,
you are noble, sagacious and prudent.	avveduta e prudente
Yet your prudence only does you harm:	per tuo sol danno sei:
less caution would be wiser.	men saggia io ti vorrei.
Why despise the ardours	A che sprezzi gli ardori
of living suitors,	dei viventi amatori
to fix your hopes and wishes	per attender conforti
on a dead man's bones and ashes?	dal cenere de' morti?

---

* This is the end of Act One in the libretto. In the score, the words 'End of Act One' are legible at the end of scene nine, and 'Act Two, scene one' instead of Scene Ten. Nevertheless the text is the same except for Penelope's two opening lines, which do not appear in the libretto.

There's no wrong to the dead in a wise
    rejoicing.
Now that he's dead and buried
your husband's love is ended,
and all your grief to him is nothing, is
    useless,
and to look for a dead man's pity is
    senseless.
True faith and loving constancy —
these are virtues most rare, and precious
to the living, but quite unmeaning
to one whose mortal senses
are in the grave. Those who have died
    we honour
with gratitude and piety.
Those who live are with the living one
    self united.
Strife will spring from great beauty,
and the cause of dissension to the dead
    is hateful,
for the life of the dead is tranquil and
    peaceful.
Withered by your lamentation
and your stern abnegation,
your sweetest flowers will die.
But widowed beauty too condemns your
    mourning;
for through the veil of sorrow,
as a gleam through water, your sun is
    shining.

Therefore love, since Love and Beauty
are a destined heavenly pair,
and Joy's arrows swiftly, surely,
pierce the heart of pining care.

Non fa torto chi gode a chi è sepolto.

L'ossa del tuo marito
estinto, incenerito,
del tuo dolor non san poco nè molto;

e chi attende pietà da morto è stolto.

La fede e la costanza
son preclare virtù; le stima amante
vivo, e non l'apprezza
perchè de' sensi privo
un huom che fu. D'una memoria grata

s'appagano i defunti,
stanno i vivi coi vivi in un congiunti.

Un bel viso fa guerra,
il guerriero costume al morto spiace,

chè non cercan gli estinti altro che pace.

Langue sotto i rigori
de' tuoi sciapiti amori
la più fiorita età,
ma vedova beltà di te si duole,

chè dentro ai lunghi pianti
mostri sempre in acquario un sì bel sole.

[10] Ama dunque, chè d'Amore
dolce amica è la beltà.
Dal piacere il tuo dolore
saettato caderà.

PENELOPE

Love is vain and fickle,
but Love is a deceiving infant,
with feathered plumes like the wind
    inconstant,
and the sweetness he's bringing
is as brief as the lightning. A single
    moment
can transform our delight to torment.
Tales of love are often, alas,
like the tales of Jason or Theseus;
all deception and inconstancy,
sorrow and dying and bitter envy.
The jealousy of Heaven that knows no
    reason
could transform even Ulysses into Jason.

Amor è un idol vano,
è un vagabondo Nume,
all'incostanze sue non mancan piume;

del suo dolce sereno
è misura il baleno. Un giorno solo

cangia il piacer in duolo.
Sono i casi amorosi
di Tesei e di Giasoni ohimè son pieni:
incostanza e rigore,
pene e morte e dolore.
Dell'amoroso Ciel splendori fissi

san cangiar in Giason anche gli Ulissi.

MELANTO

Because the inconstant breezes
sometimes disturb the sea
should the seaman in harbour
never boldly attempt to launch away?
Stars will look down from heaven
even at the blackest,
and calm comes to every tempest.

Perchè Aquilone infido
turbi una volta il mar
distaccarsi dal lido
animoso nocchier non dee lasciar?
Sempre non guarda in ciel
torva una stella,
ha calma ogni procella.

101

Therefore love, since Love and Beauty	[10] Ama dunque, chè d'Amore
are a destined heavenly pair,	dolce amica è la beltà.
and Joy's arrows swiftly, surely,	Dal piacere il tuo dolore
pierce the heart of pining care.	saettato caderà.

PENELOPE

No lover should love again	Non dee di nuovo amar
whom sorrow has destroyed;	chi misera penò:
she will waken in pain who dreams	torna stolta a penar chi prima errò.
of joy.	

Scene Eleven. *A grove. Eumæus alone.*

EUMÆUS

O wretched kings, you cannot save yourselves	Come mal si salva un Regio amante
from misadventures and sorrows!	da sventure e da mali.
Tears bedew royal sceptres,	Meglio i scettri regali
the herdsman's staff is sound and he is cheerful.	che i dardi de' pastor imperla il pianto.
Silks and satin clothes are not able	Seta vestono ed ori
to conceal care and trouble.	i travagli maggiori.
The herdsman lives more safely	È vita più sicura
than the monarch in his glory,	della ricca et illustre
although he's poor and hungry.	la povera et oscura.
O you woodlands, you hills and pastures,	Colli, campagne e boschi,
if happiness has on this earth her dwelling,	se stato human felicità contiene,
in you she's hidden, for her we sigh with longing.	in voi s'annida il sospirato bene.
You grassy meadows, in you	Herbosi prati, in voi
grows the flower of contentment,	nasce il fior del diletto,
glorious fruit you bear of joy and freedom,	frutto di libertade in voi si coglie,
and delightful to men is your sweet blossom.	son delizie dell'huom le vostre foglie.

Scene Twelve. *Irus, Eumæus.*

IRUS

A herdsman thinks his fields	Pastor d'armenti può
and woodlands are divine,	prati e boschi lodar,
for all his conversation is with swine.	avvezzo nelle mandre a conversar.
This grass which thus you nominate	Quest'herbe che tu nomini
is the diet of ca . . . my friend, of cattle	sono cibo di be . . . pastor, di bestie e
which men abominate.	non degli huomini.*
With kings I make my home,	Colà fra Regi io sto,
while you with pigs must sleep:	tu fra gli armenti qui.
your dwelling and your discourse is with sheep,	Tu godi e tu conversi tutto il dì
and with these you share opinions.	amicizie selvatiche,
I eat your precious charges, my friend,	io mangio i tuoi compagni, pastor,
your charges and your companions.	e le tue pratiche!

EUMÆUS

Irus, great greedy glutton,	Iro, gran mangiatore,
Irus, gorger of mutton,	Iro, divoratore,
Irus, ever witty, have pity	Iro, loquace!

---

* These lines were altered by Monteverdi by the insertion of the word 'pastor' and the stuttering.

On man and beast,
Hurry: hurry to the feast.

Mia pace non perturbar,
corri, corri a mangiar!*

Scene Thirteen. *Eumæus, then Ulysses in the form of an old man.*

EUMÆUS

Ulysses, O generous Ulysses,
how splendid are your conquests,
the havoc that you wrought among your
   enemies!
But perhaps the gods are angry
at the destruction of the Trojan kingdom.
Fearful is heaven's fury,
and you may be the victim.

Ulisse generoso!
Fu nobile intrapresa
lo spopolar, l'incenerir cittadi;

ma forse il Ciel irato
nella caduta del Trojano regno
volle la vita tua
per vittima al suo sdegno.

ULYSSES

Since you have named Ulysses,
his conquests and his suffering,
if you hope for his coming,
pray shelter an old man
who's destitute, who's deserted
by every help and comfort.
Some shelter for his head you may provide
   him,
and gently towards his death your staff
   may guide him.

Se del nomato Ulisse
tu vegga in questo giorno
desiato il ritorno,
accogli questo vecchio
povero ch'ha perduto
ogni mortal aiuto
nella cadente età, nell'aspra sorte;

gli sia la tua pietà scorta alla morte.

EUMÆUS

Such as I have, I offer;
My roof shall give you shelter. Beggars
   are favoured
by the mighty of heaven, as Jove's
   beloved.

Hospite mio sarai,
cortese albergo avrai. Sono i mendici

favoriti del Ciel, di Giove amici.

ULYSSES

Ulysses — I swear he lives, I swear it!
He'll find his native place,
Penelope's embrace.
Since Fortune in her heart is not relentless,
and destiny may change her first intention:
this is the truth, good shepherd.

Ulisse, Ulisse è vivo!
La patria lo vedrà,
Penelope l'havrà;
chè il Fato non fu mai d'affetto privo,
maturano il destin le sue dimore,
credilo a me pastore.

EUMÆUS

O what healing and gladness
your blessed words contain!
All my weary sadness
you have vanquished and slain.
Follow me, welcome guest:
refreshment find and rest.

Come lieto t'accoglio,
mendica Deità.
Il mio lungo cordoglio
da te vinto cadrà.
Seguimi amico pur,
riposo avrai sicur.

---

* In the libretto there is a final line which does not appear in the score: 'Corri, corri a crepar' which might be translated as 'Hurry, hurry, burst apart!'

Act Two

Sinfonia

Scene One. *Telemachus and Minerva in her chariot.*

TELEMACHUS

Happy our journeying,
leaving darkness for daylight.
Swiftly our chariot is turning
to pierce the clouds like sunlight.

[11] Lieto cammino,
dolce viaggio,
passa il carro divino
come che fosse un raggio.

TELEMACHUS AND MINERVA

Our heavenly horses
galloping follow all the stars
in their courses.

Gli Dei possenti
navigan l'aure,
solcano i venti.

MINERVA

Safely I have brought you to your father's
kingdom,
my prudent Telemachus.
Keep ever in your mind my urgent
counsels,
for if you should forget my wise
directions
you will endure great perils.

Eccoti giunto alle paterne ville,

Telemaco prudente.
Non ti scordar già mai de' miei consigli,

chè se dal buon sentier travia la mente

incontrerai perigli.

TELEMACHUS

No peril shall assail me
nor will your power fail me.

Periglio invan mi guida
se tua bontà m'affida.

Scene Two. *Eumæus, Ulysses, Telemachus.*

EUMÆUS

O great son of Ulysses,
are you really returning
to set at rest your mother's anxious
yearning?
Now reunited and sharing
all your people's ill-fortune,
you will be blest, your fallen state repairing.
Vanish all sorrow, vanish all lamentation.
Now join, O gentle stranger,
in joyful celebration, raise our voices.

O gran figlio d'Ulisse,
è pur ver che tu torni
a serenar della tua madre i giorni,

e pur sei giunto al fine
di tua casa cadente
e riparar l'altissime ruine?
Fugga, fugga il cordoglio e cessi il pianto.
Facciam, o peregrino,
all'allegrezze nostre honor col canto.

EUMÆUS AND ULYSSES

Woods and meadows freshly springing,
all bedeck themselves in pleasure,
infant breezes dance in measure,
skies rejoice to see his coming.

Verdi spiagge, al lieto giorno
rabbellite herbette e fiori,
scherzin l'aure con gli amori,
ride il ciel al bel ritorno.

TELEMACHUS

You have received me kindly and I am
grateful,
yet longing haunts me still and I am
restless.
To the ardent in spirit, waiting is
cheerless.

Vostri cortesi auspici a me son grati.

Manchevole piacer però m'alletta,

ch'esser calma non puote alma ch'aspetta.

EUMÆUS

This poor traveller beside me,
on whose weary shoulders
the weight of years is heavy,

Questo che tu qui miri
sopra gli homeri stanchi
portar gran peso d'anni e mal involto

whose rags and tatters barely cling to his body —	da ben laceri panni, egli m'accerta
he has assured me that Ulysses is coming;	che d'Ulisse il ritorno
we may hope from this day for his returning.	fia di poco lontan da questo giorno.

ULYSSES

If this should prove a lie, then let me perish,	Pastor, se nol fia ver, ch'al tardo passo
let the path of my footsteps lead to the grave,	si trasformi in sepolcro il primo sasso,
and may Death which is wooing my spirit from within me	e la morte che meco amoreggia d'intorno
swiftly carry me away where none shall know me.	hora porti a miei dì l'ultimo giorno.

EUMÆUS AND ULYSSES

Hopeful visions deceive the dreamer,	Dolce speme i cor lusinga,
joyful tidings revive the hopeless.	lieto annunzio ogni alma alletta,
To the ardent in spirit, waiting is fruitless.	s'esser paga non potè alma ch'aspetta.

TELEMACHUS

Quickly as you are able, hasten,	Vanne pur tu veloce,
Eumæus, to the palace; tell them of my arrival,	Eumete, alla Reggia e del mio arrivo
announce to the Queen my mother	fa ch'avvisata sia
that my long journey's over.	la genitrice mia.

Scene Three. *Telemachus, Ulysses. A flash of fire issues from the sky above the head of Ulysses. The earth opens and engulfs him.*

TELEMACHUS

What terror, ah heaven, what vengeance!	Che veggio, ohimè, che miro?
This ravenous earth devours her children,	Questa terra vorace i vivi inghiotte,
gaping mouths swallow human blood into her caverns,	apre bocche e caverne
the rocks no longer will	d'humano sangue ingorde, e più non soffre
support our footsteps	del viator il passo,
and our bodies are hurled into the darkness.	ma la carne dell'huom tranghiotte il sasso.
What a prodigy is here!	Che prodigi son questi?
O my country, have you learnt	Dunque, patria, apprendesti
to devour your offspring,	a divorar le genti?
are monuments prepared for the living?	Rispondono anco ai vivi i monumenti.
Is it thus, O Minerva,	Così dunque, Minerva,
that you bring me to my country?	alla patria mi doni?
Truly a country of snares,	Questa è patria comune
if we judge it by these events.	se di questo ragioni.
Though my tongue is ready,	Ma se presto ho la lingua,
yet my memory is lazy.	ho la memoria pigra.
But surely he, this wandering stranger,	Quel pelegrin ch'or hora
who to strengthen faith in his legends	per dar fede a menzogne
invoked a tombstone and wagered with death,	chiamò sepolcri et invitò la morte
by righteous heaven was punished	dal giusto Ciel punito
and deep in earth was buried? Ah, dearest father,	restò qui sepellito. Ah, caro padre,
are you no longer living,	dunque in modo sì strano
and by this strange eclipse	m'avvisa il tuo morire
does heaven announce your passing?	il Ciel di propria mano?
Heaven and earth are hostile	Ahi che per farmi guerra
and to plague me invent these signs and wonders.	fa stupori e miracoli la terra.

Ulysses rises in his own form.

But what new amazement, O heaven, is here?

Ma che nuovi portenti ohimè rimiro?

The dead are with the living
now exchanged and transmuted.
Nevermore believe that
death is bitter,
since he from death to living breath has risen.

Fa cambio, fa permuta
con la morte la vita.
Non sia più che più chiami
questa caduta amara,
se col morir ringiovanir s'impara.

ULYSSES

Telemachus, now learn
to transform bewildered wonder to joy and gaiety,
for in losing a beggar you gained a father.

Telemaco, convienti
cangiar le meraviglie in allegrezze,
che se perdi il mendico il padre acquisti.

TELEMACHUS

Though Ulysses has boasted
of immortal lineage,
yet no mortal has power
to rise from his ashes.
By magic arts you are cheating,
or the gods must be joking.

Benchè Ulisse si vanti
di prosapia celeste,
trasformarsi non puote huomo mortale,
tanto Ulisse non vale.
O scherzano gli Dei,
o pur mago tu sei.

ULYSSES

Ulysses stands here,
by the grace of Minerva,
goddess whose airy chariot flying brought you.
She changed my mortal form, that none should know me.
It was her pleasure that I should pass in safety.

Ulisse, Ulisse sono!
Testimonio è Minerva,
quella che te portò per l'aria a volo.
La forma cangiò a me come le aggrada,
perchè sicuro e sconosciuto vada.

TELEMACHUS

O father I have sighed for!

[12] O padre sospirato!

ULYSSES

O son whom I have longed for!

O figlio desiato!

TELEMACHUS

Noble source of my being!

Genitor glorioso!

ULYSSES

Pledge of joy past all telling!

Pegno dolce amoroso!

TELEMACHUS

I hail you.

T'inchino!

ULYSSES

I clasp you.

Ti stringo!

TELEMACHUS

Oh, what rejoicing,
filial pleasure and sweetness!
I weep, but not for sadness.

O mio diletto,
figliale dolcezza
a lagrimar mi sforza.

ULYSSES

Paternal loving-kindness!
with tears of joy and gladness.

Paterna tenerezza
il pianto in me rinforza.

Mankind, be ever trustful, ever hopeful;
all earthly laws are subject
to heaven's eternal edict,
whose beneficent hand guides every
   mortal.

Mortal tutto confida e tutto spera,
che quando il ciel protegge
natura non ha legge:
l'impossibile ancor spesso s'avvera.

ULYSSES

Hasten, to your mother go,
tell her what must be done.
I shall follow you soon,
but first I must resume these locks of
   snow.

Vanne alle madre, va!
Porta alla Reggia il piè.
Sarò tosto con te,
ma pria canuto il pel ritornerà.

*

Scene Four. *The Palace. Melanto, Eurimachus.*

MELANTO

Eurimachus, my royal mistress
is cold as marble,
entreaties cannot move her,
fervent prayers cannot shake her.
Though she is sick with longing,
yet her soul is steadfast.
Steeled by pride or by constancy
she feels no touch of pity;
for enemy or lover
her heart's like a diamond, naught can be
   harder.

Eurimaco! La donna
insomma ha un cor di sasso,
Parola non la muove,
priego invan la combatte;
dentro del mal d'amore
sempre tenace ha l'alma,
o di fede o d'orgoglio
in ogni modo è scoglio.
Nemica o pur amante,
non ha di cera il cor, ma di diamante.

EURIMACHUS

And yet the poet tells us,
as he complains of his mistress,
that all women are changeable and
   faithless!

E pur udii sovente
la poetica schiera
cantar donna volubile e leggiera.

MELANTO

With many vain entreaties, with ardent
   prayers.
I have sought to persuade her to take a
   lover;
but all my prayers are useless,
hateful to her is love or lover's worship.

Ho speso invan parole, indarno prieghi

per condur la Regina a nuovi amori;

l'impresa è disperata
odia non che l'amor l'esser amata.

EURIMACHUS

Those who seek shadows,
hating the sun,
torture their lovers,
cannot be won.

Peni chi brama,
stenti chi vuol,
goda fra l'ombre
chi ha in odio il sol.

MELANTO

Penelope rejoices
in her mourning, in her sorrow;
only sadness contents her;
only gladness Melanto.
She is nourished by torment and I by
   pleasure.
In loving is rejoicing,
so in perfect content I enjoy my
   treasure.

Penelope trionfa
nella doglia e nel pianto,
fra martiri e contenti,
vive lieta Melanto.
Ella in pene si nutre; io fra diletti

amando mi giocondo,
fra sì varii pensier più bello è il mondo.

---

* This is the end of Act Two in the libretto.

With kissing,	Godendo,
caressing,	ridendo
all sorrow we'll slay.	si lacera il duol.

MELANTO

Delighting,	Amiamo,
uniting,	godiamo,
we scorn what men say.	e dica che vuol.

Scene Five. *Antinous, Amphinomous, Peisander (the suitors), Eurimachus, Penelope.*

ANTINOUS

Other queens for their crowning	Sono l'altre regine
have a diadem of slaves, and you of lovers.	coronate di servi e tu d'amanti.
The tribute that your beauty demands from	Tributan questi regi
royal suitors their tears discover.	al mar di tua bellezza un mar di pianti.

ANTINOUS, AMPHINOMOUS AND PEISANDER

| Therefore love me, yes, yes, | Ama dunque, sì, sì, |
| love has the power to bless. | dunque riama un dì. |

PENELOPE

| I will not love, no, no, | [13] Non voglio amar, no, no, |
| for love brings bitter woe. | ch'amando penerò. |

THE THREE SUITORS

| Therefore love me, yes, yes, | Ama dunque, sì, sì, |
| love has the power to bless. | dunque riama un dì! |

PENELOPE

Great is the honour you do me	Cari tanto mi siete
while you so hotly pursue me,	quanto più ardenti ardete;
but do not scorch me with your amorous desire,	ma non m'appresso all'amoroso gioco,
for from afar 'tis best to feel the fire.	chè lunge è bel più che vicino il foco.

| I will not love, no, no, | [13] Non voglio amar, no, no, |
| for love brings bitter woe. | ch'amando penerò. |

PEISANDER

The green and leafy vine	La pampinosa vite
can bear no fruit for harvest	se non s'abbraccia al faggio,
unless it twines upon the tree that's nearest,	l'autun non frutta e non fiorisce il maggio;
and if the vine is barren	e se fiorir non resta
every hand will destroy it,	ogni mano la coglie,
and every foot will trample it.	ogni piè la calpesta.

AMPHINOMOUS

The cedar so fragrant carries,	Il bel cedro odoroso
unless it's grafted,	vive, se non s'incalma
no crop of cones sharp and pungent,	senza frutto, spinoso;
but if it's grafted, straightening,	ma se s'innesta poi
flourishing, fruiting grows and gives its plenty.	figliano frutti e fior gli spini suoi.

ANTINOUS

Ivy in deepest winter,	L'edera che verdeggia
with verdant emerald foliage,	ad onta anco del verno,
can shame the withered herbage,	d'un bel smeraldo eterno,
yet unsupported loses	se non s'appoggia perde
all its wandering tendrils in tangled grasses.	fra l'herbose rovine il suo bel verde.

| Therefore love me, yes, yes, | Ama dunque, sì, sì, |
| love has the power to bless. | dunque riama un dì! |

PENELOPE

I will not love, I will not!	Non voglio amar, non voglio!
As when the metal falters	Come sta in dubbio un ferro
if held between two magnets	se fra due calamite,
that in opposite directions summon and draw it,	da due parti diverse egli è chiamato,
even so with indecision	così sta in forse il core
my mind is held in prison.	nel tripartito amore.
But not again, not again	Ma non può amar
can she love, who has known	chi non sa, chi non può
its sorrowing and pain.	che pianger e penar.
Sad darkness and night	Mestizia e dolor
are the enemies of love and delight.	son crudeli nemici d'amor.

THE THREE SUITORS

Now for the feasting, now for dance and pleasure!	All' allegrezze dunque, al ballo, al canto!
Bring good cheer to our lady,	Rallegriam la Regina.
for a heart turns to love when it is merry.	Lieto cor ad amar tosto s'inchina.

Scene Six. *Dance. Here eight Moors appear and perform a Greek dance, singing the following verses.* *

MOORS

Ladies, Love bears no delay,	Dame in amor belle e gentil
so love in April while you may.	Amate allor che ride april;
When your locks are brushed with snow,	Non giunge al sen gioia, o piacer
joy and pleasure quickly go,	Se tocca il crin l'età senil
youthful beauty wastes away.	Dunque al gioir, lieto al goder.

Ladies, Love shines in your eyes,	Dame in amor belle e gentil
roses bloom in spite of thorns:	Vaga nel spin la Rosa sta,
no frozen flower to life returns,	Ma non nel gel bella è beltà:
no splendour shines from stormy skies;	Perde il splendor torbido ciel
while you linger, beauty dies.	Ciglio in rigor non è più bel.

Scene Seven. *Enter Eumæus. Eumaeus, Penelope.*

EUMÆUS

I come to give fortunate tidings.	Apportator d'alte novelle vengo!
In safety, O queen and mistress,	È gionto, o gran Regina,
Telemachus has reached us.	Telemaco tuo figlio,
Moreover, other tidings of hope	e forse non fia vana
I bring to cheer you.	la speme ch'io t'arreco:
Ulysses, my dear master,	Ulisse, il nostro Rege,
your loving husband, is living.	il tuo consorte, è vivo,
And I hope that you shortly may see	e speriam non lontano
his long-desired returning.	il suo bramato arrivo!

PENELOPE

This too-doubtful prediction	Per sì dubbie novelle
will bring a change in my fortune,	o s'addoppia il mio male
or else an increase in my affliction.	o si cangia il tenor delle mie stelle.

---

* The music for this dance is missing. The verses were specially translated for this Guide.

Scene Eight. *Antinous, Amphinomous, Peisander, Eurimachus.*

ANTINOUS

Companions, you heard it?	Compagni, udiste? Il nostro
The danger at hand, deadly and threatening,	vicin rischio mortale
demands of us an instant resolute intention.	vi chiama a grandi e risolute imprese.
Telemachus is coming, and perhaps Ulysses.	Telemaco ritorna e forse Ulisse.
Now this palace which you have violated and plundered	Questa Reggia da voi violata e offesa
awaits its lord's arrival,	dal suo signor aspetta
tardy indeed, with imminent reprisal.	tarda bensì, ma prossima vendetta.
Those who were quick to pillage	Chi d'oltraggiar fù ardito
must not now be reluctant	neghittoso non resti
to complete their aggression;	in compir il delitto. In sin ad hora
for since your pleasure by your crimes was made easy,	fù il peccato dolcezza,
surely now by a crime you must reach safety.	hora il vostro peccar fia sicurezza,
The man is mad who cringes and seeks forbearance,	chè lo sperar favori è gran pazzia
whose crimes have courted vengeance.	da chi s'offese pria.

AMPHINOMOUS AND PEISANDER

By having wronged Ulysses	Han fatto l'opre nostre
by his enmity we are stricken.	inimici d'Ulisse.
Violent ways with a foe are not forbidden.	L'oltraggiar l'inimico unqua disdisse.

ANTINOUS

Keep your resolve unshaken:	Dunque l'ardir s'accresca,
before Ulysses comes here	e pria che Ulisse arrivi
Telemachus we'll capture and we'll murder.	Telemaco vicin togliam dai vivi!

THE THREE SUITORS

Yes, yes, for love's delirium	Sì, sì, de' grandi amori
is the cause of great hatreds:	sono figli i gran sdegni;
this wounds at random, the other ruins kingdoms.	quel fere i cori e quest'abbatte i regni.

An eagle flies overhead.

EURIMACHUS

He who hears you on high	Chi dall'alto n'ascolta
now gives his answer, companions.	hor ne risponde, amici.
Thus the heavens can speak by silent omens.	Mute lingue del Ciel son gli auspici.
Above you, ah, look above you.	Mirate, ohimè mirate
Above us Jove dispatches his eagle	del gran Giove l'augello,
with predictions of ruin,	ne predice rovine,
with a promise of trouble.	ne prometto flagello.
He who fears the heavenly anger	Muova al delitto il piede
must now forswear this murder.	chi giusto il Ciel non crede.

THE THREE SUITORS

Indeed we must submit to heaven's fury,	Crediam al minacciar del Ciel irato,
for he who fears not heaven	chè chi non teme il Cielo
will pay the price most surely.	raddoppia il suo peccato.

Therefore, before her son
can arrive to help her,
let us soften the heart of Penelope
with gifts certain to please her,
because with plumes of gold Love's shafts
   are feathered.

Dunque prima che giunga
il filial soccorso,
per abbatter quel core
facciam ai doni almen grato ricorso,
perchè ha la punta d'or lo stral d'Amore.

EURIMACHUS

Gold for every condition,
gold's the only magician.
Every woman's heart, however proud
   and flinty,
softened by gold grows friendly.

L'oro sol, l'oro sia
l'amorosa magia.
Ogni cor feminil se fosse pietra

tocco dall' or si spetra.

THE THREE SUITORS

In Love's harmonious consort
sweetest singing is deep sighing.
But there's no pleasure till we hear gold's
   chiming;
true lovers must be givers.

[14] Amor è un' armonia,
sono canti i sospiri,
ma non si canta ben se l'or non suona;

non ama chi non dona.

Scene Nine. *A grove. Ulysses, then Minerva in her true form.*

ULYSSES

No man can fail who has divine
   protection,
who has the support of heaven.
For great adventures indeed I must be
   chosen,
and he must be contemptible
who is led by a god yet fears a mortal.

Perir non può chi tien per scorta il cielo,

chi ha per compagno un Dio.
A grand'imprese è ver volto son io,

ma fa peccato grave
chi difeso dal ciel il mondo pave.

MINERVA

O most courageous Ulysses,
I will arrange that your wife,
chaste Penelope,
suggests the trial which shall bring glory
   to you.
and safety and victory, and slay your
   rivals.
And so, when you have grasped your bow
   and strung it,
and hear the clap of thunder which shall
   warn you,
then boldly shoot, and with your deadly
   arrows
strike all the suitors dead and stand
   victorious.
I then shall stand beside you, and with
   celestial lightning
I shall strike down the puny mortal
   creatures.
Thus shall all of them fall to your just
   vengeance:
from the anger of heaven none gains a
   quittance.

O coraggioso Ulisse,
io farò che proponga
la tua casta consorte
giuoco che affè fia gloria e

sicurezza e vittoria e a' Proci morte.

Allor che l'arco tuo ti giunge in mano

e strepitoso tuon fiero t'invita

saetta pur che la tua destra ardita

tutti conficcherà gli estinti al piano.

Io starò teco e con celeste lampo

atterrerò l'humanità soggetto.

Cadran vittime tutti alla vendetta

che i flagelli del ciel non hanno scampo.

ULYSSES

Ever blind are we mortals,
but 'tis now my plainest duty
to obey your commands in humble
   blindness.
I will follow, O my goddess.

Sempre è cieco il mortale
ma all'or si dee più cieco.
Chi'l precetto divin devoto osserva

io ti seguo Minerva.

Scene Ten. *Eumæus, Ulysses.*

EUMÆUS

I saw, O gentle stranger, the suitors	Io vidi, o pelegrin, de' Proci amanti
tremble with dread and apprehension,	l'ardir infermarsi
their courage quite fail,	l'ardore gelar
their knees knock together,	negli occhi tremanti
their cheeks turn pale.	il cor palpitar.
Ulysses — to hear that name of terror	Il nome sol d'Ulisse,
transfixed their souls with horror.	quest'alme ree trafisse.

ULYSSES

At your story I am seized with laughter,	Godo anch'io ne so come rido
I know not why.	ne so perchè.
Laughter renews me and joy restores me,	Tutto gioisco ringiovanisco,
so happy am I.	ben lieto affè.

EUMÆUS

First let us eat, and when we have renewed our strength	Tosto ch'avrem con povera sostanza
with what I can offer, then let us hasten:	i corpi invigoriti. Andrem veloci:
we shall see the wicked suitors,	vedrai di quei feroci,
who are so impudent and proud	fieri i costumi, i gesti
in their bearing, so dishonest.	impudenti, inonesti.

ULYSSES

The evil-doer shall not live for ever;	Non vive eterna l'arroganza in terra
since Jove's anger subdues even the Olympians,	la superbia mortal tosto s'abbate
their mortal thread of life his lightning shall sever.	che il fulmine del Ciel gli olimpi atterra.

*

Scene Eleven. *Telemachus, Penelope.*

TELEMACHUS

I have spoken, O Queen, of my adventures,	Del mio lungo viaggio i torti errori
and have described them duly;	già vi narrai, Regina.
now I can refrain no longer from speaking of Helen	Hora tacer non posso della veduta Greca
and her heavenly beauty.	la bellezza divina.
When glorious Helen received me,	M'accolse Helena bella:
I gazed deep in her eyes,	io mirando stupii,
wondering how so much power	dentro a quei raggi immerso,
did not transform all the world	che di Paridi pieno
like Paris to be her lover,	non fosse l'universo;
since a single Paris is a prize	alla figlia di Leda
far too mean for Leda's daughter.	un sol Paride, dissi, è poca preda.
Small indeed was the carnage,	Povere fur le stragi
mild indeed were the flames of Troy set burning;	furon lievi gli incendi a tanto foco
the world must burn for her, all else is nothing.	che se non arde un mondo il resto è poco.
I saw in her eyes this vision,	Io vidi in que' begl'occhi,
burning, of the ruin of Troy,	dell'incendio Trojano
in a dreadful prediction,	le nascenti scintille
infant flames of destruction.	le bambine faville
Indeed, long ago,	e ben prima potea
an astrologer enamoured of those orbs and their glances	Astrologo amoroso da quei giri di foco
could have foretold disaster; and could have seen the fires	profetar fiamme e indovinar ardori

---

* This is the end of Act Three in the libretto.

that set alight the towns no less than
men's desires.
Paris now is dead, 'tis true;
ecstasy he also knew.
With his life he has paid, his debt is ended —
but for so great a pleasure,
more than one death is needed.
We must pardon young Paris for his
transgression,
for lovely Helen holds in her face and her
person,
matchless in beauty, his full absolution.

da incenerir città non men che cori.
Paride, è ver, morì,
Paride ancor gioì.
Con la vita pagar convenne l'onta,
ma così gran piacere
una morte non sconta.
Si perdoni a quell'alma il grave fallo·
la bella Greca porta
nel suo volto beato
tutte le scuse del Trojan peccato.

Alas, dangerous beauty, desire iniquitous
and accursed in remembrance,
for it was sown by hatred
among the coils of a serpent,
not in a blossoming face.
How monstrous is that love which bathes
in bloodshed!
Let memories of Helen
be buried in oblivion;
your thoughts of her are folly,
and vain your admiration.

Beltà troppo funesta, ardor iniquo
di rimembranze indegno
ti seminò lo sdegno
non tra i fiori d'un volto,
ma fra i strisci d'un angue,
chè mostro è quell'amor che nuota in
sangue.
Memoria così trista
disperda pur l'oblio,
vaneggia la tua mente,
folleggia il tuo desio.

It was not for idle folly
that I spoke of Helen, but I would tell
you
how in famous Sparta
on that day there flew
circling above our heads a bright
propitious bird,
and Helen, who is learned
in all occult science and wise in augury,
spoke rejoicing this prophecy:
'Soon we shall see Ulysses, and he will take
his revenge
on the suitors, and will restore his
kingdom.'

Non per vana follia
Helena ti nomai, ma perchè essendo

nella famosa Sparta
circondato improviso
dal volo d'un augel destro e felice,

Helena ch'è maestra
dell'indovine scienze e degli Auguri
tutta allegra mi disse
ch'era vicino Ulisse e che dovea

dar morte ai Proci e stabilirsi il Regno.

Scene Twelve. *The Suitors, Irus, Ulysses, Penelope, Telemachus, Eumæus.*

Troublesome wretch Eumæus,
evermore you are scheming
to bring about a quarrel
and to disturb our leisure;
you miserable object
and destroyer of pleasure. Why have you
brought here
this flea-ridden beggar
who will pester and trouble us
with his greedy clamour,
and will spoil all our cheer and peaceful
enjoyment?

Sempre villano Eumete,
sempre, sempre t'ingegni
di perturbar la pace,
d'intorbidir la gioia,
oggetto di dolore,
ritrovator di noia, hai qui condotto

un infesto mendico,
un noioso importuno
che con sue voglie ingorde
non farà che guastar le menti liete.

Fate has guided him hither
to the house of Ulysses
where he may rest and shelter.

L'ha condotto Fortuna
alle case d'Ulisse
ove pietà s'aduna.

ANTINOUS

Then let him stay with you and guard the pigsties,	Rimanga ei teco a custodir la gregge
and not come here to the palace	e qui non venga dove
where princes of noble blood preside and govern.	civile nobiltà comanda e regge.

EUMÆUS

Princes of noble blood are never cruel,	Civile nobiltà non è crudele,
nor is pity despised	nè puote anima grande
by a valiant heart: it grows	sdegnar pietà che nasce
from the sceptre of a monarch.	de' Regi tra le fasce.

ANTINOUS

You impudent fellow!	Arrogante plebeo!
It is not for such as you	Insegnar opre eccelse
to teach a prince his duty,	a te vil huom non tocca,
nor should a low-born churl with kings make treaty.	nè dee parlar di re villana bocca.
And you, pitiful starveling,	E tu, povero indegno,
thus do I send you packing!	fuggi da questo regno!

IRUS

Off with you, get you gone!	Partiti, movi il piè!
If you came . . . came for the din . . . ner you'll wait . . . till I have done.	Se sei qui per mangiar son pria di te.

ULYSSES

Squire of grand proportions,	Huomo di grosso taglio,
of wide and broad perspective,	di larga prospettiva,
though I am aged, and though my breath comes faintly,	benchè canuto et invecchiato sia
yet the flame in my breast burns ever brightly.	non è vile però l'anima mia.
If heaven's royal bounty	Se tanto mi concede
deigns to make me your teacher,	l'alta bontà regale
I'll tread your corpulent hulk under my feet,	trarrò il corpaccio tuo sotto il mio piede,
you contemptible creature.	mostruoso animale.

IRUS

What if now, ancient doddering soldier, greedy and artful,	E che sì, rimbambito guerriero, vecchio importuno,
what if now I should pluck the hairs out of your beard by the handful?	e che sì, che ti strappo i peli della barba ad uno ad uno!

ULYSSES

Let my life be the wager,	Voglio perder la vita
for all your huffing and puffing	se di forza e di vaglia
I'll beat you to the ground, bundle of stuffing.	io non ti vinco hor hor, sacco di paglia!

ANTINOUS

A wondrous duel from this resplendent couple,	Vediam, Regina, in questa bella coppia
royal lady, I promise	d'una lotta di braccia
as they tussle and wrestle.	stravagante duello.

TELEMACHUS

Fair fight I shall procure you,	In campo io t'assicuro,
be assured, gentle stranger.	pelegrin sconosciuto.

And I shall not take advantage
or put your feeble strength in danger.

Anch'io ti dò franchigia,
combattitor non barbuto.

ULYSSES

I accept your challenge gladly,
noble knight of the belly.

La gran disfida accetto,
cavaliero panciuto!

IRUS

Now then, coward, come on!
We'll fight to the finish, come on!

[15] Su, su dunque, alla lotta, su, su!
Alla ciuffa, alla lotta, su su!

They fight.

I'm beaten, alas, ay me!

Son vinto, ohimè!

ANTINOUS

Since he submits,
the victor must now forgive the loser.
Irus, though huge your might in appetite,
You cannot fight.

Tu vincitor perdona
a chi si chiama vinto.
Iro puoi ben mangiar,
ma non lottar.

PENELOPE

Very valiant stranger, remain and rest here,
here is safety and shelter.
From you we learn this lesson:
the heart may beat most valiantly in a
beggar.

Valoroso mendico! In corte resta
honorato e sicuro,
chè non è sempre vile
chi veste manto povero et oscuro.

AMPHINOMOUS*

Noble lady, true royalty,
Amphinomous here vows in loyalty. What
Fortune gave him,
ample and prodigal in blessings,
now is yours; to you he offers
newer riches and favours.
Token of his obedience and of the gifts he
makes you,
this royal crown is yours and craves
acceptance.
Yet where the heart is a suitor,
no gift can be greater.

Generosa Regina!
Anfinomo a te s'inchina, e ciò che diede

larga e prodiga sorte
dona a te, per te aduna
tua novella fortuna.
Questa regal corona
che di comando è segno
ti lascia in testimon di ciò che dona.

Dopo il dono del core
non ha dono maggiore.

PENELOPE

Generous in spirit,,
prodigal in kindness, your worth deserves
an empire,
for he merits no less who offers a
kingdom.

Anima generosa,
prodigo cavaliere, ben sei d'impero
degno,
chè non merita men chi dona un regno.

PEISANDER*

If my rival can tempt you
with a crown as guerdon,
I too may win your favour;
I too can give a kingdom.
Garments ornate and precious,
jewels and royal finery,
confess my proud devotion,
and praise your merits, peerless lady.

Se t'invoglia il desio
d'accettar regni in dono
ben so donar anch'io
et anch'io rege sono.
Queste pompose spoglie,
questi regali ammanti
confessano superbi
i miei ossequi i tuoi canti.

---

* Up to this point in the score, the part of Peisander was written in a tenor key and that of
Amphinomous as contralto. From here onwards, they are reversed. Here the characters are
reversed for consistency.

Noble the rivalry, and most admired the contest	Nobil contesa e generosa gara
where lovers true and generous	ove amator discreto
teach that in perfect love, to give is noblest.	l'arte del ben amar donando impara.

ANTINOUS

My true heart would possess you,	Il mio cor che t'adora
not as Queen but as woman,	non ti vuol sua Regina:
but my soul as a goddess would name you,	l'anima che s'inchina ad adorarti
to adore and acclaim you.	Deità vuol chiamarti,
And as to a goddess I offer sighs as incense,	e come Dea t'incensa coi sospiri,
my desires as priestly victims, and gold I offer	fa vittime i desiri e con quest'ori
with devotion and honour.	t'offre voti ed honori.

PENELOPE

He who makes such an offering	Non andran senza premio
surely must be rewarded,	opre cotanto eccelse,
for women's hearts are kindled	chè donna quando dona
by kindly gifts, though once they had scorned love's ardour.	se non è prima accesa allor s'accende,
To those who love sincerely,	e donna quando toglie
although at first rejected, they will surrender.	se non è prima resa al cor s'arrende.
Quickly go now, Melanto, and bring me here	Hor t'affretta Melanto e qui m'arreca
the bow of great Ulysses with his quiver;	l'arco del forte Ulisse e la faretra:
whoever proves he's able	e chi sarà di voi
to string the mighty weapon	con l'arco poderoso
and then to shoot the arrow, shall win	saettator più fiero havrà d'Ulisse
the consort of Ulysses and his kingdom.	e la moglie e l'Impero.

TELEMACHUS

Where are you, O great Ulysses?	Ulisse, e dove sei?
Oh, why do you not come to rout your enemies	Che fai che non ripari le tue perdite
and heal our sore distresses?	e in un gli affanni miei?

PENELOPE

My mouth has spoken,	Ma che promise
much against my will,	bocca facile ahi troppo
words belying what my heart had intended.	discordante dal core.
Heavenly gods, if I spoke it,	Numi del Cielo! S'io 'l dissi
'twas you released my tongue and made the promise.	snodaste voi la lingua, apriste i detti,
These must be portents and wonders of the gods,	saran tutti del Cielo e delle stelle
and of the stars above us.	prodigiosi effetti.

THE THREE SUITORS

Glorious and welcome conquest,	Lieta, soave gloria,
gracious lady, sweetest and fairest!	grata e dolce vittoria!
In Love's torment still obedient, we are healed by her gentle art,	Cari pianti degli amanti!
dear reward of a faithful heart.	Cor fedele, costante sen
Now redeemed by her gentle skill, we obey her sovereign will	cangia il torbido in seren.

This is the bow of Ulysses.
Love must teach him the art
who seeks to pierce my heart.
Amphinomous, to you I give it:
ready givers are blest:
be first to make the test.

Ecco l'arco d'Ulisse,
anzi l'arco d'Amor
che dee passarmi il cor.
Anfinomo, a te lo porgo:*
chi fu il primo a donar
sia il primo a saettar.

Sinfonia

AMPHINOMOUS

Since you became an archer,
bold Love, to wound me,
arm this weapon to help me.
If a bow first gave me wounds,
I am rescued by a bow.

Amor, se fosti arciero in saettarmi,
hor dà forza a quest'armi
chè vincendo dirò:
S'un arco mi ferì,
un arco mi sanò.

He tries to string the bow but cannot.

My fingers . . . can . . . not grasp you,
My sinews . . . can . . . not bend you.
Now that the bow defeats me
my strength is gone, even my will deserts me.

Il braccio non vi giunge,
il polso non v'arriva.
Ceda la vinta forza,
col non poter anche il desio s'ammorza.

Sinfonia

PEISANDER

But Love, pitiable infant,
is blind and cannot shoot.
All his gains are lucky chances,
his arrows are soft looks, his darts are but glances.
This bow in warlike splendour
scorns such a puny god, will not obey him.
You, glorious Mars, must lend me your mighty valour.
Then shall Mars in this battle be the victor.

Amor, picciolo Nume
non sa di saettar:
s'e' trafigge i mortali
son le saette sue sguardi, non strali,
ch'a Nume pargoletto
negano d'obbedir l'arme di Marte.
Tu, fiero Dio, le mie vittorie affretta,
il trionfo di Marte a te s'aspetta!

He tries to string the bow but cannot.

Ah, how intractable,
ah, how inflexible,
I find this bow!
Her heart so obstinate
will prove as obdurate
to me I know.

Com'intrattabile,
com'indomabile
l'arco si fa!
Quel petto frigido,
protervo e rigido,
per me sarà.

Sinfonia

ANTINOUS

Mars and Cupid defeated
yield the prize to Beauty:
He's no victor who fights unworthily.
Penelope, I'm girded
with the strength of your beauty to cheer and aid me.

Ceda Marte et Amore
ove impera beltà.
Chi non vince in honor non vincerà.
Penelope, m'accingo
in virtù del tuo bello all'alta prova.

He tries to string the bow but cannot.

My strength, my might, have failed me.
Vainly I have essayed it,
perhaps a spell has bound it. Ah, it is true then
that all things conspire
in the cause of their ruler.
Even the bow of Ulysses awaits its master.

Virtù, valor non giova.
Forse forza d'incanto
contende il dolce vanto. Ah ch'egli è vero
ch'ogni cosa fedele
ad Ulisse si rende;
e sin l'arco d'Ulisse, Ulisse attende!

---

* This line should read 'Pisandro, a te lo porgo', which is the only metrically correct solution. It is altered because of the voice switch mentioned in the previous note.

How worthless are royal titles!	Son vani, oscuri pregi
The victor in the battle is virtue alone,	i titoli de' regi.
and useless is the blood of inheritance	Senza valor il sangue
to support a sceptre	ornamento regale,
or to uphold a kingdom.	illustri scettri a sostener non vale.
Whoever is not equal	Chi simile ad Ulisse
to Ulysses in merit,	virtute non possiede
the treasures of his kingdom may not inherit.	de' tesori d'Ulisse è indegno erede.

ULYSSES

As a youthful braggart	Gioventute superba
sometimes conceals a coward,	sempre valor non serba,
just so a humble beggar	come vecchiezza humile
is not always a loser.	ad ogn'or non è vile.
Your Highness, though I am aged	Regina, in queste membra
yet my spirit incites me	tengo un'alma sì ardita
and to battle invites me.	ch'alla prova m'invita.
I claim no special favour;	Il giusto non eccedo:
I renounce the prize, and only covet the labour.	rinunzio il premio e la fatica io chiedo.

PENELOPE

Let the beggar be permitted	Concedasi al mendico
to make the arduous trial:	la prova faticosa.
a contest truly noble,	Contesa gloriosa!
with these youthful rivals, of an aged body	Contro petti virili un fianco antico
with such an ardour burning,	che tra rossori involti
so he puts them to shame and leaves them blushing.	darà 'l foco d'amor vergogna ai volti.

ULYSSES

Humbly I take the weapon,	Questa mia destra humile
arming in your cause, O heaven!	s'arma a tuo conto, o Cielo!
Make my valour victorious, mighty powers,	Le vittorie apprestate, o sommi Dei,
if by my offerings I have deserved your favours.	s'a voi son cari i sacrifizi miei.

Thunder. Minerva appears in majesty.

THE THREE SUITORS

Mighty vision and portent, prodigious wonder!	Meraviglie, stupori, prodigi estremi!

ULYSSES

Jove thundering aloud cries out for vengeance!	Giove nel suo tuonar grida vendetta!
'Tis too late for repentance.	Così l'arco saetta.

Sinfonia da guerra

Minerva! Some she will slaughter, some she will cherish.	Minerva altri rincora, altri avvilisce;
Thus her enemies perish.*	così l'arco ferisce.
We bring fear, we bring death, we bring [16] destruction!	Alle morti, alle stragi, alle ruine!

He kills the suitors with his arrows. †

---

* These lines 'Minerva! . . . perish.' are not in the libretto, and belong to bars of music which seem to have been added to the manuscript.

† This is the end of Act Four in the libretto.

Act Three

Scene One. *Irus alone, making a ridiculous entrance ('parte ridicola').*

IRUS

Oh, what pain! Oh, distress beyond endurance!
Oh, spectacle of carnage
which ever haunts remembrance!
I saw the suitors murdered,
all murdered the suitors.
The soakers, the suitors all were slaughtered. Lost are my pleasures,
the delights of the stomach and of the gullet.
Who will save me from this hunger? Who will console me?
Oh, terrible bereavement!
The suitors, Irus, you've lost them,
the suitors who were your fathers.
Well may you weep and wail,
mourning your grievous losses,
for a father is he who feeds you, is he who clothes you.
Who now will quench the fires
of your immense desires?
You'll never find — no, no, no — a friend
to fill the enormous cavity
of your ravenous belly,
or split his sides — no, no, no — with laughter
to see the drink go down your greedy gullet.
Who will save me from this thirst? Who will console me?

Unlucky day that brought my shame and ruin;
beaten first by a greybeard, a saucy beggar,
now by hunger I'm vanquished,
my sustenance is fled and vanished.

Hunger was ever my enemy:
I destroyed it, I crushed it. How can I bear to submit
and fall defeated?
Suicide would be better; and I will never suffer hunger
to gain the crown of victory.
Who escapes from the enemy has greatest glory.
Be courageous, my spirit,
vanquish your sorrow, for rather
than that villainous hunger should pronounce my doom,
freely my body I'll give to feed my tomb.

[17] O dolor, o martir che l'alma attrista!

O mesta rimembranza
di dolorosa vista!
Io vidi i Proci estinti:
i Proci, furo uccisi.
I porci, furo uccisi.* Ah, ch'io perdei

Le delizie del ventre e della gola!

Chi soccorre il digiun, chi lo consola

con flebile parola?
I Proci, Iro, perdesti,
i Proci, i padri tuoi.
Sgorga pur quanto vuoi
lagrime amare e meste,
chè padre è chi ti ciba e chi ti veste.

Chi più della tua fame
satollerà le brame?
Non troverai chi goda

empir del vasto ventre
l'affamate caverne;
non troverai chi rida

del ghiotto trionfar della tua gola.
Chi soccorre il digiun, chi lo consola?

Infausto giorno a mie ruine armato:

poco dianzi mi vinse un vecchio ardito,
hor m'abbatte la fame,
dal cibo abbandonato.

L'ebbi già per nemica,
l'ho distrutta, l'ho vinta; hor troppo fora

vederla vincitrice.
Voglio uccider me stesso e non vo' mai

ch'ella porti di me trionfo e gloria!
Che si toglie al nemico è gran vittoria.

Coraggioso mio core,
vinci il dolore! E pria
ch'alla fame nemica egli soccomba

vada il mio corpo a disfamar la tomba.

Here the score omits Scene Two ('Desert: Shades of the Suitors, Mercury') because it is 'melancholy': 'la si lascia fuori per esser maninconica'.†

---

* The play on words ('proci' — suitors, 'porci' — pigs) does not appear in the libretto.

† For the full text of this scene, and a discussion of the opera, see E. Rosand *Iro and the Interpretation of 'Il ritorno d'Ulisse in patria'* in *The Journal of Musicology,* University of California, 1989.

Scene Three. *The Palace. Melanto, Penelope.*

MELANTO

What new clamour and crying,	E quai nuovi rumori,
what a terrible slaughter,	e che insolite stragi,
what a fate for the suitors!	e che tragici amori.
Who dared — who was the rascal	Chi fu, chi fu l'ardito
that dared to bring such violence	che osò con nuova guerra
and cruelly disturb your peace and your beauty?	la pace intorbidar ch'hai tu negli occhi,
Who cast down the temples of Love	e trar disfatti a terra
which those brave souls now departed	quei tempii che ad Amor furon eretti
had pledged and dedicated?	in quei focosi petti?

PENELOPE

Poor royal queen, widowed and abandoned,	Vedova amata, vedova Regina,
yet more tears I'll shed tomorrow;	nuove lagrime appresto;
for me, O cruel fate,	insomma all'infelice
every love ends in sorrow.	ogni amore è funesto.

MELANTO

Life is shadowed by fears, even where the sceptre	Così all'ombra de' scettri anco pur sono
should give protection,	malsicure le vite,
and close to the thrones of kings	vicine alle corone
destroying hands are bolder in desecration.	son le destre esecrande ancor più ardite.

PENELOPE

The suitors perished, and though they had cried	Moriro i Proci, e queste
to the stars for shelter,	da lor chiamate stelle
these looked down uncaring	furon di quelle morti
and would bring them no succour.	assistenti facelle.

MELANTO

Penelope, Penelope,	Penelope, il castigo
The chastisement of mighty heaven	dell'immortale Fato
must waken you to scorn and fury,	non consigliar che con lo sdegno e l'ira,
for an offended monarch should rise up	chè maestate offesa
in wrath and punish justly.	esser giusta non può se non s'adira.

PENELOPE

Though my eyes with tears much burdened	Dell'occhio la pietate
may find relief in weeping,	si risente all'eccesso,
I cannot rouse my spirit	ma concitar il core
to rage and indignation; I am numb with grieving.	a sdegno et a dolor non m'è concesso.

Scene Four. *Eumæus and the above.*

EUMÆUS
entering

Joy, from your inmost being	Forza d'occulto affetto
now must banish your mourning:	raddolcisce il tuo petto.
he who single-handed	Chi con un arco solo
with his mighty weapon	isconosciuto diede
dealt out death to a hundred,	a cento morti il duolo,
that brave and powerful beggar	quel forte e quel robusto
who could bend the bow and send the arrows flying,	che domò l'arco e fe' volar gli strali,
yes, he who slaughtered the wicked thronging suitors,	colui che i Proci insidiosi e felli
by his valour and invincible strategies,	valoroso trafisse
rejoice at him, my lady, he was Ulysses!	rallegrati Regina, egli era Ulisse!

120

PENELOPE

You are a credulous shepherd	Sei buon pastor Eumete,
if you believe such stories	se persuaso credi
against the proof of your senses.	contro quello che vedi.

EUMÆUS

Yet the greybeard, the beggar,	Il canuto, l'antico,
the ragged, wandering stranger,	il povero, il mendico
he who fought with the suitors	che coi Proci superbi
and courageously slew them in their places,	coraggioso attaccò mortali risse,
rejoice at him, my lady, he was Ulysses!	rallegrati Regina, egli era Ulisse.

PENELOPE

Common folk are gullible,	Credulo è il volgo e sciocco,
and believe the clamour	e la tromba mendace
of a lying rumour.	della fama fallace.

EUMÆUS

Ulysses, I saw him, plain and clear.	Ulisse io vidi, sì,
Ulysses himself is alive and here.	Ulisse è vivo, è qui!

PENELOPE

You are stubborn and untruthful,	Relator importuno,
and your report deceitful.	consolator nocivo!

EUMÆUS

Truly Ulysses is here,	Dico che Ulisse è qui.
I saw him and I know.	Io stesso il vidi e 'l so.
That I tell you the truth will soon appear,	Non contenda il tuo no con il mio sì:
Ulysses is living, is here.	[18] Ulisse è vivo, è qui!

PENELOPE

I shall no more dispute it,	Io non contendo teco
for you are blind and obstinate.	perchè sei stolto e cieco.

Scene Five. *Telemachus and the above.*

TELEMACHUS

You are wise, Eumæus, and loyal,	È saggio Eumete, è saggio,
the truth is as he told you.	è ver quel ch'ei racconta:
Ulysses, your true husband and my true father,	Ulisse, a te consorte et a me padre
slew that multitude of hateful suitors.	ha tutte uccise le nemiche squadre.
His strange disguise, so that none should know him,	Il comparir sotto mentito aspetto,
dressed like an aged beggar —	sotto vecchia sembianza,
that was Minerva's doing, her godlike cunning.	arte fù di Minerva e fù suo dono.

PENELOPE

Often 'tis true we mortal earthly dwellers	Troppo, egli è ver, che gli huomini qui in terra
serve as the playthings of some immortal deity;	servon di gioco agli immortali Dei.
thus you too they deceive, and show no pity.	Se ciò credi ancor tu lor gioco sei.

TELEMACHUS

It was Minerva's will	Vuole così Minerva:
thus to disguise Ulysses, and deceive his enemies	per ingannar con le sembianze finte
with a false appearance.	gli inimici d'Ulisse.

121

If the mighty gods so delight in deception,	Se d'ingannar gli Dei prendon diletto
who can prove to me	chi far fede mi puote
that I am not the one to be cheated,	che non sia mio l'inganno,
as I have pined and waited?	se fu mio tutto il danno?

TELEMACHUS

But you know that Minerva	Protettrice de' Greci
is the Greeks' protectress,	è come sai Minerva,
and that Ulysses is dearer than any other.	e più che gli altri Ulisse a lei fu caro.

PENELOPE

The gods high in their heavens	Non han tanto pensiero
take little thought for mortals,	gli Dei lassù nel Cielo,
or for mortal afflictions.	delle cose mortali.
Fire they allow to burn us and ice to freeze us:	Lasciano ch'arda il foco e agghiaccia il gelo.
pleasure and sufferings come by their directions.	Figlian le cause lor piaceri e mali.

TELEMACHUS

Cast off your widow's mourning.	Togliti in pace il nero.

EUMÆUS

You must not fear. I'll call him here.	Io lo dirò: ti seguirò.

Scene Six. *The seashore. Minerva, Juno.*

MINERVA

Fury's a fire, O great goddess, scorn is a blazing flame,	Fiamma è l'ira, o gran Dea, foco è lo sdegno.
so with fury and indignation	Noi sdegnose et irate
we have destroyed by fire the Trojan nation.	incenerito abbiam di Troja il regno,
A Trojan paid the price, who first offended.	offese da un Trojan, ma vendicate;
But the worthiest Grecian is still the plaything	il più forte fra' Greci ancor contende
of his fate, of his destiny —	col Destin, con il Fato:
Ulysses, ah, most unhappy.	Ulisse addolorato.

JUNO

But no price is too high	Per vendetta che piace
that the gods require as vengeance:	ogni prezzo è leggero.
justly the Trojan empire is dissolved	Vada il Trojano impero
into ashes and forgotten.	anco in peggio di polvere fugace.

MINERVA

Through that vengeance	Dalle nostre vendette
Ulysses lives as a homeless wanderer,	nacquero in lui gli errori
all his troubles and sorrows	delle stragi dilette
are offspring of our vengeful slaughter.	son figli i suoi dolori.
Yet it befits our godhead,	Convien al nostro Nume
since he has served us well, to appease	in vindice salvar, placar gli sdegni
the fury of Neptune, god of the oceans.	del Dio dei salsi flutti.

JUNO

I will procure his pardon,	Procurerò la pace,
I will restore Ulysses	recercherò il riposo
to peace from stormy seas.	d'Ulisse glorioso.

For you, sister and consort	Per te del sommo Giove
to the Father of Heaven,	e sorella c consorte
surely the glorious gates will swiftly open.	s'aprono nove in Ciel divine porte.

Scene Seven. *Juno, Jove, Neptune, Minerva and Chorus of Gods.*

JUNO

Great Jove, soul of the gods, god of all spirits,	Gran Giove, alma de' Dei, Dio delle menti,
spirit of all creation,	mente dell'Universo,
who govern all things and dwell in all things,	tu che 'l tutto governi e tutto sei,
favour with your wise goodness my earnest prayers.	inchina le tue grazie a' prieghi miei.
Ulysses waits too long,	[19] Ulisse troppo errò.
waits and wanders too long.	troppo, ahi, troppo soffrì;
Pity him, pity and bring him home;	tornalo in pace un dì.
Through divine enmity he suffered wrong,	Fu divin il voler che lo destò.

JOVE

Your prayers are never lost	Per me non avrà mai
when you address me, O Juno,	vota preghiera Giuno,
but first we must appease	ma placar pria conviensi
the resentment of Neptune.	lo sdegnato Nettuno.
Hark to me, O god of the sea.	Odimi, O Dio del mar.
In heaven where destiny is written	Fu scritto qui dove il destin s'accoglie
fate ordained the destruction of the Trojans;	dell'eccidio Trojano il fatal punto
now the ill-starred man has reached his goal,	hor ch'al suo fine il destinato è giunto
show that resentment is unworthy a gentle breast.	sdegno otioso un gentil petto invogli.
Great Ulysses at fate's decree has acted, endured,	Fu ministro del Fato Ulisse: il forte
conquered and fought as heaven's defender.	soffrì, vinse, pugnò campion celeste.
Through him while burning Troy was cloaked in ashes,	Per lui mentre di cenere si veste
death walked abroad and strayed through the city.	cittadina di Troja errò la morte.
Great god, pardon him great god,	Nettun, pace O Nettun, Nettun, perdona
forget and pardon now, though he is guilty	il suo duolo al mortal, ch'afflitto il rese.
with the guilt that afflicts and taints every mortal.	Ecco scrive il Destin le sue difese;
Fate itself has written his acquittal:	
for the fault is not man's if heaven thunders.	non è colpa dell'huom se'l cielo tuona.

NEPTUNE

Although in icy turbulence,	So ben quest'onde frigide,
although in frosty undulance	so ben quest'onde gelide,
my stormy waters flow, my heart is moved.	ma sentono l'ardor di tua pietà.
In caverns dark and echoing,	Nei fondi algosi et infimi
in ooze too deep for fathoming,	nei cupi acquosi termini
the edicts of Jove are heard and obeyed.	il decreto di Giove anco si sa.
Reckless and bold the Phæacians incurred my anger	Contro i Feaci arditi e temerarii,
and I swore they should atone.	mio sdegno se sfogò.

My anger now is satisfied,	Pagò il delitto pessimo
for I turned their ship to stone.	la nave che restò.
Live then, let troubles cease,	Viva felice pur,
live Ulysses in peace.	viva Ulisse sicur!

Kindliest Father,	Giove amoroso
your love would rather	fa il Ciel pietoso
forgive than blame.	nel perdonar.

CHORUS FROM THE SEA

The seas give pardon	Benchè habbia il gelo,
no less than heaven	non men del Cielo
from whence it came.	pietoso è il mar.

BOTH CHORUSES

Ever, mankind, beseech him,	Prega, mortal, deh prega,
with contrition and petition, your prayers	che sdegnato e pregato un Dio si piega.
will reach him.	

JOVE

Minerva, your task is now	Minerva hor fia tua cura
to quench the rebellion	d'acquetar i tumulti
of the angry Achæans,	de' sollevati Achiri
who to avenge the murdered suitors	che per vendetta degli estinti Proci
threaten a bloody warfare	pensano portar guerra
in all the land of Ithaca.	all'Itacense terra.

MINERVA

I shall control those spirits,	Rintuzzerò quei spirti,
I shall quench their fiery anger.	smorzerò quegli ardori,
Your peace I shall establish,	commanderò la pace,
Father, all discord I shall banish.	Giove, come a te piace.

Scene Eight. *Ericlea alone.*

ERICLEA

Ericlea, should you speak?	Ericlea, che vuoi far?
Should you tell what you saw?	Vuoi tacer o parlar?
By speaking you bring comfort	Se parli tu consoli,
but silence is your duty.	obbedisci se taci.
You are tied to your bond,	Sei tenuta a servir,
yet contracted to love.	obbligata ad amar.
Should you tell what you saw?	Vuoi tacer o parlar?
But pity must give way to duty;	Ma ceda all'obbedienza la pietà;
to keep silent is best, is honesty.	[20] non si de' sempre dir ciò che si sa.

Sinfonia

If I cure her distresses — what	Medicar chi languisce, o che diletto!
jubilation!	
But 'tis vile degradation	Ma che ingiurie e dispetto
to reveal a secret thought.	scoprir l'altrui pensier;
Then in silence I'll hide it as I ought.	bella cosa talvolta è un bel tacer.
'Tis a cruel perplexity	È ferita crudele
to have power by speaking	il porter con parole
to console her in mourning and speak no	consolar chi si duole e non lo far;
word:	
yet to betray is wrong.	ma del pentirsi alfin
Wise concealment is best that waits	assai lunge è il tacer più che'l parlar.
unheard.	

This precious secret I'm keeping	Bel segreto taciuto
shortly may be revealed,	tosto scoprir si può;
yet what is once uncovered	una sol volta detto
can never be concealed.	celarlo non potrò.
Ericlea, what should you do? Should you tell what you saw?	Ericlea, che farai, tacerai tu?
Wise conccalment is best, and breaks no law.	Insomma un bel tacer mai scritto fu.

Ritornello

Scene Nine. *Penelope, Telemachus and Eumæus.*

PENELOPE

All our thoughts and our hopes the wind has taken;	Ogni nostra ragion sen porta il vento.
our dreams have not the power	Non ponno i nostri sogni
to lighten the vigils	consolar le vigilie
of a soul in desperation.	dell'anima smarrita.
Your tales may bring us laughter, not consolation.	Le favole fan riso e non dan vita.

TELEMACHUS

Blind and incredulous.	Troppo incredula!

EUMÆUS

Incredulous blindness.	Incredula troppo!

TELEMACHUS

Blind and stubborn.	Troppo ostinata!

EUMÆUS

Most stubborn blindness.	Ostinata troppo!

TELEMACHUS

The truth is certain.	È più che vero.

EUMÆUS

It must be so:	Di vero è più
it was Ulysses	che'l vecchio arciero
who strung the bow.	Ulisse fu.

TELEMACHUS

Look, he himself is coming,	Eccolo che sen viene
and in his own true likeness.	e la sua forma tiene.

EUMÆUS

Ulysses — 'tis he!	Ulisse egli è!

TELEMACHUS

Look, it is he.	Eccolo affè!

Scene Ten. *Enter Ulysses in his own form and the above.*

ULYSSES

O my beloved companion,	O delle mie fatiche
goal of my wandering footsteps,	meta dolce e soave,
haven of sweet contentment	porto caro amoroso
where I seek my refreshment.	dove corro al riposo.

Halt there, cunning enchanter,
for you must not approach me.
All your tricks and disguises cannot
   deceive me.

Fermati, cavaliero,
incantator o mago!
Di tue finte mutanze io non m'appago.

ULYSSES

And thus you greet your husband,
and thus scorn the embraces
which he has sighed for, and his fond
   caresses?

Così del tuo consorte,
così dunque t'appressi
a lungamente sospirati amplessi?

PENELOPE

True wife I am, but to the lost Ulysses.
Neither charm nor incantation
can shake my steadfast faith, my firm
   persuasion.

[21] Consorte io sono, ma del perduto Ulisse,
nè incantesimo o magie
perturberan la fè, le voglie mie.

ULYSSES

For the sake of your eyes
all else I did despise,
eternal life I renounced, and earthly
   favours,
and to keep faith unchanged, defied death's
   terrors.

In honor de tuoi rai
l'eternità sprezzai,
volontario cangiando e stato e sorte.

Per serbarmi fedel son giunto a morte.

PENELOPE

That power which gave you
the likeness of Ulysses
made me rejoice
in the slaughter of the infamous suitors.
Enough that by your deception
there grew this benediction.

Quel valor chi ti rese
ad Ulisse simile
care mi fa le stragi
degli amanti malvagi.
Questo di tua bugia
il dolce frutto sia.

ULYSSES

That Ulysses am I,
a fragment from the ashes,
a revenant from the dead.
Of the adulterous robbers
I was the avenging scourge and not the
   accomplice.

Quell'Ulisse son io
delle ceneri avanzo,
residuo delle morti,
degli adulteri e ladri
fiero castigator e non seguace.

PENELOPE

You are not the first, believe me,
who has coveted the kingdom,
and under a disguise has sought to deceive
   me.

Non sei tu 'l primo ingegno
che con nome mentito
tentasse di trovar comando o regno.

ERICLEA

I can be silent no longer.
This man is indeed Ulysses, noble lady,
for when I saw him naked at the bath I
   knew him,
finding the honourable scar on his body
where the boar once had gored him.
I too long have kept silent and I ask
   forgiveness.
Though women love to babble
and my poor tongue would fain have been
   talking,
at the command of Ulysses I told you
   nothing.

[22] Hor di parlar è tempo: è questo Ulisse.
Casta e gran donna, io lo conobbi all'ora
che nudo al bagno venne, ove scopersi

del feroce cinghiale
l'honorato segnale.
Ben ti chieggio perdon se troppo tacqui:

loquace femminil garrula lingua
per comando d'Ulisse

con fatica lo tacque e non lo disse.

Love would have me give credence to what my heart desires;

Creder ciò ch'è desio m'insegna Amore;

yet faith untouched and pure my vow requires.

serbar costante il sen comanda honore.

What must I do, O heaven?

Dubbio pensier, che fai?

My faith denies the prayers

La fe' negata ai prieghi

of the good Eumæus,

del buon custode Eumete,

of my son Telemachus,

di Telemaco il figlio,

and the prayers of my nurse

alla vecchia nutrice anco si nieghi,

also refuses, for my chaste bed

chè il mio pudico letto

gives shelter to none but Ulysses.

sol d'Ulisse è ricetto.

ULYSSES

Your chaste nature and custom I know full well.

Del tuo casto pensiero io so 'l costume

I know that your bed is so secret

So che 'l letto pudico

that no one save Ulysses ever has seen it.

che tranne Ulisse solo altro non vide.

Every night you adorn it, you and none other,

Ogni notte da te s'adorna e copre

with a coverlet of silk

con un serico drappo

that your own hands have woven, on which embroidered

di tua mano contesto, in cui si vede

with her attendant virgins

col virginal suo coro

Diana herself is depicted.

Diana effigiata.

In all my wanderings I kept this

M'accompagnò mai sempre

memory so blessed.

memoria così grata.

PENELOPE

Yes, now I can believe you, yes, now I know you.

Hor sì ti riconosco, hor sì ti credo,

As once you took possession

antico possessore

of my poor heart and passion.

del combattuto core.

Oh, forgive my reluctance,

Honestà mi perdoni,

love inspired all my doubts and my acceptance.

dono tutto ad Amor le sue ragioni.

ULYSSES

Loosen in rapture, loosen

Sciogli la lingua, sciogli

the chains that held you silent,

per allegrezza i nodi!

loosen in a sigh your sorrow that was so patient.

Un sospir, un ohimè la voce snodi.

PENELOPE

Shine in glory, O heavens,

[23] Illustratevi o Cieli,

bloom with flowers, O meadows, rejoice, you breezes.

rinfioratevi o prati, aure gioite!

Merrily birds are singing

Gli augelletti cantando,

and rivers softly murmuring for joy and sympathy.

i rivi mormorando hor si rallegrino!

Thus they mark with their music

Quell'herbe verdeggianti,

and celebrate with gentle frolic our loving ecstasy.

quell'onde sussurranti hor si consolino,

Like a phoenix new risen

già che sorta felice

from the ashes of burning Troy returns my heart's joy.

dal cenere Trojan la mia Fenice.

ULYSSES

So long sighed for, my treasure!

Sospirato mio sole!

PENELOPE

Love surpassing all measure!

Rinnovata mia luce!

127

Haven of peace and refreshment!   Porto quieto e riposo!

PENELOPE AND ULYSSES

Through long desire still dearer.   Bramato sì, ma caro.

PENELOPE

I learn to bless the torments   Per te gli andati affanni
I was compelled to suffer.   a benedir imparo.

ULYSSES

No more recall them,   Non si rammenti
joy shall forestall them.   più de' tormenti.
All is enchantment,   Tutto è piacer.
all's joyfulness.

PENELOPE

Now tears will vanish,   Fuggan dai petti
sorrows we banish.   dogliosi affetti!
All is contentment,   Tutto è goder!
all's happiness.

ULYSSES AND PENELOPE

Joyfulness, happiness, shall reign and   Del piacer, del goder venuto è 'l dì.
    bless.
Yes, beloved, yes dearest, yes, yes!   Sì, sì vita, sì, sì core, sì, sì!

The End*

---

* The libretto ends with a Chorus of Ithacans which is missing from the score.

*Anthony Rolfe Johnson and Jean Rigby as Ulysses and Penelope in David Freeman's 1989
production at English National Opera, designed by David Roger and conducted by Paul Daniel
(photo: Laurie Lewis)*

Public Vice, Private Virtue

Iain Fenlon and Peter Miller

As well as being the most compelling of all early operas, *The Coronation of Poppea* (*L'Incoronazione di Poppea*) is also the most problematic — a powerful combination that has led to much discussion. One main strand of interest has been to establish an authoritative text from the two complete (or nearly complete) and at times sharply differing scores that have survived, and from the ten or so manuscript and printed versions of the libretto that have come down to us. And while Busenello's authorship of the *Poppea* libretto is beyond reasonable doubt, a similar certainty does not surround the question of who composed the music; the most recent contribution to that debate (Alan Curtis, 1989) concludes that while most of the music in *Poppea* is Monteverdi's work, the role of Ottone (Otho in the English version) has been re-written in the surviving sources, other parts of the opera have been changed, and the whole of the final scene is a later addition, most probably by Francesco Sacrati with the assistance of Benedetto Ferrari. Yet beyond these uncertainties lies an even more intangible difficulty: what does the opera mean? As one historian has put it:

> In its most obvious terms, *Poppea* celebrates the victory of Amor; the love of Poppea and Nerone triumphs over all obstacles — over objections of state, over legality and morality. But the dark side of that victory is equally present; *Poppea* seems also to celebrate the defeat of reason. Seneca dies, Ottavia is exiled, and Ottone and Drusilla are banished from Rome. The apparent immorality of the dénouement casts a shadow over our perception of the work. Is it really love that triumphs, or is it mere lust, or Poppea's greed for power?

Only by examining the context in which *Poppea* existed for a contemporary audience can we understand this otherwise bewildering masterpiece with its evidently strange moral message. Because Venice was a city whose intellectual culture was forged as much in the wider circles of Italy and of Europe as in the grand palaces lining her canals, any attempt to understand Venetian intellectual life must properly begin there. The French invasion of Italy in 1494 and the half-century of warfare that followed destroyed the political world of the Italian Renaissance. In the second half of the sixteenth century civil wars of religion broke out in France and the Netherlands, two other highly prosperous regions. This century of depredations, disruption and princely despotism led important thinkers such as Michel de Montaigne and Justus Lipsius to two related conclusions. First, the public world, the world of politics, was about the exercise of power. Secondly, that under these circumstances the prime obligation of the citizen was that of self-preservation which could be assured only by following reason and withdrawing from the desperate conditions of civic life. The first-century Roman historian Tacitus was adopted as the guide to the political conditions of despotism, while his contemporary, the philosopher Seneca, was seen as the model for the philosophical preparation of the individual for such an existence. In his histories, Tacitus had shown how to discern and then penetrate the masks worn by princes in order to hide their true motivations. If unmasking was a necessary skill for political survival, the kind of steadfastness and fortitude Montaigne called constancy was described as the key moral virtue, and friendship its arena.

Rachel Yakar and Eric Tappy as Poppea and Nero in Jean-Pierre Ponnelle's 1977 production in Zurich, conducted by Nikolaus Harnoncourt, designed by Pet Halmen (photo: Susan Schimert-Ramme)

Seneca (Carlo Cava) condemned to death in the 1962 Glyndebourne production (photo: Guy Gravett)

Venice, in the first half of the seventeenth century, was home to a group of historians for whom Tacitus was a model. Their analysis of contemporary affairs showed a deep scepticism towards the intentions of Europe's rulers, and their writings, often deeply ironical in tone, were designed to illustrate the incompatibility of words and deeds. The most concise description of this 'Venetian style', and of the view of human nature on which it rested, is supplied by a leading Venetian rabbi, Simone Luzzatto. In his *Discourse on the condition of the Jews* (1638) he wrote that:

> The internal image of our soul is like a mosaic, which seems to be a single shape, and on closer inspection shows itself to be made up of various fragments of small stones both cheap and precious, joined and assembled. Even more so is our soul made up of various different and conflicting pieces, any one of which can appear distinctly at various times. Consequently, describing the nature and condition of a single man is very arduous and difficult; and it is more difficult still to aim to explain a man's actions in terms of a single norm or principle.

At the same time, despair with politics drove many aristocrats into the kind of social circles whose concerns were dominated by the issues of courtly life: love and manners. In the published writings of the Accademia degli Incogniti, the circle to which the librettists of both *Ulysses* and *Poppea* belonged, Tacitist wariness about appearances was applied to love and women. Beneath the surface lurked the real motives and the appearance of physical beauty was, alas, often belied by the truth. Instead, many of these writers suggested that the beauty of the soul was the real prize; they saw it expressed, for example, in the kind of powerful friendship that Montaigne himself felt and describes in his *Essays*.

'Poppea' at Glyndebourne in 1984: Seneca (Robert Lloyd) takes leave of his friends (photo: Guy Gravett)

Any contemporary audience would have read Busenello's *Poppea* as a synthesis of these differing intellectual contexts. The libretto is informed both by the Tacitist emphasis on penetrating the deceptions of princely power, and by the epistemological presupposition that this truth could only be ascertained by approaching the subject from points of view which often seemed to be conflicting, and further, by a wariness, strongly influenced by the Incogniti's beliefs, about the nature of love itself. The composer's musical descriptions also shift rapidly, and sometimes jarringly. We are presented not with a progressive development of characters, but with a series of partial revelations; these contrasts amount to a coherent narrative only when judged from afar, or after the event. The effect recalls Luzzatto's remarks, with their strong image of the mosaic-like quality of human psychology.

As the first historical opera and one, moreover, substantially based upon Tacitus, *Poppea* should be viewed (in terms of both story and style) as standing at the tail-end of nearly half a century of Venetian historical writing. It is written the way the best history was written in Venice at the time and, as a result, it can only be properly understood as a Tacitist text. To avail ourselves of Luzzatto's precepts, designed for such a purpose, we must move into this realm of confusion and seek out some of the detail in the opera before we can come to see the story as a 'single idea'.

It is instructive to start where the audience starts, at the beginning. The Prologue and the opening three scenes present the principal characters and situations. Following standard theatrical and operatic precedent, the Prologue anticipates the main theme of the story. After a brief Sinfonia, the heavens open to reveal a contest for superiority between Fortune, Virtue and Love. Virtue defends herself against Fortune, the friend of the unwise, but Love asserts pre-eminence over them both and even over the absent figure of Time. The dispute culminates in the victory of Love who, with a triumphant flourish, points forward to the drama proper. This contrast between immutable Virtue and Love follows the arguments of the Incogniti, and recalls their repeated attacks on the ease with which beautiful appearances could seduce the unwary. Many might call this reaction 'Love' but the Incogniti condemned it as a piece of deception rather than as the honest expression of the soul's yearning for companionship. With a nod from Love the heavens vanish and the scene changes.

It is dawn. Outside Poppea's palace Otho (Ottone), described by Tacitus as Poppea's cuckolded husband, is discovered with two sleeping members of Nero's guard. He has returned unexpectedly, only to discover Poppea's adulterous affair with Nero. Otho is a minor character in the ancient classical sources but in the opera he is a major figure who appears more frequently than any other, and his development as a character is an important clue to the meaning of *Poppea*. Now his outburst awakens the soldiers; they complain about the discomforts of the night, and bitterly criticise Nero's love for Poppea, which they hold responsible for the troubles of the Empire. As 'ordinary' characters from the real world, the soldiers function in much the same way as Arnalta and Octavia's nurse and page; as stock types taken from the traditions of Italian sixteenth-century spoken drama, their dramatic function is to comment on the action from which they stand apart. It is from them that we first encounter criticisms not only of Nero and Poppea, but also of Seneca, and it is from this unfavourable portrait that the audience gains its first impression of the philosopher, long before he appears.

In the third scene Poppea and Nero are seen in the early morning light, affectionately embracing. Both would have been familiar from the standard versions of the story, and from the writings of the Incogniti. In a brisk phrase Nero announces that he must leave; Poppea implores him to stay. Gently leading Nero on, Poppea extracts the promise that Octavia will be excluded from the throne, after which their own relationship can be made public. In the ensuing exchanges Poppea repeatedly, urgently seeks Nero's assurance that he will return to her; he promises to do so and they make their passionate farewells.

Poppea remains for the next scene, for which she is joined by her nurse Arnalta, a character invented by Busenello out of the traditions of the *commedia dell'arte*. As with Octavia's nurse, Arnalta initially may seem to have no dramatic rationale other then to provide comic relief but, again, it is the delineation of a seemingly minor participant's character that presents vital clues to an interpretation of the opera. Poppea confidently declares that she has nothing to fear with Love and Fortune fighting on her side. These might indeed seem to us to be strong allies, as Poppea genuinely believes, but to anyone versed in the arguments of the Incogniti they would be seen as liabilities. Although Arnalta warns her mistress of the dangers of consorting with those whose only rule of action is political, Poppea is resolutely passionate and inconstant, refuses to listen and repeatedly insists that she has no fear of the consequences of her actions. Poppea's impetuosity, characterised through a rapid succession of quickly-paced musical ideas, contrasts with the writing for Arnalta, which is generally slow-moving and calm. And so it continues, with each of Arnalta's carefully-modulated arguments provoking Poppea's vigorous responses until they culminate in final, hysterical defiance, to which Arnalta can only conclude, in sad resignation, that Poppea is out of her mind.

Thus these first four scenes of the first act form a unit, dramatically unified by being set in a single place, in which Busenello introduces the main theme of the drama, and the main characters in the action: Nero and Poppea in person, and Seneca through the unfavourable criticisms of Nero's soldiers. The composer, for his part, brings to bear the full range of his skills as a musical dramatist. At the most superficial level, individual words and images of a pictorial kind evoke traditional musical responses which come out of the traditions of the madrigal. In broader terms, one of the most distinctive features of the musical language of *Poppea* is its flexibility, its ability to move easily between declamation and aria or arioso and back again. Many earlier operas make use of the set-piece aria which stands isolated from the surrounding music; such songs are rare in *Poppea*, and when they do occur they do not fulfil such a central dramatic function as they had done in earlier works. On the contrary, the main way in which character and action are advanced is not through arias as such but through a fluid vocal style which crucially depends upon contrast, a contrast which is most characteristically achieved through subtle shifts between lyrical arioso with its use of melisma, and declamation, which is closer to speech patterns. That said, the use of measured and less measured music is not only conditioned by characterisation or plot, for in the context of the Incogniti's beliefs about song and beauty either can serve a deeply ironic purpose. Indeed, a common device in the opera is that meaning is the opposite of what the music at first appears to be saying.

That point is neatly illustrated in the confrontation between Seneca and Octavia which follows her famous lament, 'Disprezzata Regina'. Here Seneca acts as the mouthpiece of neostoicism, and his opening speech picks up the theme of the hardship of public life. Those called to service must expect anxiety and heavy responsibility; the only means of resisting these pressures is constancy of mind ('constantia'). He specifically compares virtue with beauty, rejecting the latter because of its inherent instability and uncertainty. In this context, Seneca's long virtuosic melisma on the word 'bellezza' is not merely an adaptation of a convention of madrigal-writing, but is also deeply ironic: the irony is that the concept of beauty is dramatically and directly represented in elaborate vocal ornamentation which erupts in a largely syllabic declamatory speech and is delivered by Seneca who is attacking its significance. On the surface the relationship between words and music might seem to be unexceptional, conforming to traditional methods of textual representation in music, but here it presents an ironic contrast to what we know of the characters concerned.

Octavia rejects Seneca's counsel; his philosophy provides no comfort for human sorrow. Seneca's response to this uncomprehending rebuff is to remind himself that it is the lot of public figures to suffer, and while this thought is ostensibly directed to the plight of Octavia it is clear that Seneca himself is enmeshed in this life of public rewards and private anguish. This becomes clear in the next scene, when Seneca is informed by Pallas Athene that his own death is imminent. He greets this news as a welcome relief, a response which reflects both neostoic unease with public life and a view of death as the pre-eminent expression of constancy. Seneca is then confronted by Nero's desire to divorce Octavia in favour of Poppea and, as in the earlier scene between Octavia and her page, Seneca's advice is rejected as impractical. The conflict between teacher and student is easily seen as one between reason and passion, but in the neostoic tradition that reason is allied with constancy, while feeling, like opinion, is precisely what leads to the wrong answers. All that remains is the recourse to violence, and sure enough, when Seneca attempts to pursue this argument by suggesting that the people will not tolerate Nero's behaviour, Nero responds violently. This is no academic debate argued in measured tones but the violent opposition of two philosophical positions. This sequence of scenes pitting *constantia* against

Nero (Robin Leggate) listens to Seneca (Willard White) at ENO, 1975 (photo: Mike Humphrey)

passion and will continues when Nero meets Poppea, overheard by Otho, a scene which is the opposite of his dispute with Seneca. Here again, Nero rejects constancy, which would have equipped him to deal with the decrees of destiny, and places his future in the control of Poppea's charms. Like Love's claim in the Prologue that he controls the fate of men, and Poppea's belief that Fortune and Love fight on her side, so Nero's words, when seen against the background of the discourses of the Incogniti, exude an irony visible to all except the lovers. Nero's promise to divide the imperial crown with Poppea is thus an example of what happens when will is controlled by love, entranced by beauty and deprived of constancy. The coronation of Poppea, first mooted at this juncture, is thus supported by these three things, presented as a foil to Seneca's commitment to the trio of reason, patience and constancy. As if to illustrate this incompatibility, the promised coronation actually generates Seneca's death warrant.

It is significant that the second act opens in a garden, a refuge of the mind far from the insolence and arrogance of public life. The warrant itself is reluctantly delivered by the Captain of Nero's guard (Liberto), whose genuine distress at being the messenger of death is countered by Seneca's willingness to die. His friends are summoned, and the philosopher proclaims his belief in the acceptance of death. The contrast between the heroic possessor of *constantia* and the undisciplined, wavering masses of humanity is underlined by this musical setting. Seneca's speech, after the initial command, involves no text repetition or reordering, and is delivered in a steady, lilting, evenly phrased arioso, disturbed only by the rising sequential melisma when the philosopher looks forward to his reception among the Gods. The three-voice chorus attempts to dissuade him from his resolve to die by reminding him of the pleasures of life. It is cast in three sections, and is all the more striking for being one of two sections of chorus-writing in the entire opera. The contrast with the regular and authoritative simplicity of Seneca's speech adds a further layer of meaning by confronting, through musical means, the virtues of neostoicism with an attachment to the transitory pleasures of earthly existence. Quite unlike anything else in the opera it is, simply, a *coup de théâtre*.

Nero responds to Seneca's death by celebrating the physical appearance of Poppea. He and Lucano (Lucan the poet, nephew of Seneca, and friend of Nero who will later have him executed), sing the praises of 'this beautiful face that Love has, with his own hand, inscribed in my heart'. Once again, the *constantia* and self-control of Seneca are vividly recalled in contrast with the carnal attachments of the other characters. The scenes in which Otho contemplates murdering Poppea and is in turn approached by Octavia as a hired killer are designed, like the earlier ones between Nero's lovers and their nurses, to stress the choices freely made by the characters and the consequences of those choices. The capacity to choose *constantia*, as illustrated by Seneca (and soon by Drusilla), preserves them against the uncertainties of Fate, while the choice of violence and irrationality leads only to disaster, as in the case of Octavia and, implicitly, that of Nero and Poppea. In the end, Otho's attempt on Poppea's life is deflected by the intervention of Love, who proclaims his control of human life while mocking the foolishness of those mortals who believe they are safe merely because they are asleep. Thus ends the second act. With Seneca dead, Octavia foiled and Otho a fugitive, the practical and philosophical obstacles to Poppea's coronation have been eliminated. It seems that Love has delivered on his boast. But how then is Drusilla's presence in the first five of the nine scenes of the third act to be explained, an emphasis seemingly incompatible with the swiftness and dramatic intensity which characterises the opera as a whole, and which is out of keeping with her apparent status as a minor character in the story?

Set once more in the city of Rome, Act Three establishes Drusilla as the female counterpart of Seneca and as the counterweight to the inconstancy of both Poppea and Octavia. Together with Seneca and Otho, she is the only character who displays neostoic respect for the ways of destiny. Accused by Arnalta as the murderess, she blames neither the gods nor Otho for this disastrous turn of events, but only herself. She protests her innocence, and her response to Nero's charges initiates a series of speeches in which, by implication, she is held up for comparison with Seneca. Facing the threat of torture she refuses to reveal the truth and, just as Seneca had done earlier, calls upon her friends to witness her death. Like his, it will authenticate her life and provide an example for future generations. It is Senecan *constantia* which is embodied in the figure of Drusilla.

Just before Drusilla is taken to her death, Otho appears, no longer able to endure the sight. The scene illustrates the neostoic concept of friendship. Both protest to Nero that they are guilty, neither wanting the other to suffer. Recognizing her heroism, Nero grants them both clemency, banishing Otho and leaving Drusilla alive. Otho willingly goes into exile with Drusilla and she, echoing his rejection of public life, willingly returns to Fortune all it has given her. Unlike Nero and Poppea, Drusilla is free from Fortune precisely because she is in control of herself. Before departing she announces that in her actions 'you may recognise the constant loyalty in a woman's heart', and these words must be seen as the opera's conclusion about the nature of true love. It seems clear from the sequence of scenes which opens the third act that, in their exemplification of neostoic virtue, Seneca and Drusilla were devised by Busenello as parallel characters. In this sense, there are similarities of dramatic meaning to be observed in the debate between Seneca and Nero in the first act and the three opening scenes of Act Two on the one hand, and the opening four scenes of Act Three on the other. The soliloquies, challenges, trials and, above all, firm declarations of *constantia* characterize both of them.

Busenello jerks us away from this premature dénouement, as Nero brusquely orders the banishment of Octavia. The contrast is sharp. The next scene could easily be the last for Nero and Poppea, whose dream of marriage is on the verge of becoming reality. There is no dramatic need for the coronation scene, since they have already celebrated their victory. Thematically, by contrast, the actual coronation cannot be seen as a triumph. Before that takes place we return to Arnalta, the wise and constant servant of Poppea, now raised to the status of confidante to an Empress. She knows that the future will bring her power, and she also knows how illusory is such power. At one time she was treated as a mere servant; now she will be treated with respect. She is incapable of self-deception; with renewed force she pierces the veil of false appearances, presenting ironic truths whose importance is strongly underlined in the music through sharply-differentiated responses to individual words and phrases. Thus like the Tacitist historians who gave this opera its style and mood, Arnalta uses contrasting song throughout this scene to convey her perception of the truth behind appearances.

Arnalta has survived to old age precisely because her actions are guided by prudence and her mind governed by the strict self-discipline that Montaigne, Lipsius and Venetians like Paolo Sarpi had made the criterion of personal virtue. Not for her the princely assertion of any supra-legal reason of state. Nevertheless, those who lived in a world ruled by princes and emperors had best be prepared for the worst. Like Seneca and Drusilla, she fears neither life, nor fate, nor even death. This radically affects our interpretation of the final scene, in which Poppea is crowned by Nero. It is unlikely that a contemporary Venetian audience, familiar with the rest of their story, in which she was kicked to death by Nero while pregnant with their child, would have left the theatre impressed by the constancy of the love these two manipulative creatures express for each other. The final duet, whoever wrote it, satisfied a contemporary operatic convention and it remains as one of the most beautiful but also most ironic homages to the triumph of love.

Music Examples

[1] SINFONIA I

[2] OTHO

Ca - ro tet - to, car - ro tet - to, tet - to a - mo - ro - so,
Pre - cious dwell - ing, pre - cious dwell - ing, re - fuge for lo - vers,

[3] POPPEA

Si - gnor, sem - pre mi ve - di, sem - pre, sem - - pre,
My lord, e - ver I'm with you, e - ver, e - - ver,

[4a] POPPEA

No, no, non te - mo, no, no, non te - mo, no, di no-ia al - cu - na,
Yet I'll not doubt him, no, no, I will not, no, I will not doubt him,

[4b] POPPEA

Per me guer - re - gia, guer - reg - gia A - mor,
Love is my cham - pion and fights for me,

[5] OCTAVIA

Dis - prez - za - ta re - gi - na, re - gi - na, re -
Wret - ched Em - press O - cta - via! no lon - ger, no

gi - - na, dis - prez - za - ta,
lon - - ger am I Em - press!

[6] SENECA

Tu dal des - tin ___ col - pi - ta, dal ___ des - tin col - pi - ta
But you whom fate ___ has stri - cken, you ___ whom fate has stri - cken.

[7] POPPEA

Di que - ste, di que - ste brac - cia, di que - ste brac - cia
And tell me, when I en - fold you in my em - bra - ces

gli stret - ti, stret - ti, am - ples - si? ___
in my, in my, arms I hold you? ___

[8] MERCURY

Al sub - li - me pas - sag - - - - -
the sub - lime ex - plo - ra - - - - -

- - - - - - - gio,
- - - - - - - tion,

[9] FRIENDS

Alto   Tenor

Non mo - rir, non mo - rir, Se - ne - ca,   Non mo - rir, non mo -
Do not die, do not die, Se - ne - ca,   Do not die, do not

Bass

Non mo - rir, non mo - rir, Se - ne - ca,
Do not die, do not die, Se - ne - ca,

-rir, Se - ne - ca, non mo - rir,
die, Se - ne - ca, do not die,

non mo - rir, non mo - rir,
do not die, do not die,

139

[10] VALLETTO

Sen - to un cer - to   non so che,   Che   mi piz - zi - ca, e   di - let - ta,
Some - thing pains and   trou - bles me,   plucks my heart and makes me shi - ver.

[11] Duet

LUCANO   NERO

can - tiam, _____   can - tiam, _____
we'll sing, _____   we'll sing, _____

[12] OTTONE

I   miei su - bi - ti sde - gni,   La po - li - ti - ca mia già po - co
My im - pet - u - ous an - ger   and the dan - gers that threa - tened e - ven

d'o - ra M'in - dus - se - ro a pen - sa - re D'uc - ci - de - re,
led   me   to think, ___ led me to think   I   might mur - der her.

[13] DRUSILLA

Fe - li - ce   cor   mi - o   Fe - steg - gia-mi in se - no,
My   heart is   re - joic - ing,   it's   danc - ing with - in me.

[14] POPPEA

Or che Se - ne - ca è mor - - - to, A - -
Now that Se - ne - ca's bu - - - ried, I _____

mor, A - - mor, A - - - - - mor
call, I _____ call, I _____ call

140

[15] LOVE - Aria

O scioc - chi, o fra - li   Sen - si mor-ta-li
O fool - ish frail - ty   of mor - tal sen - ses

[16] DRUSILLA

O _____ fe - li - ce, fe - li - ce Dru - sil - - la,
O _____ most hap - py, most hap - py Dru - sil - - la!

[17] OCTAVIA

A - a - a - ad - dio Ro - ma   a - a -
Ah, fare - well   Rome, I leave you,   fare - well

ad - dio pa - tria,   a - a - mi - ci, a - mi - ci   ad - di - o.
friends, I leave you,   ah,   my coun - try, my coun - try,   I leave you.

[18] ARNALTA

A - scen - de - rò del - le gran   dez - ze i   gra - di:
[I] shall climb on   high   to   share in   her new   gran - deur.

[19]

POPPEA

Pur ti mi - ro,   pur ti mi - ro, ___
I a - dore you,   I a - dore you, ___

NERO

Pur ti go - do,   pur ti go - do, ___
I de - sire you,   I de - sire you, ___

141

The coronation scene designed by Peter Whiteman for Colin Graham's 1971 production for Sadler's Wells at the London Coliseum, with Janet Baker and Robert Ferguson (photo: Stuart Robinson)

The Coronation of Poppea
L'incoronazione di Poppea

Opera in a prologue and three acts

Music attributed to
Claudio Monteverdi

and Francesco Sacrati

Libretto by G.F. Busenello

English singing version by Anne Ridler

The Coronation of Poppea was first performed at the Teatro SS. Giovanni e Paolo (Teatro Grimano), Venice, in 1643. The first performance in modern times was in Paris, in a version by Vincent d'Indy at the Théâtre des Arts, Paris, on February 5, 1913. The first performance in the United States was at Smith College, Northampton, Massachusetts, on April 27, 1927, and the first performance in Britain was later that year (December 6) by the Oxford University Opera Club, conducted and edited by Jack Westrup. The first professional performance was at Glyndebourne, on June 29, 1962 conducted and edited by Raymond Leppard, and this was the edition used by ENO for the first performance of the opera at the London Coliseum, on November 24, 1971.

There are many manuscript versions of the libretto of *L'incoronazione di Poppea*, and two printed editions, of which the last, dated 1656, appeared in Busenello's *Delle hore ociose* ('Of leisure hours') as an 'Opera Musicale'. Not all the others give an author's name, but this one seems to have been revised and corrected by Busenello himself, and to represent his final thoughts on the text. Following the critical edition of the opera by Alan Curtis (Novello, 1989), we have adopted this text for the Italian libretto, and also followed Curtis in modifying it wherever it does not tally with what Monteverdi actually set to music, as evidenced in the two source scores. One of the manuscript librettos (in the Biblioteca Comunale, Treviso) is most consistently close to the text in the scores but Curtis opts for the 1656 edition in order 'to incorporate as many as possible of Busenello's improvements, so long as they do not conflict with the music'. He lucidly sets out the problems which he encountered in making his edition in his Preface, to which all interested readers are referred. In our libretto, footnotes citing Curtis indicate important discrepancies.

The scanty stage directions and the character descriptions in the cast list come from a scenario printed for the performances in 1643. The musical titles ('ritornello', 'sinfonia') have been interpolated from the score.

The numbers in square brackets refer to the musical examples.

Fortune	Fortuna		*soprano*
Virtue	Virtù		*soprano*
Love	Amore		*soprano/* *boy soprano*
Otho	Ottone	*most noble lord*	*baritone/* *counter-tenor*
Two soldiers of Nero's Guard			*tenor, baritone*
Poppea	Poppea	*most noble lady, mistress of Nero, raised by him to be empress*	*soprano*
Nero	Nerone	*emperor of Rome*	*mezzo-soprano/* *counter-tenor/* *tenor*
Arnalta	Arnalta	*Poppea's old nurse and confidante*	*contralto/tenor*
Octavia	Ottavia	*reigning empress, who is repudiated by Nero*	*mezzo-soprano*
Nurse	Nutrice	*Octavia's nurse*	*contralto*
Seneca	Seneca	*a philosopher, Nero's tutor*	*bass*
Valletto*	Valletto	*Octavia's page*	*tenor/* *boy soprano*
Pallas Athene	Pallade	*goddess of wisdom*	*soprano*
Drusilla	Drusilla	*a lady of the court*	*soprano*
Mercury	Mercurio	*the messenger of the gods*	*bass*
Captain	Liberto	*the Captain of the Praetorian Guard, a freedman*	*baritone*
A Lady	Damigella	*Octavia's lady-in-waiting*	*soprano*
Lucano	Lucano	*a poet, Nero's friend*	*tenor*
A Lictor	Littore	*[an officer of imperial justice]*	*baritone*
Venus	Venere	*goddess of love*	*soprano*

Ensembles

Chorus of Friends (Familiari) of Seneca; Two Tribunes; Two Consuls; Chorus of Cupids

Note: it was the custom for soloists to form the chorus at this period, and to double the minor roles. Thus the Consuls could have been sung by Seneca and Mercury, which in turn could be doubled with the Lictor; or alternatively the Lictor could be doubled with the Freedman. As for the chorus of Seneca's friends, Tacitus describes the arrival of Nero's messenger while Seneca was dining with his wife and two friends, and Alan Curtis insists that this ensemble should therefore be only three voices, although it is not clear whether the highest part is for a male or female voice.

* Valletto and Liberto (like Damigella, Littore and Nutrice) are not names but descriptions; Valletto is retained in the English for the sake of the syllables.

Prologue

FORTUNE

Go, and hide your head in disgrace,
wretched Virtue;
you are so poor,
no one now believes in you:
goddess lacking a temple,
having neither believers nor altars for
worship,
you are slighted and neglected;
no one wants you or respects you;
if you stand at my side, you are always
rejected.
Once a monarch, now a beggar, you have
to barter
for your food and your clothing,
all your grand titles, your privileges, your
honour.
If I see from a distance
those who still follow Virtue,
they appear like a mirage,
like a fire in a painting,
whose flames that have no power,
neither burn nor illumine.
And your followers know they cannot hope
— can never, never hope —
to earn themselves great riches or glory or
honour,
if they have not the gift of Fortune's favour.

Deh, nasconditi o Virtù,

già caduta in povertà,
non creduta Deità,
Nume ch'è senza tempio,
Diva senza devoti e senza altari,

dissipata, disusata,
abborrita, malgradita,
ed in mio paragon sempre avvilita!

Già regina, or plebea, che per comprarti

gl'alimenti e le vesti
i privilegi e i titoli vendesti.

Ogni tuo professore,
se da me sta diviso
sembra un foco dipinto
che nè scalda, nè splende,
resta un calor sepolto
in penuria di luce.
Chi professa Virtù non speri mai

di posseder ricchezza, o gloria alcuna

se protetto non è dalla Fortuna!

VIRTUE

Go, go drown yourself, you creature,
you chimera of the masses,
made a god by fools and madmen.
For I am the one true ladder
for human nature to make its way to
heaven.
For I am the North Wind blowing,
the wind of doctrine that gives mankind
the power
rightly to steer a course straight on to
Olympus.
I tell you, and I am not given to boasting,
my nature, my incorruptible essence,
partakes of the nature of godhead.
That's more than can be said of you, dear
Fortune.

Deh, sommergiti, mal nata,
rea chimera delle genti
fatta Dea dagl'imprudenti.
Io son la vera scala
per cui natura al sommo ben ascende.

Io son la tramontana,
che sola insegno agl'intelletti umani

l'arte del navigar verso l'Olimpo.

Può dirsi, senza adulazion alcuna,
il puro incorruttibil esser mio
termine convertibile con Dio,
che ciò non si può dir di te, Fortuna.

LOVE

How can you think, foolish goddesses,
to divide the universe between you,
with its kingdoms and its people,
when Love's name is excluded? —
Deity which has by far your fame exceeded,
I can impart all virtue;
I can provide good fortune.

Che vi credete o Dee
divider fra di voi del mondo tutto
la signoria e'l governo,
escludendone Amore,
Nume ch'è d'ambe voi tanto maggiore?
Io le virtudi insegno,
io le fortune dono,

Though Love is young as a child,	questa bambina età
he rules in every age	vince d'antichità
both Time and the gods in heaven.	il tempo e ogn'altro Dio:
Eternity and I exist like twin brothers.	gemelli siam l'eternitade ed io.
You must worship me,	Riveritemi,
give me reverence,	adoratemi,
and acknowledge your ruler with due obedience.	e di vostro sovrano il nome datemi.

FORTUNE AND VIRTUE

No man would dare, nor god in high Olympus,	Uman non è, non è celeste core
to deny or invade Love's mighty empire.	che contender ardisca con Amore.

LOVE

Shortly, in a single contest,	Oggi in un sol certame,
you will both be brought low, acknowledging rightly	l'un' e l'altra di voi da me abbattuta,
that at Love's signal, the world is changed completely.	dirà che'l mondo a' cenni miei si muta.

End of the Prologue.

Hélène Demellier as Octavia in Vincent d'Indy's version of 'Poppea' at the Théâtre des Arts, Paris, in 1913 (Bibliothèque de l'Opéra)

146

Act One

Ritornello

OTHO

So I return here, I turn again to you, as lines to a centre,	E pur io torno qui, qual linea'l centro,
as flames to fire's source, or as a stream to ocean.	qual foco a sfera e qual ruscello al mare,
Though no light's shining to give me greeting,	e se ben luce alcuna non m'appare
ah, yet I'm certain that here my love is sleeping.	ah' so ben io che sta il mio sol qui dentro.
So I am returning, I turn to her, once more to my centre.	E pur io torno qui, qual linea al centro.

Ritornello

Precious dwelling, refuge for lovers, which shelters all my life and all my treasure —	[2] Caro tetto amoroso, albergo di mia vita e del mio bene
my steps now lead, my heart now moves to greet you.	il passo e'l core ad inchinarti viene.

Ritornello

Open your window, Poppea, and show me that sweet face on which ever depends my fate.	Apri un balcon, Poppea, col bel viso in cui son le sorti mie,
So banish darkness my dearest, forestalling daybreak.	previeni anima mia precorri il die.

Ritornello

Wake, and disperse for ever from our clear sky all murkiness, clouds and vapour,	Sorgi, e disgombra omai da questo ciel caligini e tenebre
fled at the blessed lifting of your sweet eyelids.	con il beato aprir di tue palpebre.

Ritornello

Carry, you dreams as you're flying, to my dear lady this message that I give you.	Sogni, portate a volo, fate sentire in dolce fantasia
Whisper gently what I have spoken sighing.	questi sospir alla diletta mia.
But — who lies here in the darkness?	Ma che veggio, infelice?
These are not phantoms, these are no ghostly shadows —	Non già fantasmi o pur notturne larve,
they surely are posted here by Nero.	son questi i servi di Nerone; ahi dunque
Ah, heavens, I have poured out my soul	agl'insensati venti
to the winds that cannot hear me,	io diffondo i lamenti.
I must beg the senseless stones to show me pity.	Necessito le pietre a deplorarmi,
I worship blocks of marble,	adoro questi marmi,
I make love to this window with my weeping,	amoreggio con lagrime un balcone,
while on the breast of Poppea Nero lies sleeping.	e in grembo di Poppea dorme Nerone.
He has posted these guards here to keep watch while he can take his pleasure.	Ha condotti costoro per custodir se stesso dalle frodi.

O how frail is the security of princes!	O salvezza di principe infelice:
These men are fast asleep, who should be watching.	dormon profondamente i suoi custodi.
Ah, treacherous Poppea!	Ah', perfida Poppea,
Is this the way you keep the promise I was given,	son queste le promesse e i giuramenti
which set my heart on fire?	ch'accessero il cor mio?
This then, this is your faith, O heaven!	Questa è la fede, o Dio!
I am Otho who faithfully followed you,	Io son quell'Ottone che ti seguì,
who longed for you, who slaved for you;	che ti bramò, che ti servì,
that Otho, who has worshipped you.	quell'Ottone che t'adorò;
Who to persuade you, to melt your heart in pity,	che per piegarti e intenerirti il core
have spangled with my tears fervent supplication,	di lagrime imperlò preghi devoti,
and sacrificed my reason to my devotion.	gli spirti a te sacrificando in voti.
Finally you yielded:	M'assicurasti al fine
you promised that folded to your breast	ch'abbracciate averei nel tuo bel seno
I should taste all the joys of passion.	le mie beatitudini amorose;
Trustful, I sowed bitter seeds of hope's deception.	io di credula speme il seme sparsi,
Now, raging, the elements have turned against me...	ma l'aria e'l cielo a'danni miei rivolto...

Scene Two. *Otho and two Soldiers, as they wake up*

FIRST SOLDIER

Who is that?	Chi parla?

OTHO

... beating down in their tempest all my sweet harvest.	.... tempestò di ruine il mio raccolto.

FIRST SOLDIER

Who goes there?	Chi va lì?

SECOND SOLDIER

What's the matter?	Camerata?

FIRST SOLDIER

O god, when will it be day?	Ohimè, ancor non è dì!

SECOND SOLDIER

Why, you're dreaming, you idiot,	Che fai?
you are talking in your sleep!	Par' che parli sognando.

FIRST SOLDIER

Surely the dawn is breaking? It's nearly morning.	Sorgono pur dell'alba i primi rai...

SECOND SOLDIER

Up and pull yourself together.	Sù, risvegliati tosto...

FIRST SOLDIER

I wasn't sleeping. I haven't slept a wink all night.	... non ho dormito in tutta notte mai.

SECOND SOLDIER

Get up now, wake up and remember we're meant to be on guard here.	Sù, risvegliati tosto, guardiamo il nostro posto.

FIRST SOLDIER

Now damn the god of love, Poppea and Nero,	Sia maledetto Amor, Poppea, Nerone,

and Rome too, and our glorious army,
for between them I get no peace and quiet,
no, not a single moment.

e Roma, e la milizia,
sodisfar io non posso alla pigrizia
un'ora, un giorno solo.

SECOND SOLDIER

Our unlucky Empress
exhausts herself with weeping,
while the Emperor slights her and courts Poppea.
There's rebellion in Armenia,
but he takes no notice.
All Pannonia's in turmoil, and he rocks with laughter.
And thus in every province
the empire moves from one disaster to another.

La nostra imperatrice
stilla se stessa in pianti,
e Neron per Poppea la vilipende;
l'Armenia si ribella,
ed egli non ci pensa
la Pannonia dà all'armi, ed ei se ne ride,
così, per quanto io veggio,
l'impero se ne va di male in peggio.

FIRST SOLDIER

What's more, our Prince is robbing all the people
to enrich those he chooses.
Thus the innocent must suffer,
while all the villains can grab the best places.

Dì pur che il Prence nostro ruba a tutti
per donar ad alcuni;
l'innocenza va afflitta
e i scellerati stan sempre a man dritta.

SECOND SOLDIER

He only listens to Seneca, that pedant —

Sol del pedante Seneca si fida.

FIRST SOLDIER

Who's as old as he's grasping,

Di quel vecchio rapace?

SECOND SOLDIER

And like a fox for cunning.

Di quel volpon sagace!

FIRST SOLDIER

So worthy a judge,
he contrives to make a fortune
by betraying his companion.

Di quel reo cortigiano
che fonda il suo guadagno
sul tradire il compagno!

SECOND SOLDIER

Shameless architect,
who raises his own fine house built on the tomb of another.

Di quell'empio architetto
che si fa casa sul sepolcro altrui!

FIRST SOLDIER

Not a word to a soul of what we've been saying,
and take care whom you trust.
You know that your two eyes don't trust each other,
even though they both look in the same direction.

Non ridir ad alcun quel che diciamo;
nel fidarti va scaltro.
Se gl'occhi non si fidan l'un dell'altro
e però nel guardar van sempre insieme.

BOTH

Eyes are wary and teach us this lesson:
loose talkers end in prison.

Impariamo, dagl'occhi
a non trattar da sciocchi.

FIRST SOLDIER

But see, the light is growing: the dawn is near.

Ma già s'imbianca l'aria e vien il dì.

Take care, take care, it's Nero, he's coming, take care, take care: the Prince is here.	Taciam, taciam, taciam, Nerone è qui.

Scene Three. *Poppea, Nero*

POPPEA

My lord — Ah, do not leave me, but let my loving arms closely encircle your body, as by your grace and beauy my heart is always surrounded.	Signor, deh non partire, sostien che queste braccia ti circondino il collo, come le tue bellezze circondano il cor mio.

NERO

Poppea, don't try to keep me.	Poppea, lascia ch'io parta.

POPPEA

Do not go, my lord, ah, do not leave me. The dawn has barely broken, yet you who truly are the daylight to me, who are the sun in my heaven, and of my life and love the joyous dayspring, you on a sudden go away and leave me. Do not say we must part. So bitter is that word that if I hear it, ah — I'll breathe my last and die, I know it.	Non partir, Signor, deh non partire. Appena spunta l'alba, e tu che sei l'incarnato mio sole, la mia palpabil luce, e l'amoroso dì della mia vita, vuoi si repente far da me partita? Deh non dir di partir, che di voce sì amara a un solo accento, ahi perir, spirar quest'alma io sento.

NERO

Your noble birth compels our secrecy, and the people of Rome must not know that we are lovers, until Octavia ...	La nobiltà de' nascimenti tuoi non permette che Roma sappia che siamo uniti in sin ch'Ottavia ...

POPPEA

Until she ...	In sin che —

NERO

shall be no longer ...	non riman' esclusa —

POPPEA

be no longer ...	non rimane —

NERO

Until Octavia is no longer Empress, and is cast off by me. Farewell beloved.	in sin ch'Ottavia non rimane esclusa col repudio da me. Vanne ben mio.

Sinfonia

A single sigh, a sigh of love, from the depth of my heart. A sigh contains a kiss and tender blessing, since we are parting. But I'll return, and quickly, I swear I shall return, light of my being.	In un sospir che vien dal profondo del sen includo un bacio o cara, ed un addio: ci rivedrem ben tosto, idolo mio.

Sinfonia

POPPEA

My lord, ever I'm with you, yet you never can see me.	[3] Signor, sempre mi vedi, anzi mai non mi vedi.

For if it's true you hide me in your heart,
and close in your breast enfold me,
you cannot with your eyes perceive me.

Perchè s'è ver che nel tuo cor io sia
entro al tuo sen celata,
non posso da' tuoi lumi esser mirata.

NERO

O be ever within me,
let your light never fail me.
Remain to make me joyful,
dear, sweetest, perfection, and ever faithful.

Adorati miei rai,
deh restatevi omai!
Rimanti, o mia Poppea,
cor, vezzo, e luce mia!

POPPEA

Ah, don't say
you must go,
for the word is so bitter, if I hear it,
ah, my soul will breathe its last, I know it.

Deh non dir
di partir,
che di voce sì amara a un solo accento
ahi perir, spirar quest'alma io sento.

NERO

Never fear, you are with me every moment,
the light of my eyes, my goddess ever
    constant.

Non temer, tu stai meco a tutte l'ore,
splendor negl'occhi e deità nel core.

POPPEA

You'll return?

Tornerai?

NERO

Though I'm away,
with you I stay.

Se ben io vo
pur teco io sto . . .

POPPEA

You'll return?

Tornerai?

NERO

From your bright eyes my heart, I swear,
never shall be parted.

Il cor dalle tue stelle
mai, mai non si divelle.

POPPEA

You'll return?

Tornerai?

NERO

Ah, no power can divide us two, it is
    decided,
just as a point is, that cannot be divided.

Io non posso da te viver disgiunto

se non si smembra la unità del punto.

POPPEA

You'll return?

Tornerai?

NERO

I'll return.

Tornerò.

POPPEA

But when?

Quando?

NERO

Yes, shortly.

Ben tosto.

POPPEA

But truly —
do you promise?

Ben tosto,
me'l prometti?

NERO

I swear it.

Te'l giuro.

POPPEA

And will you keep your promise?

E me l'osserverai?

If you don't see me here, then come to find me.	E s'a te non verrò, tu a me verrai.

POPPEA

Addio, my Nero.	Addio . . .

NERO

Poppea, addio —	Poppea, addio.

POPPEA

Farewell, my Nero.	Nerone, addio.

NERO

Poppea, addio.	Poppea, addio.

Scene Four. *Poppea, Arnalta*

Ritornello

POPPEA

Ah, Hope, cunningly you coax me, you flatter and deceive me,	[4] Speranza, tu mi vai il cor accarezzando;

Ritornello

with soft caresses please me. This royal robe you mention is very fine but — I know it's just a fiction.	il genio lusingando, e mi circondi intanto di regio sì, ma immaginario manto.*
Yet I'll not doubt him, no, no, I'll not be shaken.	No, no, non temo, no, di noia alcuna,
Love is my champion and fights for me, and smiling Fortune.	per me guerreggia Amor, e la Fortuna.

Sinfonia

ARNALTA

Ah, daughter, Heaven grant that these wanton embraces are not destined to bring about your ruin.	Ahi figlia, voglia il Cielo, che questi abbracciamenti non sìan' un giorno i precipizi tuoi.

POPPEA

But I'll not doubt him, no, no, I'll not be shaken.	No, no, non temo, no, di noia alcuna.

ARNALTA

The Empress Octavia has learnt the secret of Nero's passion, so I am trembling with terror lest every morning, every instant may bring disaster, may see your final passing.	L'imperatrice Ottavia ha penetrati di Neron gli amori, ond'io pavento e temo ch'ogni giorno, ogni punto sia di tua vita il giorno, il punto estremo.

POPPEA

Love is my champion and fights for me, and smiling Fortune.	Per me guerreggia Amor, e la Fortuna.

---

* Six additional lines for Poppea in the librettos are set in the Naples Conservatory score by 'a younger composer, possibly Francesco Sacrati' (Curtis).

To have dealings with monarchs is full of danger,	La pratica coi regi e perigliosa,
for Love and Hatred have not the power to rule them.	l'amor e l'odio non han forza in essi,
They think only of themselves, naught else can move them.	sono gli affetti lor puri interessi.

Ritornello

If Nero loves you, it's just a passing fancy;	Se Neron t'ama, è mera cortesia,
if he deserts you, all reproaches are useless.	s'ei t'abbandona, non t'en puoi dolere.
The safest way is to endure in silence.	Per minor mal ti converrà tacere.

But I'll not doubt him, no, no, I'll not be shaken.	No, no, non temo, no, di noia alcuna.

The mighty breathe an air of empty grandeur,	Il grande spira onor con la presenza,
leaving where they have passed a vain reputation,	lascia, mentre la casa empie di vento,
the smoke of useless fame as compensation.	yiputazione e fumo in pagamento.

Ritornello

Shameful it is to boast 'I am Nero's mistress'.	Perdi l'onor con dir: Neron, mi gode.
Those are useless vices sprung from ambition:	Son inutili i vizi ambiziosi!
the vices I recommend must bear fruition.	Mi piaccion più i peccati fruttuosi.

Ritornello

By him you never can be held his equal,	Con lui tu non puoi mai trattar del pari,
and if marriage is the goal you aim for —	e se le nozze hai per oggetto e fine,
you are simply praying for your own downfall.	mendicando tu vai le tue ruine.

But I'll not doubt him, no, no, I'll not be shaken.	No, no, non temo, no, di noia alcuna.

O take warning Poppea:	Mira, mira Poppea,
where the meadow is greenest and is most pleasant,	dove il prato è più ameno e dilettoso,
just there is hidden the serpent.	stassi il serpente ascoso.
The chances of our fate are past foretelling;	Dei casi le vicende son funeste;
through calm days, all unsuspected, a sudden tempest is darkly swelling.	la calma è profezia delle tempeste.

But I will not doubt him, no, no, I'll not be shaken.	Non temo, no, no, non temo di noia alcuna.
Love is my champion and fights for me, and smiling Fortune.	Per me guerreggia Amor, e la Fortuna.

You are crazy, truly crazy,
if you would trust your heart and your
future safety even
to a boy that's blind and a bald old
woman.

Ben sei pazza, se credi
che ti possano far contenta e salva

un garzon cieco ed una donna calva.

Scene Five. *The scene changes to the city of Rome. Octavia, Nurse*

OCTAVIA

Wretched Empress Octavia —
no longer am I Empress,
so despised and dishonoured by the
Emperor my husband, unhappy consort.
Alas, I am lost, bewildered, distracted —
O wretched womankind, O sex accursed.
For though the laws of Nature
had destined us to freedom,
when we are married we are bound in
fetters.
And if we bear a man-child —
O wretched womankind, O sex accursed —
we are forming the limbs of a cruel tyrant,
giving suck to a monster who will tear at
our flesh and destroy us.
So fate compels us by unwilling action
to be the agents of our own destruction.

Ah, Nero, vile and pitiless Nero,
my husband — O gods in heaven, my
husband! —
you're accursed for ever,
and are guilty of the pains I suffer.
Where, oh where are you? Oh where are
you?
In the arms of Poppea you are lying,
rejoicing, caressing, in joy and rapture.
And meanwhile, in the pain of my grief, my
tears are flowing,
and flowing they form
a great torrent of mirrors, with this
reflection,
showing beside your raptures my sore
affliction.

O Fate, if you can hear me —
Jupiter hear me now:
now you must punish Nero
with thundering bolt from Heaven.
If you do not, you are impotent,
and I blame your injustice.
Ah, I am speaking blasphemy, and I repent
it.
I must suppress and stifle,
in agonising silence, the voice of my
torment.
O heaven, O heaven, ah, quench your
righteous anger;
do not punish my fault with all your
severity.

[5] Disprezzata regina,
regina disprezzata
del monarca romano afflitta moglie,
che fo, ove son, che penso?
O delle donne miserabil sesso:
se la natura e'l Cielo
libere ci produce,
il matrimonio c'incatena serve.

se concepiamo l'uomo
o delle donne miserabil sesso,
al nostr'empio tiran formiam le membra,
allattiamo il carnefice crudele
che ci scarna e ci svena,
e siam forzate per indegna sorte
a noi medesme partorir la morte.

Nerone, empio Nerone,
marito, o Dio, marito

bestemmiato pur sempre,
e maledetto dai cordogli miei,
dove ohimè, dove sei?

In braccio di Poppea,
tu dimori felice e godi, e intanto
il frequente cader de' pianti miei

pur va quasi formando
un diluvio di specchi in cui tu miri,

dentro alle tue delizie, i miei martiri.

Destin, se stai lassù,
Giove ascoltami tu,
se per punir Nerone
fulmini tu non hai,
d'impotenza t'accuso,
d'ingiustizia t'incolpo;
ahi, trapasso tropp'oltre e me ne pento,

sopprimo e seppelisco
in taciturne angoscie il mio tormento.

O Ciel, O Ciel, deh l'ira tua s'estingua,

non provi i tuoi rigori il fallo mio.

Octavia, O you who are the only
  Empress
set over all the people . . .

Ottavia, o tu dell'universe genti
unica imperatrice . . .

My words were all unthinking, and spoken
  lightly;
I am guiltless at heart, my tongue alone
  is guilty.

Errò la superficie, il fondo è pio,
innocente fu il cor, peccò la lingua.

Listen, listen
to your faithful old nurse, I shall advise you.

. . . odi, odi,
di tua fida nutrice, odi gli accenti.

Since Nero's quite lost his senses
in Poppea's sweet caresses,
you should now choose a man, nobly born,
  who would not disgrace you,
and who would be happy to embrace you.
If the crime he commits so pleases Nero,
you should also find pleasure in taking
  vengeance.

Se Neron perso ha l'ingegno,
di Poppea ne' godimenti,
scegli alcun, che di te degno

d'abbracciarti si contenti.
Se l'ingiuria a Neron tanto diletta,
abbi piacer tu ancor nel far vendetta.

Ritornello

And if honour lost should grieve you,
or the pangs of conscience pain you,
just reflect on what I've been saying:
every wrong will then delight you.

E se pur aspro rimorso
dell'onor t'arreca noia,
fa riflesso al mio discorso,
ch'ogni duol ti sarà gioia.

What you say is repulsive.
Never talk so again. I won't allow it.

Così sozzi argomenti
non intesi più mai da te, nutrice!

Do reflect on what I've been saying:
every wrong will then delight you.
But think it shame to endure the offence in
  silence:
for true honour consists in taking
  vengeance.
If queens should go astray from the paths
  of virtue,
there is this advantage:
if a simpleton learns it, he'll not believe
  it,
if a wise man should hear, he'll not betray
  it,
and a secret unspoken is still unbroken.
So the sin is secure on every quarter:
on one side a deaf man, and a mute one on
  the other.

Fa riflesso al mio discorso,
ch'ogni duol ti sarà gioia.
L'infamia sta gl'affronti in sopportarsi,

e consiste l'onor nel vendicarsi.

Han poi questo vantaggio

delle regine gli amorosi errori,
se li sa l'idiota non li crede,

se l'astuto li penetra, li tace,

e'l peccato taciuto e non creduto
sta segreto e sicuro in ogni parte,
com'un che parli in mezzo un sordo, e un
  muto.

No, dear Nurse, believe me,
if a woman is betrayed by the passion
of a husband who's unfaithful,
pitiful is her lot, but not disgraceful!
But it is certain that man,
her husband, will be disgraced,
if by him the marriage-bed shall be
  dishonoured.

No, mia cara nutrice:
la donna assassinata dal marito
per adultere brame,
resta oltraggiata si, ma non infame!
Per il contrario resta
lo sposo inonorato,
se il letto marital li vien macchiato.

Daughter, respected lady,
you do not understand the duty, the mystery
  of vengeance.
Though the offence is a mere slap in the
  face,
revenge yourself by stabbing and by
  slaughter.
If he wounds your feelings,
then you must wound his honour,
but even so you will not
(to speak the truth) be properly avenged.
For Nero wounds your heart in its affection,
but you can only wound his reputation.
Do reflect on what I've been saying:
every wrong will then delight you.

Figlia e signora mia, tu non intendi
della vendetta il principal arcano.

L'offesa sopra il volto
d'una sola guanciata
si vendica col ferro e con la morte.

Chi ti punge nel senso,
pungilo nell'onore,
se bene, a dirti il vero,
nè pur così sarai ben vendicata;
nel senso vivo te punge Nerone,
e in lui sol pungerai l'opinione.
Fa riflesso al mio discorso,
ch'ogni duol ti sarà gioia.

But if there exists no god, no honour,
my own self shall be god and honour,
and all my sins myself with my own hand
  will punish.
But alas, though I'm guiltless of sin or
  transgressing,
yet innocence must share my heart with
  weeping.

Se non ci fosse né l'onor, né Dio,
sarei Nume a me stessa, e i falli miei
con la mia stessa man castigherei,

e però lunge da gli errori intanto,

divido il cor tra l'innocenza e'l pianto.

Scene Six. *Seneca, Octavia, Valletto*

Here is the most unhappy lady,
exalted to empire,
then reduced to the lowest.
O, you are empress
of all nations and all people,
with a title excelling in illustrious rank
  your forebears, though noble.
These useless tears now filling your eyes
are all unworthy of a royal empress.
Be thankful, show gratitude to Fortune,
for when she strikes you harshly,
your virtues shine more brightly.
The flint that is not stricken
cannot produce the sparks of fire.
But you whom Fate has so harshly
  stricken
produce in your own person heavenly
  virtues
ever faithful to duty,
glories more prized by far than outward
  beauty.
Though the graces of feature, of form and
  bearing,
shine in a noble aspect,
glowing with delicate and brilliant
  colours,
the robber Time soon steals away these
  glories.
But in a soul that's constant, virtue defies
  misfortune.
Though by fate mistreated,
its soul is never defeated.

Ecco la sconsolata,
donna assunta all'impero
per patir il servaggio: o gloriosa
del mondo imperatrice,
sovra i titoli eccelsi
degl'insigni avi tuoi conspicua e grande,

la vanità del pianto
degl'occhi imperiali è ufficio indegno.
Ringrazia la Fortuna,
che con i colpi suoi
ti cresce gl'ornamenti.
La cote non percossa
non può mandar faville;
[6] tu dal destin colpita

produci a te medesma alti splendori

di vigor, di fortezza,
glorie maggiori assai che la bellezza.

La vaghezza del volto, i lineamenti,

ch'in apparenza illustre
risplendon coloriti e delicati,

da pochi ladri dì ci son rubati.

Ma la Virtù costante

usa a bravar le stelle, il fato, e'l caso,
giammai non vede occaso.

You would promise that I shall find	Tu mi vai promettendo
healing from this poison,	balsamo dal veleno,
and gain renown through torment.	e glorie da tormenti;
You must excuse me for saying, worthy Master,	scusami, questi son, Seneca mio,
that your words are quite useless,	vanità speciose,
quite remote from reality.	studiati artifici,
They cannot bring comfort to the unhappy.	inutili rimedi agl'infelici.

My lady, please allow me.	Madama, con tua pace,
I am fit to burst with fury.	io vo' sfogar la stizza, che mi move
I am choking at this canting philosopher, this bogus prophet.	il filosofo astuto, il gabba Giove.
I'm burning with contempt,	M'accende pure a sdegno
while he is spinning out his feeble inventions.	questo miniator de' bei concetti.
I cannot stand and listen,	Non posso star al segno,
while he with his golden words holds others spellbound.	mentr'egli incanta altrui con aurei detti.
Gravely he tells his tales, spun from his own mind:	Queste del suo cervel mere invenzioni,
as mysteries he sells them, but they are moonshine.	le vende per misteri, e son canzoni!
My lady, if he sneezes, or if he yawns	Madama, s'ei sternuta o sbadiglia
— ee, ah, oh, ee —	— e — a — o — e —
he thinks that he should draw moral conclusions,	presume d'insegnar cose morali,
and gets in such a tangle . . .	e tanto l'assottiglia,
I can't help laughing, and even my boots are splitting.	che moverebbe il riso a' miei stivali.
This scurrilous philosophy, where'er she rules us,	Scaltra filosofia, dov'ella regna,
is contradicting everything she tells us.	sempr'al contrario fa di quel ch'insegna.
When the people are ignorant,	Fonda sempre il pedante
there is greater profit to the pedant.	su l'ignoranza d'altri il suo guadagno,
He argues with such cunning,	e accorto argomentando
he sees Jove not as deity but his assistant.	non ha Giove per dio, ma per compagno,
And his teachings are framed in a manner so confusing	e le regole sue di modo intrica,
that at last not even he knows what he is saying.	ch'al fin ne anch'egli sa ciò chei si dica.

I know that Nero now is planning to divorce me	Neron tenta il ripudio della persona mia
so he can wed Poppea. Let him enjoy her,	per isposar Poppea. Si divertisca,
if such shameful acts can give him pleasure.	se divertir si può sì indegno esempio.
Pray for me, I beg you; pray to the Senate and the people;	Tu per me prega il popol e'l senato,
and in the meantime, my vows I'll offer in the temple.	ch'io mi riduco a porger voti al tempio.

If you do not bring help to our Empress,	Se tu non dai soccorso
then by my life I swear it —	alla nostra regina, in fede mia,

I'll set fire to your toga and your beard;
and your precious books too; by my life
I swear it.

che vo' accenderti il foco e nella toga*
e nella libreria. In fede mia.

Scene Seven. *Seneca*

SENECA

The grand imperial purple, the robe of
princes,
is full of thorns and twined about with
brambles;
these are woven in the garment worn by
our rulers
for their perpetual torment.
And the coronets that glitter serve but
one purpose —
to crown their heads with anguish.
Of the grandeur of empire
we see the outward showing and all its
glories,
but ever invisible are its miseries.

Le porpore regali e imperatrici,

d'acute spine e triboli conteste,

sotto forma di veste

sono il martirio a prencipi infelici;
le corone eminenti

servono solo a indiademar tormenti.
Delle regie grandezze
si veggono le pompe e gli splendori,

ma stan sempre invisibili i dolori.

Scene Eight. *Pallas Athene, Seneca*

ATHENE

Seneca, I see in Heaven a dreadful portent
which is threatening you with utter ruin.
Perhaps today you must prepare for dying.
If so, then Mercury shall bring you a
warning.

Seneca, io miro in Cielo infausti rai
che minacciano te d'alte ruine;
s'oggi verrà della tua vita il fine
pria da Mercurio avvisi certi avrai.

SENECA

Swiftly then let death come;
with courage unswerving I'll defeat black
misfortune and all death's darkness.
And when the whirl of earthly days is
ended,
death will show me the dawning of life
everlasting.

Venga la morte pur; costante e forte
vincerò gli accidenti e le paure;

dopo il girar delle giornate oscure

è di giorno infinito alba la morte.

Scene Nine. *Nero, Seneca*

NERO

Seneca, I must tell you:
I have fully determined
to remove Octavia
from her place as my consort.
And I shall wed Poppea.

Son risoluto insomma,
o Seneca, o maestro,
di rimover Ottavia
dal posto di consorte,
e di sposar Poppea.

SENECA

My lord, at the heart of the sweetest
pleasure
very often repentance lies hidden.
For desire is an evil adviser,
hating our statutes, and always foe to
reason.

Signor, nel fondo alla maggior dolcezza

spesso giace nascosto il pentimento.
Consiglier scellerato è'l sentimento
ch'odia le leggi e la ragion disprezza.

---

* "While all libretti except the one printed at Naples read 'toga', both scores have 'barba' instead. Since the change was more likely effected by a costume designer than by a poet or composer, we have restored 'toga'." (Curtis)

Our statutes are just for servants, and if I wish it's easy	La legge è per chi serve, e se vogl'io,
to abolish old ones and make some new ones.	posso abolir l'antica e indur le nove;
For power is divided: Jove rules Heaven,	è partito l'impero, è'l Ciel di Giove,
but the kingdom below is ruled by Nero.	ma del mondo terren lo scettro è mio.

SENECA

Any will that's unruly is not a true one,	Sregolato voler non è volere,
and — allow me to say it — it's merely madness.	ma (dirò, con tua pace) egli è furore.

NERO

Reason's rule is for those who are destined to be obedient,	La ragione è misura rigorosa
but not those who can command them.	per chi ubbidisce e non per chi comanda.

SENECA

Quite the opposite, for the unreasonable order	Anzi l'irragionevole comando
is destructive of all obedience.	distrugge l'ubbidienza.

NERO

No more discussion: I want it as I've decreed it.	Lascia i discorsi, io voglio a modo mio.

SENECA

Do not offend the people or the Senate.	Non irritar il popolo e'l senato.

NERO

As for the people and the Senators, I scorn them.	Del senato e del popolo non curo.

SENECA

Care at least for yourself then, and for your honour.	Cura almeno te stesso e la tua fama.

NERO

I'll tear the tongue out of any man who blames me.	Trarrò la lingua a chi vorrà biasmarmi.

SENECA

The more you try to gag them, the more they'll babble.	Più muti che farai, più parleranno.

NERO

Octavia is both frigid and infertile.	Ottavia è infrigidita ed infeconda.

SENECA

When a man has no case, he must invent one.	Chi ragione non ha, cerca pretesti.

NERO

When a man is in control, his will is reason.	A chi può ciò che vuol, ragion non manca.

SENECA

Yet in an unjust action there's no safety.	Manca la sicurezza all'opre ingiuste.

NERO

But he is always the soundest who is the strongest.	Sarà sempre più giusto il più potente.

But who abuses power grows ever weaker.   Ma chi non sa regnar, sempre può meno.

NERO

But might is right in peacetime . . .   La forza è legge in pace . . .

SENECA

But might without justice . . .   La forza accende gli odi . . .

NERO

. . . and a sword in wartime . . .   . . . e spada in guerra . . .

SENECA

. . . will kindle hatred and evil passions . . .   . . . e turba il sangue . . .

NERO

. . . and it feels not the slightest need of reason.   . . . e bisogno non ha della ragione.

SENECA

Reason governs gods and mortals.   La ragione regge gl'uomini e gli Dei.

NERO

You will goad me to frenzy. Despite your preaching,	Tu mi sforzi allo sdegno; al tuo dispetto,
and despite the people,	e del popolo in onta, e del senato,
despite the Senate and Octavia, gods in heaven and in the abysses,	e d'Ottavia, e del cielo, e dell'abisso,
just or unjust my action,	siansi giuste od ingiuste le mie voglie,
I've decided that today Poppea I'll take as Empress.	oggi, oggi Poppea sarà mia moglie!

SENECA

Kings should ever be seen as faultless;	Siano innocenti i Regi,
or if they sin, let them sin in search of glory.	o s'aggravino sol di colpe illustri;
If they're innocent no longer,	s'innocenza si perde,
then let the crime be in pursuit of conquest.	perdasi sol per guadagnar i regni,
For the sin that's committed	ch'il peccato commesso
to enhance the glory of empire	per aggrandir l'impero
is by itself remitted.	si assolve da se stesso;
But if a woman's charms have power to sway you	ma ch'una femminella abbia possanza
and lead you into error,	di condurti agli errori,
that sin's unworthy of a ruler, a demi-godhead:	non è colpa da rege o semideo:
it's a sin for a peasant.	è un misfatto plebeo.

NERO

Out of my sight at once, sir,	Levamiti dinnanzi,
you impudent philosopher,	maestro impertinente,
not fit to be a teacher.	filosofo insolente!

SENECA

The inferior side ever is the victor.	Il partito peggior sempre sovrasta,
Virtue is treason, when force opposes reason.	quando la forza alla ragion contrasta.

Scene Ten. *Poppea, Nero, Otho (unseen)*

POPPEA

In this night we have passed, my lord, now tell me,
did you find they were sweet, my loving kisses,
and did they give you great pleasure?

Come dolci, signor, come soavi
riuscirono a te la notte andata
di questa bocca i baci?

NERO

The dearer, the more tormenting!

Più cari i più mordaci.

POPPEA

And also the apples of my two breasts?

Di questo seno i pomi?

NERO

Give them a finer name than apples, your lovely breasts . . .

Mertan le mamme tue più dolci nomi.

POPPEA

And tell me, when I enfold you
in my embraces, in my arms I hold you . . .

[7] Di queste braccia
gli stretti amplessi?

NERO

Dearest Poppea, ah, if only once again I clasped you . . .
Poppea, my passion chokes me,
gazing upon your lips,
with my eyes I devour them,
and feel again that fiery spirit
which with my kisses — O dearest, in you I kindled.
My fate no more in heaven with all its glories is fixed,
but on your lips it hangs, upon your lips with their bright rubies.

Idolo mio, deh, in braccio ancor t'avessi!
Poppea, respiro appena;
miro le labbra tue,
e mirando ricupero con gl'occhi
quello spirto infiammato,
che nel bacciarti, o cara, in te diffusi.
Non è, non è più in cielo il mio destino,
ma sta de' labbri tuoi nel bel rubino.

POPPEA

My lord, words that you utter seem so perfect,
I in my soul repeating
those sweet sounds never lose them,
and their echo returning
must cause my loving spirit to swoon in rapture.
First as your words I can hear them,
then as kisses enjoy them.
Uttering precious — ah, precious — language,
your tongue is so enchanting and so beguiling,
that (not contented that you soothe my senses)
your words then pierce to my heart and there imprint your kisses.

Signor, le tue parole son sì dolci,
ch'io nell'anima mia
le ridico a me stessa,
e l'interno ridirle
necessita al deliquio il cor amante,
Come parole le odo,
come baci le godo;
son de' tuoi cari detti
i sensi sì soavi e sì vivaci,
che, non contenti di blandir l'udito,
mi passano a stampar sul cor i baci.

NERO

This splendid crown is the symbol
by which I order men's fortunes and govern a mighty empire,
this I wish to divide between us,
and then I shall be happy,
when you own the name and style of Empress.

Quell'eccelso diadema ond'io sovrasto
degl'uomini, e de' regni alla fortuna,
teco divider voglio,
e allor sarò felice
quando il titolo avrai d'imperatrice;

161

But this is foolish, O Poppea,
Rome's too small to be worthy of your
  great name,
and all Italy's narrow for your kingdom.
It is a style far too lowly for your beauty
to be known as the Queen and wife of
  Nero.
And your wonderful eyes which excel all
  else
do not win praise that equals their
  deserving,
in their modesty do not tempt heaven
  with boasting.
When their beauty should win them
  praise unbounded,
the people gaze silently and are
  dumbfounded.

ma che dico, o Poppea!
Troppo piccola è Roma ai merti tuoi,

troppo angusta è l'Italia alle tue lodi,
e al tuo bel viso è basso paragone
l'esser detta consorte di Nerone;

ed han questo svantaggio i tuoi
  begl'occhi,
che, trascendendo i naturali esempi,

e per modestia non tentando i cieli,

non ricevon tributo d'altro onore,

che di silenzio e di stupore.

POPPEA

With a hope that's sublime my heart is
  singing,
because you so commanded,
and you have given courage to my
  humility.
But there is much that may prevent and
  hinder
that most glorious triumph which you
  have promised.
Seneca, your learned master,
philosopher and Stoic,
that omniscient teacher,
who would persuade all the court and
  people
that your sceptre depends on his
  approval . . .

A speranze sublimi il cor innalzo

perchè tu lo comandi,
e la modestia mia riceve forza;

ma troppo s'attraversa, ed impedisce

di sì regie promesse il fin sovrano,

Seneca, il tuo maestro,
quello stoico sagace,
quel filosofo astuto,
che sempre tenta persuader altrui

ch'il tuo scettro dipende sol da lui . . .

NERO

What — what?

Che, che?

POPPEA

That your sceptre depends on his
  approval.

Ch'il tuo scettro dipende sol da lui.

NERO

That decrepit and crazy . . .

Quel decrepito pazzo . . .

POPPEA

Yes? Yes?

Quel, quel!

NERO

He dares to say it?

. . . ha tanto ardire?

POPPEA

He dares to say it.

Ha tanto ardire.

NERO

You there — Go at once,
quickly, to Seneca, and give him my
  royal order
that he today must perish.
Solely on me, depends the rule of
  empire,
not on the fancies or on the words of
  others.

Olà, vada un di voi
a Seneca volando, e imponga a lui,

ch'in questo giorno ei mora;
vo' che da me l'arbitrio mio dipenda,

non da concetti e da sofismi altrui.

I should deny my manhood and the
   powers of my spirit,
if I thought that unworthily and basely I
   were swayed
by the influence of others.
Poppea, pluck up your courage, for
   nothing appals us.
Yes, I promise, today you shall see Love
   victorious.

Rinnegherei per poco

le potenze dell'alma, s'io credessi
che servilmente indegne
si movessero mai col moto d'altre.
Poppea, sta di buon core,

oggi vedrai quel che sa far Amore.

Scene Eleven. *Otho, Poppea, Arnalta (unseen).*

Ritornello

OTHO

While others may drink deeply
of the sweet wine, I only see the vessel.
If Nero comes, the door stands open
   wide;
meanwhile Otho stands outside it.
Nero at table enjoys the best of eating;
while in rigorous fast, Otho is dying.

Ad altri tocca in sorte
bere il licor, e a me guardar il vaso,
aperte stan le porte

a Neron, ed Otton fuori è rimaso;
siede egli a mensa a satollar sue brame,
in amaro digiun mor'io di fame.

Ritornello

POPPEA

Some men are born unlucky;
their complaint should be made to
   themselves, not others.
Although your state's unhappy,
I'm not the cause, Otho; I cannot help
   it.
It is Fate throws the dice and awaits the
   ending;
events for good or evil are in Fate's
   keeping.

Chi nasce sfortunato
di se stesso si dolga, e non d'altrui;

del tuo penoso stato
aspra cagion, Otton, non son nè fui;

il destin getta i dadi e i punti attende:

l'evento, o buono o reo, da lui dipende.

Ritornello

OTHO

The harvest that I sighed for,
that my hope promised me, the fruit of
   longings,
is garnered by other fingers.
It shall be mine no more — Love has
   decreed it.
While Nero covers your breast with
   caresses,
I bathe my lips with tears, mourning my
   losses.

La messe sospirata
dalle speranze mie, da' miei desiri,

in altra mano è andata,
e non consente Amor che più v'aspiri;

Neron felice i dolci pomi tocca,

e solo il pianto a me bagna la bocca.

Ritornello

POPPEA

Your head was shorn by Fortune,
yet she, in her bounty gives flowing
   locks to others;
if she fulfils their wishes,
then they were born under a luckier
   planet.
You must not therefore blame me for
   your misfortune,
but blame yourself and your unlucky
   destiny.

A te le calve tempie,
ad altri il crine la Fortuna diede;

s'altri i desiri adempie
ebbe di te più fortunato piede.

La disventura tua non è mia colpa,

te solo dunque e'l tuo destino incolpa.

163

OTHO

Your heart, though hard and stony,
lovely Poppea, I hoped might feel some
   pity,
might be by Love's touch melted,
seeing the proof of my pain and my
   great misery.
But that hard flint you keep within your
   bosom
is the tomb where, unpitied, my hopes
   lie buried.

Sperai che quel macigno,
bella Poppea, che ti circonda il core,

fosse d'amor benigno
intenerito a pro' del mio dolore,

or del tuo bianco sen la selce dura

di mie morte speranze è sepoltura.

Ritornello

POPPEA

No more of these reproaches.
You must endure your martyrdom in
   silence,
and no longer attempt to persuade me.
To imperial decree Poppea owes submission.
Stifle your sorrow, and quench fires of
   anger.
By leaving you I hope to gain an Empire!

Deh, non più rinfacciarmi,
porta, deh porta il martellino in pace,

cessa di più tentarmi,
al cenno imperial Poppea soggiace;
ammorza il foco omai, tempra gli sdegni;

io lascio te per arrivar ai regni.

OTHO

Now I see that ambition,
of all the vices, is the ruling Empress.

E così l'ambizione
sovra ogni vizio tien la monarchia.

POPPEA

And now you see that my reason
condemns your wild complaints of me as
   madness.

Così la mia ragione
incolpa i tuoi capricci di pazzia.

OTHO

And this is the reward of my devotion?

È questo del mio amor il guiderdone?

POPPEA

No more.

Modestia.

OTHO

And this is the reward of my devotion?

È questo del mio amor il guiderdone?

POPPEA

No more, no more.

Olà, non più.

OTHO

And this is the reward of my devotion?

È questo del mio amor il guiderdone?

POPPEA

No more. I turn to Nero.   *

Non più, son di Nerone.

---

* The Naples score has two further speeches, set to music by a later composer.

OTHO

Ahi, ahi, he who has trusted
in outward beauty,
raises a building over the airy void
tries to catch the wind in his fingers,
and to hold the waves steady, to make the
   smoke obey him.

Ahi, ahi, chi si fida
in un bel volto,
fabbrica in aria, e sopra il vacuo fonda
tenta palpare il vento
ed immobili afferma il fumo, e l'onda.

continued

Scene Twelve. *Otho*

OTHO

Be warned, my soul: Otho, come to your senses.
You know the weaker sex
has nothing in its nature
of true humanity, save outward beauty.
Otho, come to your senses.
Poppea is greedy for power,
and if she wins it, then my life will be forfeit.
Otho, come to your senses.
Fearing that Nero
will somehow come to learn
that we once were lovers,
she will soon try to destroy my reputation,
she will exert her power to find some man
to accuse me of deceit and call me traitor.
For the great will always take pleasure
in destroying a guiltless life and honour.
Yes, I must forestall her malice,
attacking with steel or poison.
I no longer will feed this snake in my bosom.
To such a pass you've brought me,
I who have faithfully loved you,
O treacherous, treacherous Poppea!

Otton, torna in te stesso,

il più imperfetto sesso
non ha per sua natura
altro d'uman in sè che la figura.
Otton, torna in te stesso.
Costei pensa al comando, e se ci arriva
la mia vita è perduta …

Otton, torna in te stesso …
           … ella temendo
che risappia Nerone
i miei passati amori,
ordirà insidie all'innocenza mia,
indurrà con la forza un che m'accusi
di lesa maestà, di fellonia.
La calunnia, da' grandi favorita,
distrugge agl'innocenti onor e vita.
Vo', vo', prevenir costei
col ferro o col veleno,
non mi vo' più nutrir il serpe in seno.

A questo, a questo fine
dunque arrivar dovea
l'amor tuo, perfidissima Poppea!

Scene Thirteen. *Drusilla, Otho*

DRUSILLA

Still brooding on Poppea?
You are for ever thinking or speaking of her.

Pur sempre di Poppea,
o con la lingua, o col pensier discorri.

OTHO

I drive her from my heart; see her no longer;
but then her name sounds whenever I am speaking.
I cast her to the winds, but she returns —
she who betrayed my heart's affections.

Discacciato dal cor viene alla lingua,
e dalla lingua è consegnato ai venti

il nome di colei
ch'infedele tradì gl'affetti miei.

DRUSILLA

I see that Love's tribunal
can sometimes tell what's just.
You never pitied me;
now others laugh at you in your sorrow.

Il tribunal d'Amor
talor giustizia fa:
di me non hai pietà,
altri si ride, Otton, del tuo dolor.

---

* Footnote continued

ARNALTA

Poor unhappy young fellow!
Compassion moves my heart to see you suffer.
Poppea feels no pity,
and she will not show mercy.
But I, when I was young,
could not bear it when my lovers
were weeping and distracted.
For pity's sake, to make them happy, I gave them what they wanted.

Infelice ragazzo!
Mi move a compassion il miserello;

Poppea non ha cervello
a non gl'aver pietà;
quand'ero in altra età
non volevo gl'amanti
in lacrime distrutti,
per compassion gli contentavo tutti.

I offer you myself,
most beautiful Drusilla:
take me, such as I am.
I here renounce all others,
and only yours I'll be, my sweet Drusilla.
Forgive me, O god forgive me
for discourtesy shown you and unkindness.
Though you do not reproach me for my error,
I accuse myself of blindness.
Here then my soul I offer, full of repentance.
Long as I live, I'll be yours, never parted,
who lately was so unheeding and stony-hearted.
Now, now, repenting of the wrong that's over,
from henceforth I shall be servant and lover.

A te di quanto son,
bellissima donzella
or fo libero don;
ad altri mi ritolgo,
e solo tuo sarò, Drusilla mia.
Perdona, o dio, perdona
il passato scortese mio costume;
benchè tu del mio error non mi riprenda,
confesso i falli andati,
eccoti l'alma mia pronta all'emenda.
Fin ch'io vivrò, t'amerà sempre, o bella;
quest'alma che ti fu cruda, e rubella;
già, già pentita dell'error antico
mi ti consacra omai servo ed amico.

DRUSILLA

You so quickly can bury
former passion?
It's really true, you say it's true
that you will firmly pledge your heart to me?

Già l'oblio seppellì
gl'andati amori?
È ver, Otton, è ver,
ch'a questo fido cor il tuo s'unì?

OTHO

Drusilla, I swear it's true.

Drusilla, è ver, sì, sì.

DRUSILLA

Otho, I fear that you deceive me; you are lying.

Temo, che tu mi dica la bugia.

OTHO

No, no, Drusilla, no.

No no, Drusilla, no.

DRUSILLA

I'm still afraid. I can't be sure.

Otton, non so, non so.

OTHO

Now by my faith I swear I don't deceive you.

Teco non può mentir la fede mia.

DRUSILLA

You love me?

M'ami?

OTHO

I long for you.

Ti bramo.

DRUSILLA

Do you love me?

M'ami? M'ami?

OTHO

Yes, truly I long for you.

Ti bramo. Ti bramo.

DRUSILLA

You love, all in a moment?

E come in un momento?

OTHO

The fires of passion are suddenly enkindled.

Amor è foco, e subito s'accende.

DRUSILLA

Such unexpected sweetness — joyful happiness and gladness.	Sì subite dolcezze
Joy is filling my heart, but I'm still doubtful.	gode lieto il mio cor, ma non l'intende.
Do you love me?	M'ami? M'ami?

OTHO

I truly desire you:	Ti bramo. Ti bramo.
your beauty should assure you that I love you.	Ti dican l'amor mio le tue bellezze.
Upon my heart I have your form imprinted.	Per te nel cor ho nova forma impressa,
You this miracle wrought: only believe it.	i miracoli tuoi credi a te stessa.

DRUSILLA

I'm rejoicing: my heart's filled with gladness.	Lieta men vado: Otton, resta felice;
I leave you, for I must go to find the Empress.	m'indrizzo a riverir l'imperatrice.

OTHO

Calm the storms of your heart — doubt me no longer.	Le tempeste del cor tutte tranquilla:
Now to you I belong, and to no other.	d'altri Otton non sarà che di Drusilla;
Despite myself, although with loving words I name Drusilla,	e pur al mio dispetto, iniquo Amore,
my heart is crying — it is crying *Poppea*.	Drusilla ho in bocca, ed ho Poppea nel core.

The end of Act One.

Aimée Lecouvreur as the Nurse, and Madeleine Sibille as Octavia, in Jean Mercier's production for the Opéra-Comique in 1937 (photo: Lipnitzki)

Act Two

Scene One. *The scene changes to Seneca's villa. Seneca, Mercury*

SENECA

Solitude, I love and bless you:
hermitage for the spirit;
for the thoughtful, a refuge;
a rare prize to every thinker,
who may seek and discover
the truth of things celestial,
under the forms they wear of things
    terrestrial.
To you hastens my soul, freely retiring,
and far from court and courtiers,
who with insolent pride and foolish
    concerns
disgust me and try my patience,
here among the trees and green bushes
I rest in the bosom of this healing
    silence.

Solitudine amata,
eremo della mente,
romitaggio a' pensieri,
delizia all'intelletto,
che discorre e contempla
l'immagini celesti
sotto le forme ignobili terrene,

a te l'anima mia lieta sen viene,
e lunge dalla corte,
ch'insolente e superba

fa della mia pazienza anatomia,
qui tra le frondi e l'erba
m'assido in grembo della pace mia.

MERCURY

Trusted friend of the gods,
you see that in your favourite lonely
    refuge
I have chosen to find you.

Vero amico del Cielo
appunto in questa solitaria chiostra

visitarti io volevo.

SENECA

But when, ah tell me when,
have I deserved a visit from a god?

E quando, e quando mai
le visite divine io meritai?

MERCURY

Sovereign virtue, which you possess in
    plenty,
can deify a mortal,
and you therefore are worthy of a message
from the goddess Athene.
I Mercury am sent to warn you
that the end of your earthly existence
is swiftly approaching.
You will pass to a heaven that's everlasting.

La sovrana virtù, di cui sei pieno,

deifica i mortali,
e perciò son da te ben meritate
le celesti ambasciate.
Pallade a te mi manda,
e t'annunzia vicina l'ultim'ora
di questa frale vita,
e'l passaggio all'eterna ed infinita.

SENECA

O now thrice happy am I.
Until this moment I have been living
the life of common mortals;
but when this life is over,
I shall live with the immortals.
You, courteous godhead, you come to
    say that my life is ended?
This confirms what I have written,
assures the truth of my teaching.
To leave this life is welcome, is blessed
    even,
if the summons is brought us by a
    message from heaven.

O me felice, adunque,
s'ho vivuto sinora
degl'uomini la vita,
vivrò dopo la morte
la vita degli dei.
Nume cortese tu'l morir m'annunzi?

Or confermo i miei scritti;
autentico i miei studi;
l'uscir di vita è una beata sorte,

se da bocca divina esce la morte.

MERCURY

Gaily therefore make ready
for the celestial journey,
the sublime exploration.

Lieto dunque t'accingi
al celeste viaggio,
[8]   al sublime passaggio,

I shall instruct you clearly how you may follow	t'insegnerò la strada,
the path that leads to the heavens, to the celestial regions.	che ne conduce allo Stellato Polo;
Seneca — now thither I am swiftly flying.	Seneca, or colà sù io drizzo il volo.

Scene Two. *Captain of Nero's Guard (a freed slave), Seneca*

CAPTAIN

The imperial order admits of no denial;	Il comando tiranno esclude ogni ragione,
its only message is either violence or death.	e tratta solo o violenza o morte.
I'm bound to recite it,	Io devo riferirlo, e nondimeno,
and although I am only the messenger,	relatore innocente,
I feel that I am sharing in the evil	mi par d'esser partecipe del male,
which in this sentence I'm bringing.	ch'a riferire io vado.
Seneca, I'm truly sorry to have found you,	Seneca, assai m'incresce di trovarti,
even though I had sought you.	mentre pur ti ricerco.
Ah, don't fix your eyes on me so sternly,	Deh, non mi riguardar con occhio torvo
although I come like a crow with tidings of sorrow.	se a te sarò d'infausto annunzio il corvo.

SENECA

My friend, a long while since,	Amico, è già gran tempo,
I have armed myself with courage	ch'io porto il seno armato
against the blows of ill fortune.	contro i colpi del Fato.
The scandals of the epoch which we live in	La notizia del secolo in cui vivo,
have by no means escaped my observation.	forestiera non giunge alla mia mente;
If to death you must call me,	se m'arrechi la morte,
do not ask my forgiveness:	non mi chieder perdono:
laughing I receive tidings of such goodness.	rido mentre mi porti un sì bel dono.

CAPTAIN

The Emperor . . .	Nerone . . .

SENECA

No more, no more . . .	Non più, non più . . .

CAPTAIN

. . . has sent me to you.	. . . a te mi manda.

SENECA

No more. I understand you; I shall obey you swiftly.	Non più. T'ho inteso, ed ubbidisco or ora.

CAPTAIN

How can you understand till I have spoken?	E come intendi me pria ch'io m'esprima?

SENECA

The manner of your speech, and the person who has sent you,	La forma del tuo dire e la persona
are both of them cruel and most threatening tokens	ch'a me ti manda, son due contrassegni
that I for death am destined.	minacciosi e crudeli
This I've long known, and long predicted.	del mio fatal destino;
The Emperor has sent you to me:	già, già son indovino.
to die he now commands me,	Nerone a me t'invia
and I shall soon obey him.	a imponermi la morte,
I'll only so long delay it	ed io sol tanto tempo
as will give me the time	frappongo ad ubbidirlo

169

to express my gratitude for what he has done.	quanto bast' a formar ringraziamenti
For he, believing that heaven had forgotten all about me, wished to make it aware that I am living, and thus to free the airy skies and nature from the load — the intolerable burden — of my unwanted and too-prolonged existence. But when once Nero has achieved my death, it won't content him fully. When a vice has been fed, it's yet more hungry. One way to crime that's opened, lets in thousands. It is ordained by heaven: untold abysses near the first are gaping.	alla sua cortesia, che mentre vede dimenticato il Ciel de' casi miei, gli vuol far sovvenir ch'io vivo ancora, per liberar e l'aria, e la natura dal pagar l'ingiustissima angheria de' fiati e giorni alla vecchiaia mia. Ma di mia vita il fine non sazierà Nerone; l'alimento d'un vizio all'altro è fame, il varco d'un eccesso a mille è strada, ed è lassù prefisso, che cento abissi chiami un sol abisso.

CAPTAIN

My lord, you have guessed rightly. So die, and die contented. For as the glow at sunset still illumines the day although the sun shines no longer, so shall it be in future, for other men will borrow the light of your wisdom. So die, and die contented.	Signor, indovinasti; mori, e mori felice, che, come vanno i giorni all'impronto del sole a marcarsi di luce, così alle tue scritture verran per prender luce in scritti altrui. Mori, e mori felice.

*

SENECA

Go now, go to find Nero. If you find him before the day is ended, you may tell him that I'm dead; that I'm buried.	Vanne, vattene omai, e se parli a Nerone avanti sera, ch'io son morto e sepolto gli dirai.

Scene Three. *Seneca, Friends* †

SENECA

Companions, the moment is now approaching when we must calmly follow that great ideal which I have so commended. Death is but a brief anguish: then the breath of life goes, leaving the body, like a pilgrim who leaves the hostel that held him many years a stranger, and takes its flight to Olympus,　　$ where peace and perfect joy are his for ever.	Amici, è giunta l'ora di praticare in fatti quella virtù che tanto celebrai. Breve angoscia è la morte; un sospir peregrino esce dal core, ov'è stato molt'anni, quasi in ospizio, come forestiero, e se ne vola all'Olimpo, della felicità soggiorno vero.

---

* Eight more lines of Busenello's text, followed by a repetition of 'Mori felice', were set anonymously about 1650 in the Naples score.

† According to Curtis, this is an ensemble for three voices only, possibly (as in Tacitus) Seneca's wife and two friends.

$ All librettos have 'e sen vola' but both scores have this text.

Do not die, Seneca, do not die.
I for my part would not die,
I do not wish to die.

[9] Non morir, non morir, Seneca
io per me morir non vo'.

Ritornello

Earthly life is far too joyful,
earthly skies are blue and smiling;
every sorrow is but fleeting,
every bitterness a trifle.

Questa vita è dolce troppo,
questo ciel troppo è sereno,
ogni amar, ogni veleno
finalmente è lieve intoppo.

Ritornello

When the night is past and over,
I am sure to waken with morning;
from the tomb there's no returning
it will hold me fast forever.

Se mi corco al sonno lieve
mi risveglio in sul mattino
ma un avel di marmo fino
mai non dà quel che riceve.

No I do not wish to die.
Do not die, Seneca, no.

Io per me morir non vo',
non morir, Seneca, no.

Ritornello

SENECA *

All of you go now, make sure my bath is
    ready.
For if our life is like
a river flowing onward,
I would wish that a river of my innocent
    blood should flow,
to redden the path before me of my
    death,
which I soon must follow.

Itene tutti a prepararmi il bagno,

che se la vita corre
come il rivo fluente
in un tepido rivo

questo sangue innocente io vo' che vada

a imporporarmi del morir la strada.

Scene Four. † *The scene changes to the city of Rome. Valletto, Lady-in-waiting*

VALLETTO

Something pains and troubles me,
plucks my heart and makes me shiver;
do explain, what can it be?
Is it love that makes me suffer?
I would do — I would say —
I would say — I would do —
I don't know what I am doing,
I don't know what I am saying.

[10] Sento un certo non so che,
che mi pizzica, e diletta,
dimmi tu che cosa egli è,
damigella amorosetta.
Ti farei, ti direi,
ti direi, ti farei,
ma non so quel ch'io vorrei.

Ritornello

When you're near, my heart is beating,
when you go, my thoughts depress me,
for delight is all too fleeting,
and your breasts do so obsess me.

Se sto teco il cor mi batte,
se tu parti io sto melenso,
al tuo sen divino latte,
sempre aspiro e sempre penso.

Ritornello

LADY

Cunning fellow, this must follow —
these are games Love plays with you.

Astutello, garzoncello,
bamboleggia Amor in te,

---

* Ten more lines of Busenello's text for Seneca were 'set anonymously, about 1650.'
(Curtis)
† Some librettos (including the 1656 edition) give a nineteen-line scene here for
Seneca and a (twice repeated) *coro di Virtù*. It appears in neither score, so it is omitted,
and the scenes renumbered accordingly.

What he wishes you to do
is to lose your head completely.
Let Love and you make sport with
  babes like angels,
but you know you are both of you
  scoundrels.

se divieni amante, affè,
perderai tosto il cervello.
Tresca Amor per sollazzo coi bambini,

ma siete Amor e tu, due malandrini.

VALLETTO

Is this truly Love beginning?
And does it really bring such sweetness?
I would give, to relish your true
  perfections,
cherries and candies, and cakes and such
  confections.
But if this honey which delights me with
  its taste
were changed to bitter,
you'd make it sweet again?
Tell me you would, my darling, tell me
  you would.

Dunque amor così comincia?
È una cosa molto dolce?
Io darei, per godere il tuo diletto,

i ciliegi, le pere, ed il confetto.

Ma se amaro divenisse

questo miel che sì mi piace,
l'addolciresti tu?
Dimmelo, vita mia, dimmelo, dì!

LADY

I'd make it sweet — yes, yes,

L'addolcirei, sì, sì.

LADY AND VALLETTO†

My darling, my treasure,
we'll go now, rejoicing,
rejoicing, delighting.
Delay sharpens longing,
increases my pleasure.

O caro, godiamo,
godiamo, cantiamo,
andiamo a godere.
Allunga il morire
chi tarda il piacere.

Scene Five. *Nero, Lucano**

NERO

Seneca is dead and buried,
so sing Lucano, we'll sing . . . making
  rapturous verses
to give her praise unstinted,
whose features on my heart Love's hand
  has printed.
We'll sing, we'll sing, sing praises —

Or che Seneca è morto,
cantiam, Lucano, amorose canzoni

in lode d'un bel viso,
che di sua mano Amor nel cor m'ha
  inciso.
[11] Cantiam, cantiam, Lucano —

LUCANO

We'll sing, we'll sing, your Highness —

Cantiam, cantiam, Signore —

BOTH

— to that marvellous goddess,
who shines in glory, whose breath inspires
  her lovers;
— of those features, so blessed . . .
that from the snow in winter
can bring the burning wonder,
whence there shows, whence there glows
  the bright pomegranate.
We'll sing those lips so luscious,
where the spice of Arabia and India
breathes perfume, and pearls bring beauty.

— di quel viso ridente,
che spira glorie ed influisce amori;

— di quel viso beato . . .
e seppe su le nevi,
con nova meraviglia,
animar, incarnar la granitiglia.

Cantiam di quella bocca,
a cui l'India e l'Arabia
le perle consacrò, donò gli odori.

---

† The words for this duet do not appear in any of the librettos, nor in the Venice
score, which is the sole source for the music. They have been supplied by Alan
Curtis, 'based on suggestions by Giovanni Morelli'.

* Variously in different sources 'with his court', or with Petronio and Tigellino. An
anonymous composer (c. 1650) added lines for them to sing, and another verse for Nero.

172

Sweetest, ah, my fate . . .   Bocca, ahi destino . . .

Beauty, beauty when she's speaking or   Bocca, bocca che se ragiona o ride
    smiling
can with a hidden weapon wound us   con invisibil arme punge, e all'alma
and so strangely offers felicity while she   dona felicità mentre l'uccide.
    is slaying.
Beauty which then will offer   Bocca, che se mi porge
voluptuous kisses so tenderly to me,   lasciveggiando il tenero rubino
and intoxicate my heart with nectar   m'inebria il cor di nettare divino.
    straight from heaven.
You fall, my lord,   Tu vai, Signor
into ecstasies, and love's delicious   nell'estasi d'amor deliciando,
    pleasures;
from your eyes fall like rain   e ti piovon dagl'occhi
the drops of your tender passion,   stille di tenerezza,
tears of surpassing sweetness.   lacrime di dolcezza.

Heavenly, heavenly mistress,   Idolo, idolo mio,
I would worship and praise you.   celebrarti io vorrei,
But all my words are faint flickering   ma son minute fiaccole, e cadenti,
    tapers
when compared to the shining of your   di rimpetto al tuo sole i detti miei.
    sun's splendour.

Ritornello

Rubies glowing and priceless are your   Son rubin preziosi
    lips
where Love sits smiling,   i tuoi labbri amorosi,
while my heart always faithful   il mio core costante
is hard as a diamond in constancy.   è di saldo diamante,
And thus my faithful heart and your   così le tue bellezze, ed il mio core
    great beauty
are fashioned of precious stones by Love   di care gemme ha fabbricato Amore.
    for his greater glory.

Ritornello

Scene Six. *Otho*

My impetuous anger,   [12] I miei subiti sdegni,
and the dangers that threatened,   la politica mia già poco d'ora
even led me to think that I might   m'indussero a pensare
murder her . . . Poppea!   d'uccidere . . . Poppea?
O thrice accursed thought,   O! Mente maledetta,
why are you so hard to banish?   perchè se' tu immortale, ond'io non posso
For I cannot forget you or destroy you.   svenarti, a castigarti?
I thought, I spoke of killing you, my   Pensai, parlai d'ucciderti, ben mio,
    darling.
How perversely,   il mio genio perverso,
when my spirit was denied the affection   rinnegati gl'affetti,
which once you gave me freely,   ch'un tempo mi donasti,
I slipped, I sank, I fell   piegò, cadè, proruppe
into a thought so hateful and wicked.   in un pensier sì detestando e reo?
You gods, I pray you change this sinful   Cambiatemi quest'anima deforme
    spirit.
Give me instead a spirit   datemi un altro spirto meno impuro
that is less corrupted, O you powers!   per pietà vostra, o dei!
I disown you, my mind,   Rifiuto un intelletto,

which has such impious thoughts;
which had planned with a hellish and
  bloody stratagem
to murder her who was my dearest, to
  see her blood flow.
Now vanish into darkness,
O wretched memory, as I recall you.

che discorre impietadi,
che pensò sanguinario, ed infernale

d'uccidere il mio bene, e di svenarlo.

Isvieni, tramortisci,
scellerata memoria, in ricordarlo.

Ritornello

Scorn me as you are able;
hate me with all your powers;
I like a sunflower would turn to your
  eyes' shining.

Sprezzami quanto sai,
odiami quanto vuoi,
voglio esser Clizia al sol de' lumi tuoi.

Ritornello

I will love, hoping nothing,
in defiance of fortune.
Love unrequited be my joy and satisfaction.

Amerò senza speme
al dispetto del fato,
fia mia delizia, amarti disperato.

Ritornello

I shall endure my torments,
offspring of your great beauty.
I shall be damned, it's true, but 'twill be
  in heaven.

Blandirò i miei tormenti,
nati dal tuo bel viso,
sarò dannato, sì, ma in paradiso.

Ritornello

Scene Seven. *Octavia, Otho*

OCTAVIA

You that owe to my ancestors
your rank and position,
if you feel any gratitude for favours given,
I beg you help me, help, I beg you.

Tu che dagli avi miei
avesti le grandezze,
se memoria conservi
de' benefici avuti, or dammi aita.

OTHO

Majesty, your prayer
is a command to me from Fate.
I am ready to obey you, gracious
  Empress,
anything you ask me,
yes, even though it brought about my
  ruin.

Maestade che prega
è destin che necessita; son pronto
ad ubbidirti, o regina,

quando anco bisognasse
sacrificare a te la mia ruina.

OCTAVIA

Know then, my wish is that your dagger
should cancel the debt you owe me
by writing in the blood of Poppea. Yes,
  you must kill her.

Voglio che la tua spada
scriva gli obblighi miei
col sangue di Poppea; vuo' che l'uccida.

OTHO

I must kill — whom?

Che uccida chi?

OCTAVIA

Poppea.

Poppea.

OTHO

Must kill her? Must kill Poppea?

Poppea? Che uccida Poppea?

OCTAVIA

Poppea, I said. Why are you drawing back
from what you just promised?

Poppea, perchè? Dunque ricusi
quel che già promettesti?

From what I promised?
I only spoke in commonest politeness,
a purely formal answer — automatic.
To what penance — to what criminal act
— have you condemned me?

Io ciò promisi?
Urbanità di complimento umile,
modestia di parole costumate,
a che pena mortal mi condannate!

OCTAVIA

What's that you're saying? You are
saying to yourself?

Che discorri fra te?

OTHO

I am trying to think what way
will be safest and most secret
for a mission so deadly.

Discorro il modo
più cauto, e più sicuro
d'un impresa sì grande.

O gods, O gods, O heavens,
in such a fearful moment,
now take my life, I pray you; end my
existence.

O Ciel, o dei, o dei,
in questo punto orrendo
ritoglietemi i giorni e i spirti miei.

OCTAVIA

What are you muttering?

Che mormori?

OTHO

I'm praying. I'm offering prayers to
Fortune
to give me the ability to serve you.

Fo voti alla Fortuna,
che mi doni attitudine a servirti.

OCTAVIA

This work you are to do will be the
better
the sooner it is finished.
So act without delaying.

E, perchè l'opra tua
quanto più presta fia tanto più cara,
precipita gl'indugi.

OTHO

So soon then I am to die?

Sì tosto ho da morir?

OCTAVIA

Why are you constantly talking to
yourself?
But I tell you, you shall feel
the force of royal anger
if you do not act quickly on my order;
you will pay for your slowness with
your neck, sir.

Ma che frequenti
soliloqui son questi? Ti protesta
l'imperial mio sdegno,
che se non vai veloce al maggior segno,
pagherai la pigrizia con la testa.

OTHO

What if Nero should find out?

Se Neron lo saprà?

OCTAVIA

Go and change your appearance.
Borrow some woman's clothing to disguise
you,
and when you have chosen your moment
with care,
go boldly to the deed.

Cangia vestiti.
Abito muliebre ti ricopra,
e, con frode opportuna,
sagace esecutor t'accingi all'opra.

OTHO

Give me time, oh wait a little,
till I can stir up my emotions to hatred
and make my heart inhuman.

Dammi tempo, ond'io possa
inferocire i sentimenti miei,
disumanare il core . . .

Go, act without delay.

Precipita gl'indugi.

Give me time, oh wait a little,
till I teach my hand to strike as a
  barbarian.
For I cannot change all in a moment
the spirit of a lover
to the craft of a pitiless executioner.

Dammi tempo, ond'io possa
imbarbarir la mano,

assuefar non posso in un momento
il genio innamorato
nell'arti di carnefice spietato.

If you do not obey me
I shall pretend to Nero
that you approached me
and tried to assault me;
and I'll make sure, before this day is
  over,
you will suffer the torture, till death
  shall end it.

Se tu non m'ubbidisci,
t'accuserò a Nerone,
ch'abbi voluto usarmi
violenze inoneste,
e farò sì, che ti si stanchi intorno

il tormento, e la morte in questo giorno.

I shall obey you, my honoured Empress,
  and swiftly.

Ad ubbidirti, imperatrice, io vado.

O gods, O gods, O heavens,
in such a fearful moment,
now take my life, I pray you; end my
  existence.

O Ciel, o Ciel, o dei,
in questo punto orrendo
ritoglietemi i giorni e i spirti miei.

Scene Eight. *Drusilla, Valletto, Nurse*

My heart is rejoicing,
it's dancing within me.
For the storm is gone by, and now comes
  the sunlight.
Otho soon will be coming,
and he will say again that he adores me.
I laugh and sing for joy:
Otho adores me.
I laugh and sing for joy: Otho adores me.

[13] Felice cor mio,
festeggiami in seno,
dopo i nembi, e gl'orror godrò il sereno.

Oggi spero ch'Ottone
mi rinconfermi il suo promesso amore.
Felice cor mio,
festeggiami in seno,
festeggiami nel sen, lieto mio core.

Now tell me, Nurse, tell me, how much
  payment would you make
if for one day you could be bright and
  youthful like Drusilla?

Nutrice, quanto pagheresti un giorno

d'allegra gioventù, com'ha Drusilla?

All the riches in the world I
  would make over.
The envy of others' fortune,
hatred of one's own self,
the soul's flagging powers,
infirmity of the senses —
these four are the ingredients,
or rather the elements,
of this miserable dotage,
hoary-headed and trembling,
a walking graveyard to give its own
  bones a shelter.

Tutto l'oro del mondo io pagherei.

L'invidia del ben d'altri,
l'odio di sè medesma,
la fiacchezza dell'alma,
l'infermità del senso,
son quattro ingredienti,
anzi i quattro elementi
di questa miserabile vecchiezza,
che canuta, e tremante,
dell'ossa proprie è un cimiterio andante.

Don't take so gloomy a view, you're still a youthful woman; your sun is not yet setting, although no more you'll see a rosy dawning.	Non ti lagnar così, sei fresca ancora; non è il sol tramontata se ben passata è la vermiglia aurora.

Ritornello

NURSE

For womankind, the day reaches its evening just at the hour of noon; from midday on, you will see their beauty fading soon. In time the taste grows sweet of fruit once hard and bitter; but when it's ripe it decays: the best is over.	Il giorno femminil trova la sera sua nel mezzo dì. Dal mezzogiorno in là sfiorisce la beltà, col tempo si fa dolce il frutto acerbo e duro, ma in ore guasto vien quel ch'è maturo.

Ritornello

Believe what I can tell, all you young people, sparkling in your prime. The springtime is when Love will make his home with you; do not let green April pass, nor May, the month to marry, for in July you sweat too much to start a journey.	Credetel pure a me, o giovanette fresche in sul mattin, primavera è l'età che Amor con voi si stà; non lasciate che passi il verde april o'l maggio si suda troppo il luglio a far viaggio.

VALLETTO

Let's go to Octavia straightway, my venerable grandma . . .	Andiam a Ottavia, omai signora nonna mia, . . .

NURSE

Just you wait until I catch you.	Ti darò una guanciata!

VALLETTO

Monumental antiquity!	. . . venerabile antica,

NURSE

You're a bundle of iniquity.	Bugiardello!

VALLETTO

To aged Charon, his intimate companion.	. . . del buon Caronte idolatrata amica.

NURSE

Enough, you cheeky little rascal, enough, enough.	Che sì, bugiardello insolente, che sì, che sì.

VALLETTO

Let's go, for you're not only long past midday, but past midnight as well.	Andiam, che in te è passata la mezza notte, non che il mezzo dì.

Scene Nine. *Otho, Drusilla.*

OTHO

I don't know where I'm going. My heart's insistent beating, and the steps that I take, distract each other.	Io non so dov'io vada; il palpitar del core, ed il moto del piè non van d'accordo.

Air as it enters my body, drawn in as I
   am breathing,
finds in my heart such anguish
that it is altered into tears of sorrow;
thus it is, while I suffer,
the air in my breast weeps too for pity.

L'aria che m'entra in seno quand'io
   respiro
trova il mio cor sì afflitto,
ch'ella si cangia in subitaneo pianto;
e così mentr'io peno,
l'aria per compassion mi piange in seno.

DRUSILLA

My Otho, where are you going?

E dove, signor mio?

OTHO

Drusilla, Drusilla!

Drusilla, Drusilla!

DRUSILLA

Tell me, where are you going?

Dove, signor mio?

OTHO

You only, only for you I'm looking.

Te sola io cerco.

DRUSILLA

Here I am: what's your pleasure?

Eccomi a' tuoi piaceri.

OTHO

Drusilla, I must confide in you
a secret of great gravity.
You promise you'll be silent and will
   help me?

Drusilla, io vo' fidarti
un secreto gravissimo; prometti
e silenzio e soccorso?

DRUSILLA

If you should need my blood or my
   possessions,
if they could help you or serve you,
they are yours more than mine.
Disclose to me the secret;
then with my vow of silence
I'll give you as my pledges my faith and
   courage.

Ciò che del sangue mio, non che
   dell'oro,
può giovarti e servirti,
è già tuo più che mio.
Palesami il secreto,
che del silenzio poi
ti do l'anima in pegno, e la mia fede.

OTHO

You never need be jealous now
of Poppea.

Non esser più gelosa
di Poppea.

DRUSILLA

Not now?

No, no.

OTHO

Of Poppea.

Di Poppea.

DRUSILLA

My heart is rejoicing,
it's dancing within me.

Felice cor mio,
festeggiami in seno.

OTHO

Listen, listen.

Senti, senti.

DRUSILLA

It's dancing within me.

Festeggiami in seno.

OTHO

Listen.
I very shortly must perform a dreadful
   task,
must plunge my sword into Poppea's
   body.

Senti, io devo
or ora per terribile comando

immergerle nel sen questo mio brando.

Now to disguise myself,
doing so fearful a murder,
I want to borrow some clothes of yours.

Per ricoprir me stesso
in misfatto sì enorme
io vorrei le tue vesti.

DRUSILLA

Take my clothes, take my life, all I have
is yours.

E le vesti e le vene io ti darò . . .

OTHO

If I succeed with my plan,
we'll henceforth live united,
ever, we shall know love's perfection.
But if death is my fortune,
then give me funeral rites befitting pious
sorrow
as memorial, O Drusilla.
If my danger should force me to fly,
fearing the royal wrath of those in
power,
then help me in my misfortune.

Se occultarmi potrò vivremo poi
uniti sempre in dilettosi amori;

se morir converrammi,
nell'idioma d'un pietoso pianto

dimmi esequie, o Drusilla!
Se dovrò fuggitivo
scampar l'ira mortal di chi comanda,

soccorri a mie fortune.

DRUSILLA

All my garments and my lifeblood
I would give, oh most gladly.
But do go carefully, watchful of danger.
And now remember always
that all my fortune and my possessions —
those too I would give,
they'll be yours in all your wanderings.
And you shall find Drusilla
will prove such a noble mistress
that none in ancient times could show
her equal.
Let's go now.
My heart is rejoicing,
it's dancing within me.
Let's go, let's go now.
I'll change dresses, and my own hand
shall transform you to a woman.
But first I want to know in every detail
why you have undertaken this fearful
murder.

E le vesti e le vene
ti darò volentieri;
ma circospetto va', cauto procedi.
Nel rimanente sappi
che le fortune e le ricchezze mie

ti saran tributarie in ogni loco;
e proverai Drusilla
nobile amante, e tale,
che mai l'antica età non ebbe uguale.

Andiam pur.
Felice cor mio,
festeggiami in seno.
Andiam pur, ch'io mi spoglio.
E di mia man travestirti io voglio.

Ma vuo' da te saper più a dentro e a fondo
di così orrenda impresa la cagione.

OTHO

Let's go. Let's go together.
You will hardly believe it, when you
have heard it.

Andiam, andiamo omai,
che con alto stupore il tutto udrai.

Scene Ten. *The scene changes to Poppea's garden. Poppea, Arnalta*

POPPEA

Now that Seneca is buried,
I call on you, O Love.
Steer my hopes to a safe harbour,
make me Empress to Nero.

Or che Seneca è morto,
[14] Amor ricorro a te,
guida mia speme in porto,
fammi sposa al mio re.

ARNALTA

You are harping for ever
on this theme of marriage.

Pur sempre sulle nozze
canzoneggiando vai.

POPPEA

Of that, yes, Arnalta, I am always
thinking, and of nothing else.

Ad altro, Arnalta mia, non penso mai.

The most destructive passion	Il più inquieto affetto
is a mad ambition.	è la pazza ambizione;
But if you should achieve the crown and sceptre,	ma se arrivi agli scettri, alle corone,
do not forget your nurse:	non ti scordar di me,
keep me always at your side.	tiemmi appresso di te,
Be sure you never trust in any courtier;	nè ti fidar giammai di cortigiani,
for there are two examples	perchè in due cose sole
where Jove himself is powerless:	Giove è reso impotente:
he cannot introduce death into heaven,	ei non può far che in Cielo entri la morte,
nor can he find a courtier who is honest.	nè che la fede mai si trovi in corte.

No, never doubt,	Non dubitar, che meco
you'll always just as now be near me.	sarai sempre la stessa,
Be sure there will be no one other than you	e non fia mai che sia
to whom I trust my secrets.	altra che tu la secretaria mia.
I call on you, O Love,	Amor, ricorro a te,
steer my hopes to a safe harbour	guida mia speme in porto,
make me Em . . .	fammi sposa . . .
Ah, I think sleep is drawing me to close my eyes,	Par che'l sonno m'alletti
here in the lap of stillness.	a chiuder gl'occhi alla quiete in grembo.
Here in the garden, Arnalta, make me a bed,	Qui nel giardin, o Arnalta,
and I shall find refreshment;	fammi apprestar del riposare il modo,
for when one's sleepy, fresh air is pure enjoyment.	ch'alla fresc'aria addormentarmi godo.

Come quickly here, girls.	Udiste ancelle, olà!
Hullo. D'you hear me?	Udiste ancelle, olà!

If I should sleep so soundly	Se mi trasporta il sonno
that I don't wake as usual,	oltre gli spazi usati,
do you then come and wake me,	a risvegliarmi vieni,
and let nobody enter the garden	nè conceder l'ingresso nel giardino
except for Drusilla, or some other of my people.	fuor ch'a Drusilla, o ad altre confidenti.

Rest quietly, Poppea,	Adagiati, Poppea,
rest quietly, my dearest mistress,	acquietati, anima mia:
in peace here, and in safety.	sarai ben custodita.
Forgetfulness shall gently	Oblivion soave
dissolve all thoughts and feelings,	i dolci sentimenti
while you're sleeping, my daughter.	in te, figlia, addormenti.
You mischievous eyes, close tightly,	Posatevi occhi ladri,
when open, how you threaten,	aperti deh che fate,
if, when you're closed, you steal all hearts!	se chiusi anco rubate?
Sleep safely, sleep sound, Poppea.	Poppea, rimanti in pace;
Lovely eyelids veiling brightness,	luci care e gradite,
be drowsy now, and shrouded in darkness.	dormite omai, dormite.
You lovers, come admire	Amanti, vagheggiate
this miraculous picture,	il miracolo novo
for luminous and bright as ever, here our sky is shining,	è luminoso il dì, sì come suole,
and yet beside you, the sun is soundly sleeping.	e pur vedete addormentato il sole.

Scene Eleven. *Love*

Ritornello

Sleeping — she's rashly sleeping.	Dorme, l'incauta, dorme,
She does not know	ella non sa,
that soon we'll see	ch'or or verrà
the murderer approaching.	il punto micidiale;
So all humanity rests in oblivion,	così l'umanità vive all'oscuro,
and with its eyes tight fastened	e quando ha chiusi gl'occhi
thinks it may lead its life free and in safety.	crede essersi dal mal posta in sicuro.

Aria

O foolish frailty	[15] O sciocchi, o frali
of mortal senses,	sensi mortali
for while you lie in careless drowsy oblivion,	mentre cadete in sonnacchioso oblio
your sleep is guarded by ever-watchful heaven.	sul vostro sonno è vigilante Dio.

Ritornello

You'd be for ever	Siete rimasi
playthings of Fortune,	gioco de' casi
helpless in danger, while evil powers molest you,	soggetti al rischio, e del periglio prede,
if Love, strongest and greatest, did not help you.	se Amor, genio del mondo, non provvede.

Ritornello

Sleep well, Poppea,	Dormi, Poppea,
you earthly goddess:	terrena dea;
you will escape the onslaught of those who hate you,	ti salverà dall'armi altrui rubelle,
through Love that moves the sun and other stars.	Amor, che move il sole e l'altre stelle.

Ritornello

And now he's nearer,	Già s'avvicina
intent on murder;	la tua ruina;
but you'll not come to harm, you'll meet no danger;	ma non ti nuocerà strano accidente,
though Love's body is small, no power is stronger.	ch'Amor picciolo è, sì, ma onnipotente.

Scene Twelve. *Otho, Love, Poppea, Arnalta*

OTHO

Look at me — look what a transformation!	Eccomi trasformato
I am Otho no longer — I am changed to Drusilla. But no,	d'Otton in Drusilla; no
not changed to Drusilla,	non d'Otton in Drusilla,
but to a serpent so full of rage and venom	ma d'uom in serpe, al cui veleno, e rabbia
as never yet has been seen or heard of.	non vide il mondo, e non vedrà simile.
But what's here, O unhappy?	Ma che veggio infelice?
You're sleeping, dearest Poppea,	Tu dormi anima mia?
you closed your eyes here,	Chiudesti gl'occhi
to open never more?	per non aprirli più?
Eyes once so precious,	Care pupille,
kind Sleep has shut you tight,	il sonno vi serrò

in order that you might not witness this unnatural murder,
this cruel action by one who was your lover.
Alas, my spirit trembles, transfixed with horror,
my heart leaves its usual station,
it sinks into my shuddering entrails,
searching for a dark recess to hide in,
or shaken with its sobbing,
it tries to find a way out of my body,
for it would not be a part of such an outrage.
But why linger, why hesitate?   †
She hates me and despises, should I still love her?
I have promised Octavia; if I withdraw now,
I know that my own death must surely follow.
Life for a courtier has no place for mercy,
and he who cares for aught
except his own success, deserves his ruin.
The deed is done in secret,
and the stain on my conscience
will be washed in deep oblivion.
Poppea, I'll kill you. My love, my faith, my scruples, I renounce you.

affinchè non vediate
questi prodigi strani:
la vostra morte uscir dalle mie mani.

Ohimè, trema il pensiero, il moto langue,
e'l cor fuor del suo sito
ramingo per le viscere tremanti
cerca un cupo recesso per celarsi,
o involto in un singulto,
ei tenta di scampar fuor di me stesso,
per non partecipar d'un tanto eccesso.

Ma che tardo? Che bado?
Costei m'aborre, e sprezza, e ancor io l'amo?

Ho promesso ad Ottavia: se mi pento

accelero a miei dì funesto il fine.

Esca di corte chi vuol esser pio.

Colui ch'ad altro guarda,
ch'all'interesse suo, merta esser cieco.

Il fatto resta occulto,
la macchiata coscienza
si lava* con l'oblio,
Poppea, t'uccido; Amor, rispetti: addio.

LOVE

Wretched villain, foolish madman,
enemy to Love's divinity.
How do you dare to offend my godhead?
I should strike you down with lightning,
but you're not worthy of a death
by the hand of an immortal.
You go unharmed, and my sharp arrows will not pierce you.
No tribute shall Love accept from scoundrels.

Forsennato, scellerato,
inimico del mio nume,
tanto adunque si presume?
Fulminarti io dovrei,
ma non merti di morire
per la mano degli Dei.
Illeso va da questi strali acuti,

non tolgo al manigoldo i suoi tributi.

POPPEA

Drusilla, what are you doing?
Why are you holding that weapon?
I was fast asleep, here in the garden.

Drusilla, in questo modo?
Con l'armi ignude in mano,
mentre nel mio giardin dormo soletta?

ARNALTA

Quickly, quickly, come quickly —
all servants quickly — all the women quickly —
you must catch Drusilla — hurry, hurry.
Do not hesitate to kill so vile a monster.

Accorrete, accorrete,
o servi, o damigelle,

inseguir Drusilla, dalli, dalli,
tanto mostro a ferir non sia chi falli.

LOVE

I've defended Poppea.
I'll make her Empress.

Ho difesa Poppea.
vuo' farla imperatrice!

Sinfonia

---

† Later librettos have ten additional lines here, but no music survives for them.

* Monteverdi seems to have omitted 'finalmente', although it is in the libretto.

Act Three

Scene One. *The scene changes to the city of Rome. Drusilla*

DRUSILLA

O most happy Drusilla. O my hope — what do I hope for?	[16] O felice Drusilla, o che sper'io?
Let that hour come quickly which I long for.	Corre adesso per me l'ora fatale,
Fatal hour, when my rival is to die. She will die, my hated rival,	perirà, morirà la mia rivale,
and he, dearest Otho, will belong to Drusilla.	e Otton finalmente sarà mio.
O my hope — what do I hope for?	O che spero, che sper'io?
But if my garments	Se le mie vesti
have done their duty,	avran servito
if they have covered him and disguised him,	a ben coprirlo,
then, if you gods allow it,	con vostra pace, o dei,
my garments I'll praise, and give them worship.	adorar io vorrò gl'arnesi miei.
O most happy, most happy Drusilla.	O felice Drusilla, o che sper'io?

Scene Two. *Arnalta, Drusilla, Lictor [with other guards]*

ARNALTA

There is the wicked woman.	Ecco la scellerata
As she hoped to escape notice,	che, pensando occultarsi,
she has changed her clothing.	di vesti s'è mutata.

DRUSILLA

What accusation . . .	E qual peccato . . .

LICTOR

Hold your tongue — or you die.	Fermati, morta sei.

DRUSILLA

For what offences am I condemned to death?	E qual peccato mi conduce a morte?

LICTOR

You still deny it, wretched guilty woman?	Ancor t'infingi, sanguinaria indegna?
While Poppea was sleeping,	A Poppea dormiente
you attempted to kill her.	macchinasti la morte.

DRUSILLA

Ah, dear companion! Ah, evil fortune!	Ahi caro amico, ahi sorte,
Ah, my innocent garments!	ahi miei vesti innocenti!
There's no one else to blame here except Drusilla.	Di me dolermi deggio e non d'altrui,
Credulous, yes, and careless; far too rash and foolish.	credula troppo, e troppo incauta fui.

Scene Three. *Arnalta, Nero, Drusilla, Lictor [with other guards]*

ARNALTA

My lord, here is the criminal	Signor, ecco la rea
who attempted to kill	che trafigger tentò
the lady Poppea,	la matrona Poppea;
when innocently sleeping	dormiva l'innocente
all alone in her garden;	nel suo proprio giardino,
this woman burst upon her with weapon ready.	sopraggiunse costei col ferro ignudo,

If your devoted servant
had not luckily awakened,
that cruel blow had ended her existence.

se non si risvegliava
la tua devota ancella,
sopra di lei cadeva il colpo fiero.

NERO

How could you dare to do this, and
who induced you,
and plotted this act of treason?

Onde tanto ardimento? E chi t'indusse

rubella al tradimento?

DRUSILLA

I am innocent of treason.
This is known by my conscience, and
known in heaven.

Innocente son io,
lo sa la mia coscienza e lo sa dio.

NERO

No, no, confess it, confess it plainly.
Were you driven by hatred,
or were you compelled to do it by
another,
or did you lust for riches?

No, no confessa omai,
s'attentasti per odio
o se ti spinse l'autoritade,

o l'oro al gran misfatto.

DRUSILLA

I am innocent of treason.
This is known by my conscience, and
known in heaven.

Innocente son io,
lo sa la mia coscienza e lo sa dio.

NERO

Then whip her, scourge her, scald her:
make her reveal the person
who planned it and helped her.

Flagelli, funi e fochi
cavino da costei
il mandante e i correi.

DRUSILLA

Wretched that I am, I'd suffer
the fiercest of torments
before I would tell that which I must
keep secret.
So on my shoulders
must fall the sentence of doom, and I
must bear it.
Oh, all you who hold the worthy name
of lovers,
ah, model yourselves on me:
this is the faithful office of a true friend.

Misera me, piuttosto,
ch'un atroce tormento
mi sforzi a dir quel che tacer vorrei,

sopra me stessa toglio
la sentenza mortal, e il monumento.

O voi ch'al mondo vi chiamate amici,

deh, specchiatevi in me:
questi del vero amico son gl'uffici.

ARNALTA

What's this chatter, you trollop?

Che cinguetti ribalda?

LICTOR

Are you still busy plotting?

Che vaneggi assassina?

NERO

Are you talking of treason?

Che parli traditrice?

DRUSILLA

Conflicting and disputing within me
in fiercest battle
are love and innocence.

Contrastano in me stessa
con fiera concorrenza
amor e l'innocenza.

NERO

Soon the cruellest tortures
will prove to you the strength of Nero's
anger,
unless your obstinate spirit yields
and will confess your rebellious treason.

Prima ch'aspri tormenti
ti facciano sentir il mio disdegno,

or persuadi all'ostinato ingegno
di confessar gl'orditi tradimenti.

DRUSILLA

My lord, I was the miscreant who tried to murder	Signor, io fui la rea, ch'uccider volli
the innocent Poppea.	l'innocente Poppea.
My brain and my hand only *	Quest'alma, e questa mano
were accomplices in murder.	fur le complici sole;
As to my motive — a hatred deriving from old times —	a ciò m'indusse un odio occulto antic
enquire no more, for it's the truth I tell you.	non cercar più, la verità ti dico.

NERO

Take the woman to where	Conducete costei
the executioner awaits her.	al carnefice omai,
Tell him to find some method	fate ch'egli ritrovi,
before her final dying	con una morte a tempo,
to prolong for her the bitterest agony,	qualche lunga amarissima agonia
and poison the ending of this monster.	ch'inasprisca la morte a questa ria.

DRUSILLA

O my dearest beloved,	Adorato mio bene
think of me still when buried,	amami almen sepolta
and on my tomb I pray you,	e sul sepolcro mio
weep in the days to come	mandino gl'occhi tuoi
tears which shall spring from your heart most sincerely;	sol una volta dalle fonti del core
tears if not of love, at least of pity.	lacrime di pietà, se non d'amore;
For I go, as truest friend and faithful lover,	ch'io vado fida amica e vera amante
to die with evil felons,	tra i manigoldi irati
and with my own blood to cover your sinful actions.	a coprir col mio sangue i tuoi peccati.

NERO

You're too slow, my attendants.	Che si tarda, o ministri,
Take her away for torture,	con una atroce fine
let her suffer	provi, provi costei
a thousand deaths before she dies, a thousand torments.	mille morti oggi mai, mille ruine.

Scene Four. *Otho, Drusilla, Nero, Guards*

OTHO

No, no. Let this terrible sentence	No, no questa sentenza
fall on me, only on me, for I am guilty.	cada sopra di me, che ne son degno.

DRUSILLA

No, for I was the miscreant	Io fui la rea ch'uccider
who tried to murder the innocent Poppea.	volli l'innocente Poppea.

OTHO

Heaven and all the gods must be my witness	Siatemi testimoni, o cieli,
that she is wholly guiltless.	o dei, innocente è costei.

---

* According to Curtis, in whose edition the music for these four lines was published for the first time, there are reasons why this beautiful passage may not be by Monteverdi. If they are omitted, however, he argues that Nero might be expected to go on looking for a way to blame Octavia. Drusilla's confession satisfies Nero, even if it is perhaps odd that he accepts this invented motivation of 'un odio occulto antico'.

My brain and my hand only
were accomplices in murder.
As to my motives — a hatred of long
standing —
do not question, for it's the truth
I tell you.

Quest'alma, e questa mano
fur le complici sole;
a ciò m'indusse un odio occult'antico;

non cercar più, la verità ti dico.

OTHO

She is guiltless, I swear it.
It was I who was disguised in the clothes of
Drusilla,
and went at the command of the Empress
Octavia
to carry out the murder of Poppea.
Therefore my lord, on me must fall
the judgement.

Innocente è costei.
Io con le vesti di Drusilla andai,

per ordine d'Ottavia imperatrice

ad attentar la morte di Poppea.
Dammi, signor, con la tua man la morte.

DRUSILLA

But I, I was the miscreant
who tried to murder the innocent Poppea.

Io fui la rea ch'uccider
volli l'innocente Poppea.

OTHO

Jove and the Goddess of Vengeance
now must strike me with lightning,
for in just retribution
the terrible scaffold I know awaits me.

Giove, Nemesi, Astrea
fulminate il mio capo,
che per giusta vendetta
il patibolo orrendo a me s'aspetta.

DRUSILLA

For me, it's waiting.

A me s'aspetta.

OTHO

For me, it's waiting.

A me s'aspetta.

DRUSILLA

For me.

A me.

OTHO

For me, it's waiting.
Deal me, my lord, by your own hand
the sentence.
If you're unwilling that I should have
the honour
of a death so illustrious,
then let me live deprived of your favour,
and spend my weary days far from your
presence.
If you wish to torment me,
then my own conscience will provide the
scourges.
If to lions and bears you wish to throw
me,
merely leave me to brood upon my
actions:
these will devour my flesh, every morsel.

A me s'aspetta.
Dammi, signor, con la tua man la
morte;
e se non vuoi che la tua mano adorni;

di decoro il mio fine,
mentre della tua grazia io resto privo,
all'infelicità lasciami vivo.

Se tu vuoi tormentarmi
la mia coscienza ti darà i flagelli,

s'a leoni, ed a gl'orsi espormi vuoi

dammi in preda al pensier de le mie
colpe,
che mi divorerà l'ossa, e le polpe.

NERO

Live then, but go to the remotest deserts,
and stripped of all your titles and your
fortune,
existing as a miserable beggar,

Vivi, ma va ne' più remoti lidi
di titoli spogliato, e di fortune,

e serva a te mendico, e derelitto,

186

in caverns and scourgings find retribution.
And you, who dared such danger,
O noble Roman lady,
to shield this man from punishment,
and have lied for the sake of his safety,
live for the honour of my royal mercy,
live for the glory of your noble courage.
Henceforth, to your own sex in every era
let your great loyalty provide a shining pattern.

di flagello, e spelonca il tuo delitto.
E tu ch'ardisti tanto,
o nobile matrona,
per ricoprir costui
d'apportar salutifere bugie,
vivi alla fama della mia clemenza,
vivi alle glorie della tua fortezza,
e sia del sesso tuo nel secol nostro

la tua costanza un adorabil mostro.

DRUSILLA

Let me go into exile,
ah, gracious lord, allow it.
If I go with him, how happy a journey!

In esilio con lui
deh, signor mio consenti
ch'io tragga i dì ridenti.

NERO

Go then, if so you wish it.

Vanne, com'a te piace.

OTHO

My lord, my lord, I am not punished, nor am I banished.
For with her I shall find perfect happiness and blessing,
joy unceasing.

Signor, non son punito, anzi beato;

la virtù di costei sarà ricchezza,

e gloria a' giorni miei.

DRUSILLA

So long as I am with you,
nothing else I desire now.
I shall return to Fortune
what was once my deserving,
so you may believe that the heart of woman
contains a faith unswerving.

Ch'io viva, o mora teco:
altro non voglio.
Dono alla mia fortuna
tutto ciò che mi diede,
purchè tu riconosca in cor di donna

una costante fede.

NERO

I have decreed and decided,
by imperial edict
to repudiate Octavia.
From Rome I order that she be exiled,
never to return here.

Delibero e risolvo
con editto solenne
il ripudio d'Ottavia,
e con perpetuo esilio
da Roma io la proscrivo.

Let her be taken to the nearest harbour;
let a seaworthy vessel
quickly prepare to leave here,
and then commit her to the fancy of the winds and the billows.
Such treatment they deserve who offend me.
Now hurry to obey me.

Sia pur condotta al più vicino lido
le s'appresti in momenti
qualche spalmato legno
e sia commessa al bersaglio de'venti.

Convengo giustamente risentirmi.

Volate ad ubbidirmi.

Scene Five. *Poppea, Nero*

POPPEA

My lord, surely today I'm beginning —
I'm born again to this new existence with you.
Sighs I am breathing deeply, so deeply,
to assure and persuade you
that reborn for your love I'm dying for you,
and that dying or living, each hour I adore you.

Signor, oggi rinasco, e i primi fiati
di questa nova vita,

voglio che sian sospiri
che ti facciano fede
che, rinata per te, languisco e moro,

e morendo e vivendo ogn'or t'adoro.

187

Drusilla's not the guilty one who tried to take your life.	Non fu Drusilla, no, ch'ucciderti tentò.

Then who, then who was guilty?	Chi fu, chi fu il fellone?

Our friend, the noble Otho.	Il nostro amico Ottone.

Otho alone?	Egli da sè?

Octavia gave the order.	D'Ottavia fu il pensiero.

Why now you have reason to proceed with divorcing her; to reject her, divorce her.	Or hai giusta cagione di passar al ripudio.

This day as I have promised, my consort I shall make you.	Oggi, come promisi, mia sposa tu sarai.

So dear a day — such a precious day — I never thought to see.	Sì caro dì veder non spero mai.

By the great name of Jove, and by my honour, you shall today, I swear it, be Empress of Rome's great empire. On the royal command you may believe it.	Per il nome di Giove e per il mio, oggi sarai, ti giuro, di Roma imperatrice, in parola regal te n'assicuro.

On the royal . . .	In parola . . .

On the royal command.	In parola regal.

On the royal command . . .	In parola regal?

You may believe it.	In parola regal te n'assicuro.

Idol whom my heart worships, surely the time is come when I may taste my joy?	Idolo del cor mio, giunta è pur l'ora ch'io del mio ben godrò.

No more shall destiny delay our union.	Ne più s'interporrà noia e dimora.

No more.	Ne più.

No more shall destiny delay our union.	Ne più s'interporrà noia e dimora.

There's no heart in my breast,	Cor nel petto non ho:
you have robbed me.	me'l rubasti —

NERO

You have robbed me, yes.	Me'l rubasti, sì, sì.

POPPEA

This heart you stole away, with your	Dal sen me lo rapì de' tuoi begl'occhi —
bright glances.	

NERO

This heart you stole away with your	Dal sen me lo rapì de' tuo' begl'occhi
bright glances,	
your eyes so calm and lucid.	il lucido sereno —

POPPEA

Through you my dearest, I own a heart	Per te, ben mio, non ho più cor in seno.
no longer.	
Hold me tightly enfolded.	Stringerò tra le braccia innamorate
Thus I clasp you by whom I am wounded.	chi mi trafisse, ohimè!
Our happy hours shall never now be ended,	Non interrotte avrò l'ore beate,
and if in you I'm lost,	Se son perduta in te,
in you I shall be found.	in te mi cercarò,
Then I shall try	in te mi trovarò,
to be lost again, my dearest.	e tornerò a riperdermi, ben mio.
For always it is my longing thus to be	Che sempre in te perduta esser vogl'io.
lost in you.	

Scene Six. *Octavia* *

OCTAVIA

Ah, farewell, Rome, I leave you.	[17] Addio Roma, addio patria, amici addio.
Farewell, friends, I leave you.	
Ah, my country, I leave you.	
Though I'm blameless, I am banished	Innocente da voi partir conviene.
for ever.	
Now I go into exile in bitter sorrow,	Vado a patir l'esilio in pianti amari,
I shall sail, quite despairing, the cruel	navigo disperata i sordi mari.
oceans.	
Breezes which from hour to hour	L'aria, che d'ora in ora
will receive my sighs,	riceverà i miei fiati,
will surely bear them with my name	li porterà, per nome del cor mio,
upon them	
to seek out and to kiss the walls of my	a veder, a baciar le patrie mura,
city.	
And meanwhile, alone and friendless,	ed io starò solinga,
I shall wander and mark out my path	alternando le mosse ai pianti, ai passi,
with weeping;	
I shall teach compassion to rocks and	insegnando pietade ai tronchi, ai sassi.
bushes.	
Now I call you to look, you cruel people, †	Remigate oggi mai perverse genti,
for I am leaving for ever, this my	allontanarmi dagli amati lidi.
beloved homeland.	
Ah, sacrilegious sorrow,	Ahi, sacrilegio duolo,
you will not let me weep,	tu m'interdici il pianto

---

* Curtis notes that Scenes Six and Seven are reversed in both scores, and in the
Naples 1651 libretto. He surmises that Anna Renzi, who created the role of
Octavia, may have insisted on the change in sequence so that she would not be
'upstaged when followed by the male comic who played Arnalta'.

† 'Remigate . . . lidi': Curtis notes that these lines only appear in one of the librettos
(Naples 1651) and are probably not by Busenello. They are in both scores.

although I'm leaving my country,	mentre lascio la patria,
nor may I shed a tear, though I must sever	nè stillar una lacrima poss'io,
from family, and friends, and country — for ever.	mentre dico ai parenti e a Roma: addio.

Scene Seven. *Arnalta*

ARNALTA

Now today will Poppea	Oggi sarà Poppea
be honoured in Rome as Empress.	di Roma imperatrice;
I then her Nurse and attendant	io che son la nutrice,
shall climb on high to share in her new grandeur.	[18] ascenderò delle grandezze i gradi:
No, no, no longer shall I mix with the herd.	no, no, col volgo io non m'abbasso più:
Those who would speak as familiars,	chi mi diede del tu,
all now with honey-sweet voices	or con dolce armonia
will warble softly: 'Your Ladyship is gracious. Your Ladyship's kind.'	gorgheggierammi 'il Vostra Signoria'.
In the street if they meet me, they'll greet me: 'Oh, how young you are looking.'	Chi m'incontra per strada
'Yes, you look so young, and as beautiful as ever' —	mi dice 'bella donna, e fresca ancora',
though really I know I look	ed io pur so che sembro
like the ugly witches we hear about in stories —	delle Sibille il leggendario antico;
but all of them will flatter me,	ma ognun così m'adula,
thus thinking they can win me	credendo guadagnarmi
to intercede for favours from Poppea.	per interceder grazie da Poppea:
And I, pretending not to perceive the falsehood,	ed io fingendo non capir le frodi,
from bumpers of deception I'll drink their praises.	in coppa di bugia bevo le lodi.
I was born a servant, and I shall die a lady.	Io nacqui serva, e morirò matrona;
I do not wish to die,	mal volentier morrò;
but if I were born again,	se rinascessi un dì,
I'd be born as a lady, and die a servant.	vorrei nascer matrona e morir serva.
For those in high position	Chi lascia le grandezze,
draw weeping their final breath;	piangendo a morte va;
but servants greet their death	* ma chi servendo sta,
as something happier than what they're leaving,	con più felice sorte,
and perceive in their dying, an end to their grieving.	come fin degli stenti ama la morte.

Finale composed by Francesco Sacrati (and Benedetto Ferrari?)

Scene Eight. *The scene changes to Nero's royal palace. Nero, Poppea, Consuls, Tribunes, Love, Venus in Heaven, Chorus of Cupids*

NERO

Ascending, O dearest treasure,	Ascendi, o mia diletta,
from your high station,	della sovrana altezza
now climb to yet dizzier heights of glory,	all'apice sublime,
caressed by heavenly spirits,	blandita dalle glorie
whose purpose is to serve you and to cherish.	ch'ambiscono servirti come ancelle.

---

* This line is not set to music in either of the scores although it is in all the libretto.

Cries of welcome, acclamations resound
  from the earth and from the heavens.
You must reckon among your triumphs,
with the choicest trophies,
O beloved Poppea, the love of Nero.

Acclamata dal mondo e dalle stelle,

scrivi del tuo trionfo
tra i più cari trofei,
adorata Poppea, gl'affetti miei.

Now my spirit, bewildered
by such a dazzling brilliance,
all but loses the power,
my lord, to truly thank you.
Upon this lofty summit
where you have placed me,
to pay my homage fully,
my humble strength and my spirit fail me.
If Nature had ever conceived
such overwhelming emotions,
she would have made a second heart to feel
  them.

Il mio genio confuso,
al non usato lume,
quasi perde il costume,
signor, di ringraziarti.
Se quest'eccelse cime,
ove mi collocasti,
per venerarti a pieno,
io non ho cor che basti.
Doveva la natura,
al soprapiù degli eccessivi affetti,
un core a parte fabbricar ne' petti.

Passacaglia

Now to shine in your eyebeams
the sun has shrunk in size,
and to be housed in your bosom,
morning has left the sky.
And to make you supreme over women
  and deities,
Jove all the stars in heaven has lavished
  on your features
and so consumed perfection.

Per capirti negl'occhi
il sol s'impicciolì,
per albergarti in seno
l'alba dal ciel partì,
e per farti sovrana a donne e a dee,

Giove nel tuo bel viso,

stillò le stelle e consumò l'idee.

By permission, may my spirit go
from this labyrinth of loving praises,
of praise so overwhelming,
and make obeisance to you as it is
  fitting:
my king, my husband and my lord, my
  blessing.

Dà licenza al mio spirto,
ch'esca dall'amoroso laberinto
di tante lodi e tante,
e che s'umilii a te, come conviene,

mio re, mio sposo, mio signor, mio bene.

Look there, they are coming now,
the Consuls and the Tribunes,
to do you homage, O dearest.
At sight of you, already the Senate and
  the people
at length begin to know they are truly
  blessed.

Ecco vengono i consoli e i tribuni
per riverirti, o cara:
nel solo rimirarti,
il popolo e'l senato

omai comincia a divenir beato.

Sinfonia

To you, our Sovereign and Empress,
We come, to carry out the will of Rome,
  our Mother.
At her command, we crown you.
To you Asia, to you Africa, pay homage.
To you our Europe and the sea
which joins and encircles our mighty
  Empire,
consecrate humbly and offer this
for your crowning and your reward and
  honour.

A te, sovrana augusta
con il consenso universal di Roma —

indiademiam la chioma.
A te l'Asia, a te l'Africa s'atterra;
a te l'Europa, e'l mar che cinge e serra
quest'impero felice,

ora consacra e dona
questa del mondo imperial corona.

CUPIDS

Descend, my companions, swiftly on pinions flying, seek out the married lovers; come flying to the fortunate lovers.	Scendiam, compagni alati, voliam ai sposi amati.

LOVE

And to attend us, resplendently are shining the highest deities.	Al nostro volo risplendano assistenti i sommi Divi.

CUPIDS

And now we see from the farthest pole come rays flaming more brightly.	Dall'alto polo se veggian fiammeggiar raggi più vivi.

LOVE

Since the Consuls and the Tribunes, Poppea, chose to crown you over all regions of empire, now Love comes to crown you, among women most happy, as the queen above all other beauties. Venus, Mother, by your permission, you are like Poppea in heaven, she is Venus here on earth.	Se i consoli e i tribuni, Poppea, t'han coronato sopra provincie e regni, or ti corona Amor, donna felice, come sopra le belle imperatrice. Madre, sia con tua pace tu in cielo sei Poppea, questa è Venere in terra.

VENUS

I must take pleasure, my dear son, in all that is pleasing to you. Then bestow on Poppea the title of a goddess.	Io, io mi compiacio o figlio di quanto aggrada a te; diasi pur a Poppea il titolo di Dea.

CHORUS OF CUPIDS WITH LOVE AND VENUS

Now with gladness let praises be
   sounded
on earth and in heaven, all creatures
   rejoice,
let your joy be unbounded.
Let every region throughout the Empire
re-echo with the cry: 'Hail Nero and
   Poppea!'
	Or cantiamo giocondo,
	
	in terra e in Cielo, il gioir sovrabbondi,
	
	e in ogni clima, in ogni regione
	si senta rimombar 'Poppea e Nerone'.

NERO AND POPPEA

I adore you. I desire you. I embrace you, now I bind you. No more grieving, no more sorrow, O my dearest, my dearest treasure.	[19] Pur ti miro, pur ti godo, pur ti stringo, pur t'annodo più non peno, più non moro, o mia vita, o mio tesoro.

POPPEA

I am yours.	Io son tua.

NERO

I am yours.	Tuo son io.

BOTH

You alone are my soul, tell me so. Yes, my { love, heart, my life, yes.	Speme mia, l'idol mio, tu sei pure, dillo dì. Sì, mio { ben, cor mia vita, sì.

The end of the opera.

The Revival of Monteverdi's Operas in the Twentieth Century

Jeremy Barlow

In the nineteenth century scarcely anyone had heard a note of Monteverdi's music, yet the three pages devoted to him in the first edition of *Grove* (1880) begin 'MONTEVERDE, CLAUDIO, the originator of the Modern style of Composition . . .' and leave no doubt of his historical significance (even if the writer, like many others before and since, believed the composer's bolder harmonic progressions to be careless mistakes, and stated that 'it would be absurd to suppose that such evil-sounding combinations could have been introduced deliberately'). The article reflected a growing interest in Monteverdi among musicologists; in Germany a year later a scholarly edition of *Orfeo* was published, edited by Robert Eitner. Actual performances of *Orfeo* and the other two operas (at first in concert versions) date from the early years of this century and were initiated through the efforts and enthusiasm of the French composer Vincent d'Indy. His arrangement of *Orfeo* was first performed in Paris in 1904; versions of *Poppea* and *Ulysses* were given in 1908 and 1925 respectively. All three operas were translated into French and contained enormous cuts; the lengthy *Poppea* and *Ulysses* are reduced by d'Indy to slender volumes. D'Indy stated that the function of his editions was not musicological, but 'simply to facilitate concert or even stage performance'. His first staged performance of *Orfeo* took place in Paris in 1911.

In the preface to his edition of *Poppea* (1908), d'Indy chided the Italians for lack of interest in their own composer, writing that the opera had 'remained ignored even — one might say, above all — in its country of origin'. However, the very next year saw a concert performance of *Orfeo* in Milan, based on a new edition by the critic and now forgotten composer Giacomo Orefice; it was dissatisfaction with this edition (which, like d'Indy's, contains many cuts) that led Malipiero to produce the most useful and influential of the early editions; first a vocal score of *Orfeo* (1923), and then full scores of all three operas, as part of his complete Monteverdi edition (1926-42). Britain had to wait until 1924 for a concert performance in London of *Orfeo* (d'Indy's version), although the following year the opera was given as the first production of the Oxford University Opera Club (sung in English), using a much more complete edition prepared by the youthful musicologist Jack Westrup.

D'Indy was the first in a long line of twentieth-century composers to produce versions of the Monteverdi operas. The main factors which appear to have fired their imaginations are the apparently incomplete scores, the archetypal qualities perceived in both the subject matter and the historical, pioneering role of the operas, and, in the case of the Italians, an element of national interest and pride. More important names to have been involved include, in order of seniority, d'Indy (all three operas, 1904-1926), Respighi (*Orfeo*, 1935), Malipiero (all three operas, 1923 onwards), Orff (*Orfeo*, or in his title, *Orpheus*, several versions, 1923-40), Hindemith (*Orfeo*, 1943), Krenek (*Poppea*, 1935), Dallapiccola (*Ulysses*, 1942), Maderna (*Orfeo*, 1967), Berio, as the director of a project involving five young Italian composers (*Orfeo*, 1984), and Henze (*Ulysses*, 1982). All these versions, except the Hindemith and Berio, have been available to the public, and most, as might be expected, reflect a desire to recreate and revitalise the operas in the composers' own terms. Exceptions are the editions by d'Indy, Malipiero, and also Hindemith; the latter was the first editor to envisage, and eventually (in Vienna, 1954) to organise, a performance entirely with period instruments. Although d'Indy did not aim at a personal re-interpretation of the scores and believed that his harmonic realisation of the continuo 'conformed to the style in use in seventeenth-century Italy', his arrangements, as stated above, did not have a musicological basis and now seem very dated. Malipiero's editions, although rendered obsolete by subsequent research and developments in musicological practice, have stood the test of time much better; his vocal score of *Orfeo* is still useful today if one disregards the continuo realisation.

Musicologists' editions include Eitner (*Orfeo*, 1881), Goldschmidt (*Poppea*, 1904), van den Borren (*Poppea*, 1914), Haas (*Ulysses*, 1922), Westrup (*Orfeo*, 1925), Redlich (*Orfeo*, 1936 and *Poppea*, 1958), Dart (*Orfeo*, 1950), Stevens (*Orfeo*, 1967), Tarr (*Orfeo*, 1974), Bartlett (*Poppea*, 1988 and *Orfeo*, 1990) and Curtis (*Poppea*, 1989). Several of the musicologists have had dual careers as performers; Dart, Stevens and Curtis have all directed performances of their own editions. A majority of these editions have been published; only Westrup, Redlich (*Orfeo*), Dart and Bartlett (*Poppea*) remain unavailable.

The dividing line between musicologists and performers becomes further blurred when one considers the many conductors with a strong interest in Monteverdi who have produced their own editions for particular productions or recordings; of the 26 recordings listed in the discography, only five conductors have used editions other than their own. Conductors' editions include Wenzinger (*Orfeo*, 1955), W. Goehr (*Poppea*, 1960), Leppard (*Orfeo*, 1965, *Poppea*, 1966 and *Ulysses*, 1979), Harnoncourt (*Orfeo*, 1968, *Ulysses*, 1971 and *Poppea*, 1974), Glover (*Orfeo*, 1975), Norrington (*Ulysses*, 1978), Gardiner (*Orfeo*, 1985), Daniel (*Ulysses*, 1989), and Pickett (*Orfeo*, 1991) (see also the discography). Of these, only the Wenzinger, Goehr and Leppard (*Poppea*) editions have been made available in editions for sale to the public.*

Despite the fact that the Monteverdi revival goes back to the beginning of the century, it is really only since the 1967 quatercentenary of his birth that he has been fully accepted as a mainstream classical composer, rather than an important historical figure (compare, for example, the number of recordings before and since then in the discography). It was at about that time too that musicians such as David Munrow and Nikolaus Harnoncourt began to make original instrument performances of renaissance and baroque music the norm rather then the experimental exception. Now it is the composers re-interpreting the operas, such as Henze and Berio, who have become the experimenters, consciously swimming against the tide of historical 'authenticity'.

The methods of realising Monteverdi's operas have been transformed by the increasing availability of copies of period instruments, and by the increasing skill of their performers; skill not just in instrumental technique, but in the case of the continuo players (keyboards and plucked string instruments), ability at realising the correct chords in an appropriate style from a bass line. Almost all the vocal solos in the Monteverdi operas are scored just on two staves — vocal line and bass — with (apart from in *Orfeo*) no instrumental indications. Until recently, any modern score of a Monteverdi opera had to indicate which instruments should play the chords implied by this top-and-bottom score, and also to write out the chords to be played. Today, plenty of harpsichordists and some lutenists can realise a continuo accompaniment at sight from a bass line, and conductors can acquire, from the

---

* For more detailed lists and descriptions of Monteverdi editions up to the mid-1980s, see *The New Monteverdi Companion*, ed. Arnold and Fortune, 1985, and, for *Orfeo* in particular, the Cambridge Opera Handbook on the opera, 1986, with its excellent article 'The rediscovery of *Orfeo*' by Nigel Fortune.

most recent research and editions, the knowledge to make an informed choice of continuo instruments. Leppard's scores of *Orfeo* and *Poppea* from the 1960s indicate precisely which instruments are to play the continuo and what notes they are to play; Curtis's edition of *Poppea* (1989) and Bartlett's of *Orfeo* (1990) have editorial figures added to the bass line, but no chordal realisations or editorial instrumental indications in the music. Edward Tarr's edition of *Orfeo* (1974) represents an intermediate stage; he provides skeletal chords, not intended to be played as they stand, but to be used as a basis for embellishment and re-arrangement by the performers.

Yet the introduction of period instruments into the operas has not been a clear cut revolution because the many different instruments needed have not all become available, with players, at the same time; the harpsichord was revived early in the century, whereas the cornett did not become widely available until the late 1960s. The design, construction and resulting sound of the instruments appropriate to Monteverdi, such as the lute, harpsichord, recorder and viol, have changed greatly over the past 25 years, as instrument makers, instead of building 'improved' versions incorporating nineteenth- and twentieth-century technology, have gone back to copying originals more or less faithfully. These copies have led to an increasing awareness of the difference in sound between renaissance and baroque versions of the same instrument. Until recently (and even now), early string players have tended to use baroque violins and 'Corelli' bows c.1700 as instruments suitable for anything from Monteverdi to early Mozart (understandably, for economic reasons); yet the renaissance violin and bow suitable for *Orfeo* produces as different a sound from the mid-baroque violin as the latter does from a modern instrument. One only has to compare the classic recordings of *Orfeo* conducted by Wenzinger in 1955 and by Gardiner 30 years later, to hear how the sound world of supposedly 'authentic' performances has changed. It continues to change; Pickett's 1991 recording sounds still lighter-textured than Gardiner's. This lightening of texture has taken place in early music performances generally, and has a particular justification in *Orfeo*. Some performers in the past have been misled by the size of Monteverdi's instrumental forces to envisage some kind of operatic spectacular; thanks to Iain Fenlon's research we now know that the work may have been performed in a relatively small room. The traditional view, questioned by Fenlon, is that the venue was either the Galleria degli Specchi or the Galleria dei Fiumi in the ducal palace. Even these are nothing like a theatre; Philip Pickett visited the palace as background research for his recording, and feels that the smaller Galleria dei Fiumi would have been a particularly appropriate setting: it measures approximately 10 x 30 metres!

Discussion on the performance of the Monteverdi operas now centres on four main points: the completeness of the original scores and the extent to which they represent Monteverdi's intentions; the extent to which one can reconstruct his intentions if the scores *are* incomplete; the value of attempting to reconstruct the composer's intentions in terms of instrumental sound, when we listen with twentieth-century ears in the very different performing environment of a modern opera house, with its associated repertory and performing styles which we cannot eliminate from our consciousness; and finally the value of attempting to recreate the music of the original production, when little may be known about its staging and cast, and when discrepancies between the earliest surviving scores and librettos suggest that contemporary revivals may have altered the music either to incorporate lessons learned from the première or to suit a new occasion, employed new singers with vocal ranges necessitating transpositions, and made use of different instrumental forces.

A distinction needs to be made between *Orfeo*, where the published edition of 1609 (reprinted in 1615) had Monteverdi's authority, and the other two surviving operas, where only manuscript sources of the music survive, of arguable authority and completeness. Much of the controversy over *Ulysses* and *Poppea* has focused on the incompleteness of the scores, and whether Monteverdi's methods in *Orfeo*, composed nearly 35 years previously for a court performance with lavish funding, can be applied to them, since they were composed for performances in the early public opera houses, with consequent economic restraints on orchestral forces.

Here I have constructed, from their writings, a dialogue between performers and musicologists on the controversial issues of embellishment and orchestration when attempting a historical realisation; this is followed by statements of aims from some of the composers who have re-interpreted the operas. Finally, the views of two music critics, separated by 22 years, illustrate Dallapiccola's point that interpretative editions or 'musical translations' may have, like literary translations, a limited life span.

Embellishment in 'Orfeo'

Nikolaus Harnoncourt (1968)
For improvisatory embellishments by the singers there are indeed many instructional works, but there are also contemporary voices, particularly regarding the works of Monteverdi, warning that nothing, or as little as possible, should be added to the musical text. Indeed, Monteverdi has written out more embellishments than any other composer of his time, and it is quite obvious that where he did not write any embellishments he did not want any sung [...] In our opinion embellishment should be applied even *more* sparingly in a gramophone recording than in a concert, since every improvisation is fundamentally something unique which, when heard again — especially when heard again repeatedly — becomes ridiculous.

(Sleeve notes to 1968 recording; see discography)

Edward H. Tarr (1974)
We have avoided suggesting ornamentation [of the continuo realisation in this edition], for two reasons. In the first place, we wish to encourage well-schooled performers to invent their own ornaments. In the second place, the sound of a large number of continuo instruments playing in unison an ornament written out by the editor is hardly in keeping with the improvisatory nature of baroque performance. We have avoided suggesting ornamentation in the vocal parts for similar reasons[...] More ornamentation should probably be expected from the leading singers, especially Orpheus, than from those singing minor roles. In no case should ornamentation interfere with declamation during narrative passages.

(Introduction to Tarr's edition of *Orfeo*, Editions Costallet, Paris)

John Eliot Gardiner (1985)
During this recording[...] we never fixed or standardised ornaments, which were prompted, rather, by the mood and skill of each singer and, to some extent, by the relative status of the character sung: the more godlike the character (for example, Orpheus, or, still more, Apollo), the more elaborate and extravagant the embellishment! Nor were the solo obbligato players restrained in any way from ornamenting their lines, even against a simultaneous simple statement of a ritornello by the ripieno player.

(Sleeve note to 1985 recording; see discography)

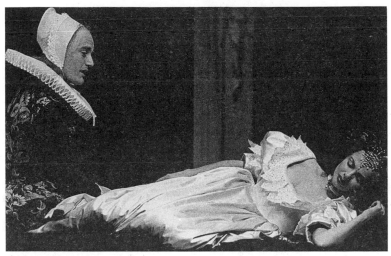

Eirian James as Poppea and Christopher Eillett as Arnalta in Jonathan Hales' 1986 production for Kent Opera, conducted by Ivan Fischer and designed by Roger Butlin (photo: Robert Workman)

Instrumentation in 'Ulysses' and 'Poppea'

Raymond Leppard, describing his realisation of the bass line in Act One, scene nine, the quarrel between Seneca and Nero, in 'Poppea' (1988):
It seems to me suitable for Nero to be accompanied by harpsichord and 'cello playing *staccato* chords, Seneca by harp, reed organ and bass playing softly and sustained until he begins to lose his temper. When the music moves into connected, regular metre ('Force is law in time of peace'), the strings can enter and, reflecting the character of the continuo instruments, I used the upper strings for Nero and the lower for Seneca.

(*Authenticity in Music*, Faber Music, London, 1988)

Alan Curtis (1989)
The true 'realisation' of a baroque opera score can only occur in performance. There were, and still are, very good reasons why an artistic, imaginative, and therefore correct continuo performance was not, should not, and cannot properly be written out.

To a greater extent than any other well-known opera, *Poppea* is a sung play [. . .] Busenello's libretto is highly dramatic and could [. . .] sustain the interest of a modern audience even without music. What is more, the vocal lines [. . .] are themselves so intensely charged with drama that the piece could be successfully performed with only continuo accompaniment. The 'orchestra' in fact supplies only incidental music: ritornellos or sinfonias mostly 10-20 seconds in length, intended to[. . .] provide variety, but not primarily in the anachronistic sense of supplying 'instrumental colour'. It is the voice that counts[. . .] Historical evidence does not support the addition of instruments other than continuo to perform simultaneously with voices in *Poppea*.

[The chordal continuo usual in seventeenth-century Venice consisted of] two harpsichords and one or two instruments of the lute family[. . .] The organ was not normally used in the theatre at this time, and the harp seems to have been more in use for chamber music than for opera.

(Introduction to Curtis's edition of *Poppea*, Novello, London, 1989)

Nikolaus Harnoncourt (1984)
In contrast to the all-too-liberal arrangers, there are those representing the opposite extreme: super purists who only want to realise the handed-down, skeletal score and reject any additions. This sort of loyalty to the work does not serve the intention of the composer, since it negates the presuppositions on which he has based his work. It is just as incorrect to reveal only the 'skeleton' which was written down by Monteverdi as to cover it with inappropriate 'flesh' of a much later age — as frequently happens.

(Article on *Ulysses* reprinted in *The Musical Dialogue*, translated by Mary O'Neill, published by Christopher Helm, Bromley, Kent, 1989; the German original was published by Residenz Verlag, Salzburg and Wien, 1984)

Alan Curtis (1989)
This is not to say that d'Indy, Krenek, Ghedini, Malipiero, Goehr, Leppard, Harnoncourt, et al were wrong[. . .] It is all 'a matter of taste'. It is high time, however, that the public be made aware of the historical facts (too often obscured by so-called musicologists), and that modern arrangements (whether or not for 'original' instruments) be no longer allowed to masquerade as 'realisations', or as having anything whatever to do with the composer's intentions. Seventeenth-century operas scores are not 'sketches' in need of completion, or 'skeletons' needing to be filled out. They are, in the majority of cases, full scores in need only of intelligent, sensitive editing and interpretation.

(Introduction to Curtis's edition of *Poppea*; see above)

Paul Daniel (1989)
We can add or take away instruments as the scene or even the phrase progresses to mirror those subtleties [of performance], and must avoid at all costs the attempts in earlier editions to strait-jacket the music into a pre-determined metrical or orchestral shape[. . .] the only criterion we can have in rehearsing is Monteverdi's own — simply that the singer must 'speak through singing'. There is always the temptation, in some cases justified, to add to this music. Taking my cue from Monteverdi's instructions in an earlier score that a similar band of solo strings, harpsichords and chitarrone could be 'doubled or extended, if the size of the room suggests this', I have added to the tiny pit band (imposed on the composer by financial constraints) only one harp and two recorders, but none of the string orchestra or trombones, cornetts and other wind, for which I believe Monteverdi would have written more, or certainly different, music if he had had the chance. Other additions are totally alien to the style. The tendency to add *sinfonia* and *ritornelli* to divide the opera's scenes is an anachronism, belonging certainly to *Orfeo* but not to the 1640s.

(Programme note for the ENO production of *Ulysses*, 1989)

Composers on Recreating the Operas

Luigi Dallapiccola on 'Ulysses' (1942)
Should transcriptions of old works be the province of musicologists or practising musicians? [. . .] Today I am more convinced than ever that both scholars and performers can and should make their own editions. These editions will co-exist and complement one another, in the same way that the various popular translations of Homer and Virgil complement the countless pure philological studies which elucidate doubtful points and compare texts.

Just as literary translations (with very rare exceptions) have a limited life span, because they more or less reflect the taste of their times and disappear to

Anne Collins (Arnalta) and Sandra Browne (Poppea) at ENO in 1975 (photo: Mike Humphrey)

make room for others more in conformity with the taste of later generations, so it is and so it should be with musical translations. And no one will deny that a similar fate is reserved for interpretations. The work of the philologist and the historian, on the other hand, seems to suffer from far fewer limitations than the 'free' translator. This is natural, for the historian is not pre-occupied with the taste of a particular epoch; he has other aims and aspirations. Because his work is restricted to a small circle of specialists and adepts, he doesn't have to make concessions to a wider, less accomplished public.

Among the concessions I have felt compelled to make, let me first mention the many long cuts, always designed to keep alive the dramatic interest. I haven't followed the example of Vincent d'Indy, who eliminated the whole mythological apparatus except the character of Minerva, because he considered it extraneous to the plot [. . . but] I have lightened the dialogue, thereby reducing the exceedingly long opera (originally four-and-one-half hours of music) to a more normal length. I have added several brief instrumental episodes, derived from Monteverdi's thematic material, at the beginning and end of certain scenes which lacked a sinfonia, and sometimes at the end of scenes to accompany the exit of a character.

. . . I felt that the harmonisation should maintain great simplicity and dignity. If I have broken this rule, the very rare exception will be noted just at those points where the character, in a transport such as the 'awakening of Ulysses', renounces words and bursts into a cry more expressive than any gesture or word.

I have used the large modern orchestra, for a very simple reason: old instruments aren't available, nor are performers skilled in seventeenth-century bowing technique. And apart from such practical considerations, only with the large orchestra could I characterise the principal roles, by using particular groups of instruments. This, too, is part of my concept of 'musical translation'.

(Reprinted in *Dallapiccola on Opera*, translated and edited by Rudy Shackleford, first published by Toccata Press, 1987; previously published in Italian by Il Saggiatore, Milan, 1980)

Bruno Maderna on 'Orfeo' (1967)

There are many editions of *Orfeo*, old and new, scholarly ones and performing ones. So many that the first question to arise is why I wanted to undertake a new one. The likely answer is that I did it for love; I had been waiting for years for a chance to 'interpret' *Orfeo*. Besides this essential motive, I had another compelling reason for the project: in none of the editions I happened to study (almost all of them) or listen to did I find that vivid sense of colour and imaginative energy in the realization of the bass line and the instrumental parts which, to my mind, are among the 'divine Claudio's' foremost characteristics. Some editions are very fine at the philological level, but puny, timid things, almost fearful of too much ardour. Others (often the so-called 'performing' editions), flagrantly disregarding cultural history, give way to outbursts of rhetoric and sentimentality which well and truly show up the personal inadequacy of many musicians once they are unshielded by 'technique' or 'aesthetics'.

There is no doubt that the task of rendering *Orfeo* in its integral beauty is an arduous if not impossible one today. Especially because true counterpoint, the true madrigal style and the true modal system have, alas, long since ceased to be taught, nor is there any analysis or teaching of the 'chromatic style' which so fashioned and agitated the musical world of the Renaissance, and led it to the transformation from modality to tonality.

(Translated from the introduction to Maderna's version of *Orfeo*, Zerboni, 1967).

Thomas Allen and Kathleen Kuhlmann in the 1985 Salzburg production of Henze's realisation of 'Ulysses', conducted by Jeffrey Tate, produced by Michael Hampe and designed by Mauro Pagano (photo: Salzburger Festspiele/Weber)

Hans Werner Henze on 'Ulysses' (1981)

My feeling for Greece, my picture of Greece, is probably influenced more by Hölderlin and Monteverdi than by Homer and Badoaro. I think there's a lot of Italy in this music, a lot of the country where Greek philosophy and art have remained vital and effective forces not just beyond the Renaissance but up to the present day, affecting people's lives more than they may be aware. And so there could be no question of my adopting a historicist approach when approaching the score of *Ulysses*, no question of carefully feeling my way and then holding back. Of course, the Vienna and Venice manuscripts (neither of which is in Monteverdi's hand) contain only the vocal lines and bass. Entire numbers are missing and the music of several scenes has disappeared — one thinks in particular of the Moorish Dance, the Suitors' funeral procession and Neptune's entrance music. All I could do was imagine Monteverdi's music by picturing it in my own mind: starting out from the sound of the orchestra, the voices and atmosphere and using only my own imagination, I tried to report the cultural climate of that first performance at the Teatro San Cassiano in Venice in autumn 1641, pretending that I was actually there, in order to translate what I heard and experienced into our modern spatial and instrumental sound world (while also adapting it to our modern listening habits), allowing the piece in that way to shine forth in all its old naturalness and vitality. In adopting this approach I always refer and appeal to Monteverdi's writings and to the melodic, rhythmic and harmonic forms and ideas which, present in the extant *Ulysses* fragment, are therefore prescribed by it.

(translated from the German in 'Musiktheater' booklet on Henze's version of *Ulysses*, Schott, Mainz, 1981)

Luciano Berio on 'Orfeo'

BERIO: For many years now I've had in mind a version of *Orfeo* that would come out of a group project, the product of a genuine musical collective rather than a single composer. Why *Orfeo*? Because Monteverdi's *Orfeo* represents a meeting point in the middle of that extraordinary thoroughfare and market place within which music was created and circulated at the end of the sixteenth century; it is above all a bid to combine and fuse the different forms of *representation*. It was, incidentally, the first ever example of a synthesis involving a convergence of the past, the present — with its own standard musical features — and a future. What this means is that the musical imprints of *Orfeo* are infinite. The very myth on which it is based is at the roots of our culture. Incidentally — and it's an aspect which tends to be overlooked — *Orfeo* is a great machine of musical seduction: when *Orfeo* 'enchants' Charon, we should perceive it as a central symbolic core of the opera. Our own project should also be viewed as an intensely vigorous act of musical seduction. Like *Orfeo* in relation to its period, we too need to make a fusion of the most diverse expressive and representational tools. The problem of instrumentation: you all know that the first printed edition of the score listed precise details of where and how particular instruments were deployed. 'This ritornello *was* performed by four violas [. . .]': a sentence like this is important, because it gives us to understand that those *ritornelli*, in another context, would have been played with different instruments. I think this was the first time in the history of musical theatre that instruments are given a dramatic function, used to emphasise or rather to 'colour' certain situations: the reed and pipe organs, the chittarones, the trombones are so many musical characters.

So, an *Orfeo* transposed to our own reality could become the basis for a project at different levels: the pedagogical level, the creative level, and the level of the ideal. We live in a musical world that is very interconnected and centrifugal, where the latest technology, along with standard features, tendencies, schools and innovations all come together. I should like our *Orfeo* to make the greatest possible contribution to the search for that inner musical unity of which we have so much need.

There's another very important question: the finale. You all know that the concluding climax of *Orfeo* is a replacement finale, substituted instead of the original finale (Orpheus torn to pieces by the Bacchantes) because of censorship. A tragic finale of which only the text is extant, but which I would like to reinstate; Orpheus's entry into Paradise accompanied by Apollo is, even musically, somewhat awkward.

FRANCO PIPERNO But how? It would mean cutting out the whole last act.

BERIO Not cutting it out. More a matter of modifying the musical and dramatic structure — of course, of steering clear of producing something 'after the style of', a bogus Monteverdi. I'd suggest coming in and out of Orpheus's final lament, 'Rendetemi il mio ben'. A little before the end, the musical landscape should begin to change, to become troubled. We have to create a passage into unease, a piece which gradually swells out and explodes into the finale. As far as the staging is concerned, it would need very little, just lighting effects.

NINO PIRROTTA And how do you envisage the tragic finale with the Bacchantes reinstated?

BERIO What we'll do will be radical, completely new, entirely reinvented. What has to emerge is a veritable musical hurricane, with the Monteverdian elements utterly transformed. A last act should involve everything and everyone, instruments and voices, bands and computer synthesisers. A short circuit, so to speak, of different standard features to produce a new event.

(Translated from an edited transcript of a round table interview with Berio, supplied by David Osmond-Smith.)

Richard Lewis (Nero) and Magda Laszlo (Poppea) at Glyndebourne in 1962 (photo: Guy Gravett)

The critic's view: changing attitudes to realising Monteverdi

Raymond Leppard's version of 'Poppea' was first performed at Glyndebourne in 1962; it was revived there in 1984 as part of the 50th anniversary season

Peter Heyworth (The Observer, July 1, 1862)
Mr Raymond Leppard, who has realised *Poppea* for Glyndebourne from a manuscript that contains nothing but the vocal and bass lines, has scored it for the chaste combination of strings, harpsichords, a pair of organs, lutes, harp and guitar, and only in the final scene has he weakened so far as to permit a couple of trumpets. All that is, musicologically speaking, as it should be. But I must confess that my ears found this nexus of sound monotonous and Mr Leppard's attempts to escape monotony self-conscious. And when to this is added an almost total lack of ensembles, choruses and instrumental numbers, it can readily be seen that this is an opera that puts all its eggs in one basket. Fortunately they are all of superb quality.

Winton Dean (The Musical Times, August 1984)
In 1962 Raymond Leppard's realization of Monteverdi's *L'incoronazione di Poppea* was a defensible compromise. The opera was seldom performed, and then only in grotesquely inflated versions. There was need to capture an audience and that was done. Now that we know it with the vocal pitches Monteverdi intended, and can appreciate the marvellous flexibility of his treatment of text and character, such temporizing is no longer tolerable. It is surprising that Leppard took no account of this. The score is said to have been revised, but its weaknesses are more obtrusive than ever: plushy scoring, souped-up extra string parts at emotional moments, organ fantasies, three disastrous octave transpositions. It evokes the image of Respighi rather than the Baroque, and is as outdated as Hagen's rehash of Handel's operas in the 1920s.

Postscript

Denis Stevens (1978)
Nero and Poppea, each a treasure to the other, sing [at the end of the opera] the most beautiful of all Monteverdi's duets ['Pur ti miro'] in the sure knowledge that his music itself is the treasure, shining brilliantly through no matter what arrangement, orchestration, or adaptation might be foisted upon it.

(*Monteverdi: Sacred, Secular, and Occasional music,* Associated University Presses, London)

Alan Curtis (1989)
Thus it would seem that the entire final scene [. . .] was written by a younger composer than was the main body of the opera [. . .] This is the conclusion I reluctantly arrived at roughly two decades ago — reluctantly, because it was a shock particularly to image 'Pur ti miro' [. . .] 'the most beautiful of all Monteverdi's duets', with which the eminent scholar Denis Stevens poignantly closes his brief Monteverdi biography, as the work of some other composer. [. . .] One must now judge not the case of Ferrari *versus* Monteverdi but rather of Ferrari *versus* Sacrati [. . .] In any case, the widely believed legend of 'Pur ti miro' forming the climax, the glowing sunset of Monteverdi's long career, if not yet perhaps conclusively put to rest, has at least been shown to be most unlikely.

(Introduction to Curtis's edition of *Poppea*; see above)

Grateful acknowledgements to Jonathan Burton, Kathy Hill, David Osmond-Smith, Philip Pickett and Rosy Runciman who supplied me with material for this chapter.

Discography by Jeremy Barlow

1. Several of the recordings have appeared with a variety of labels and numberings; where alternatives exist, I have listed only the most widely available in Britain. All record numbers before 1981 are for 12 inch discs unless otherwise stated; all numbers from 1981 are for compact discs.
2. Where a single name is given under 'Conductor/Edition', the conductor is also the editor of the score.

Date	Label/Number	Conductor/Edition	Orchestra/Chorus
L'ORFEO			
1939	HMV DB 5370-81 (78)	Calusio/ Benvenuti	Not named
1950	VOX VBX 21 (mono)	Koch/not known	Berlin Radio
1955	ARCHIVE APM 14057-8 (mono)	Wenzinger	Hitzacker Festival Orch./ Hamburg Music High School Choir
1968	ERATO STU 70440-2	Corboz/Tarr	Lausanne Complesso Strumentale
1968	TELDEC 8.35020/A-B (CD reissue)	Harnoncourt (first version)	Vienna Concentus Musicus/ Munich Capella Antiqua Chorus
1973	ARCHIVE 2565 030-2	Jürgens	Hamburg Camerata Accademica and Wind Ensemble/Hamburg Monteverdi Chorus
1980	JUBILATE JU.85-810-2	Heinrich (edition reconstructs original ending)	Orchestra, Choirs and Soloists from the 20th Bad Hersfield Festival, 1980
1981	TELDEC 8.35807/A-B	Harnoncourt (second version)	Zurich Opera House
1983	EMI CDC.747142-3	Rogers and Medlam	London Baroque, London Cornett and Sacbut Ensemble/ Chiaroscuro
1985	ERATO ECD 88134-5	Corboz/edition	Lyons Opera Orchestra/Paris Chapelle Royale Vocal Ensemble
1985	ARCHIV 419 251-2-2	Gardiner	English Baroque Soloists, His Majesties Sagbutts and Cornetts/Monteverdi Choir
1991	DECCA L'OISEAU LYRE 433-545-2	Pickett	New London Consort

3. All recordings are in Italian.

4. I have not attempted to distinguish performances on period instruments from those on modern instruments; as mentioned above, the use of the former has been introduced piecemeal, with designs that have in many cases altered greatly over the period of the recordings.

Orfeo	Euridice	La Musica	Messaggera
De Franceschi	Vivante	Vivante	Nicolai
Meili	Trötschel	Fleischer	Lammers
Krebs	Mack-Cosack	Guilleaume	Deroubaix
Tappy	Schwartz	Staempfli	Sarti
Kozma	Hansmann	Hansmann	Berberian
Rogers	Petrescu	Petrescu	Reynolds
Seipp	Liebermann	Bühler	Blanke-Roeser
Huttenlocher	Yakar	Schmidt	Linos
Rogers	Kwella	Kirkby	Laurens
Quilico	Michael	Alliot-Lugaz	Watkinson
Rolfe Johnson	Baird	Lynne Dawson	Von Otter
Ainsley	Gooding	Bott	Bott

Date	Label/Number	Conductor/Edition	Orchestra/Chorus

IL RITORNO D'ULISSE IN PATRIA

Date	Label/Number	Conductor/Edition	Orchestra/Chorus
1964	VOX DLBX 211; TURNABOUT TV 37016-8	Ewerhart	Santini Chamber Orchestra
1971	TELEFUNKEN SKBT-T.23/1-4 or (GK) 6.35024/A-D	Harnoncourt	Vienna Concentus Musicus
1979	CBS 79332/A-C	Leppard	London Philharmonic/ Glyndebourne Chorus

Date	Label/Number	Conductor/Edition	Orchestra/Chorus

L'INCORONAZIONE DI POPPEA

Date	Label/Number	Conductor/Edition	Orchestra/Chorus
1952	CONCERT HALL CHS. 1184 (mono)	W. Goehr	Zurich Tonhalle Orchestra/ unnamed chorus
1963	VOX STOPBX 50113-1/3	Ewerhart	Santini Chamber Orchestra
1963	HMV ANGEL SAN 126-7	Pritchard/ Leppard	Royal Philharmonic Orchestra/ Glyndebourne Festival Chorus
1966	CAMBRIDGE CRS B 1901	Curtis	Instrumental soloists with Oakland Symphony Orchestra (strings, trumpets) and Chorus
1974	TELDEC 8.35247/A-D (CDs)	Harnoncourt (first version)	Vienna Concentus Musicus
1980	FONIT CETRA LMA.3008/A-D	Curtis	Il Complesso Barrocco
1981	TELDEC 8.35807/D-F	Harnoncourt (second version)	Zurich Opera House Monteverdi Ensemble
1984	CBS M3K 39728/A-C	Malgoire	La Grande Ecurie et la Chambre du Roy
1988	VIRGIN CLASSICS VCT 790775-2/A-C	Hickox/Bartlett	City of London Baroque Sinfonia
1988	NUOVA ERA 6737-39	Zedda	Bassano Pro Arte Orchestra
1990	HARMONIA MUNDI HMC 901330-2	Jacobs	Not named; based on Montpellier Opera production

Ulisse	*Penelope*	*Telemaco*	*Minerva*
English	Lehane	Whitesides	Fahberg
Eliasson	Lerer	Hansen	Hansmann
Stilwell	Von Stade	Power	Murray

Poppea	*Nerone*	*Ottavia*	*Seneca*
Gahwiller	Brueckner-Ruggeberg	Helbling	Kelch
Buckel	Mielsch	Zareska	Wollitz
Laszlo	Lewis	Bible	Cava
Bogard	Bressler	Hayes	Beattie
Donath	Söderström	Berberian	Luccardi
Balthrop	Watkinson	Bierbaum	Cold
Yakar	Tappy	Schmidt	Salminen
Malfitano	Elwes	Gal	Reinhart
Auger	Jones	Hirst	Reinhart
Dessi	Ligi	Tabiadon	Caforio
Borst	Laurens	Larmore	Schopper

Bibliography

The Letters of Claudio Monteverdi (translated and introduced by Denis Stevens; London/New York, 1980) contains some of the greatest letters by any composer and make a great introduction to his ideas and the practical problems he encountered when composing opera. *The New Monteverdi Companion* (ed. Arnold and Fortune, London, 1985) is a fine introduction to different aspects of his work, with essays by distinguished specialists. For a study of the background to Monteverdi's later operas, Ellen Rosand's magnificent *Venetian Opera in the 17th Century: The Creation of a Genre* (California, 1991) must be recommended as the most recent study of the way opera developed in its early years, and it has to some extent superseded earlier books such as Robert Donnington's *The Rise of Opera*.

Books devoted to individual operas include most notably *Claudio Monteverdi: Orfeo* (ed. Whenham, one of the Cambridge Opera Handbooks, 1986), and *The Song of the Soul: Understanding 'Poppea'* by Iain Fenlon and Peter Miller (Royal Musical Association monograph, 1992). E.H. Tarr's edition of *Orfeo* (Editions Constellat/United Music Publishers, 1974) has been the basis of our work on the opera in this Guide. Alan Curtis's edition of *Poppea* (London, 1989) opens with his important introduction on sources, and performing practice, and closes with appendices of all the variants to the main score. There is no similar edition of *Ulysses*.

Contributors

Iain Fenlon is a Fellow of King's College, Cambridge.

Anne Ridler, poet and translator, has translated librettos for operas by Monteverdi, Cavalli, Mozart and Handel, which have been performed by Kent Opera, English National Opera and Opera Factory.

John Whenham is Senior Lecturer in Music at the University of Birmingham.

Tim Carter is Reader in Music at Royal Holloway and Bedford New College.

Peter Miller is a Fellow of Clare Hall, Cambridge, and studies the political and cultural thought of early modern Europe.

Paolo Fabbri is Professor of Musical Aesthetics at the University of Ferrara. He is deputy director of the Rossini Foundation in Pesaro, and a member of the editorial board for the publication of the complete works of Rossini and Andrea Gabrieli. He is co-director of music studies at the Istituto di Studi Rinascimantali in Ferrara, and he was awarded the Dent Medal in 1989 by the Royal Musical Association.

Jack Sage is Emeritus Professor of the University of London, and former Head of the Department of Spanish, King's College, London.

Jeremy Barlow is both a musicologist and a performer, specialising in popular and dance music from the sixteenth to the eighteenth centuries. His edition and reconstruction of *The Beggar's Opera* has recently been published by Oxford University Press; he has also directed a recording of the work for Hyperion Records.

6 | 36 | | 0